The Life and Legends
of Calamity Jane

The Oklahoma Western Biographies
Richard W. Etulain, General Editor

Also by Richard W. Etulain (*a selective listing*)

AUTHOR
Owen Wister
Ernest Haycox
Re-imagining the Modern American West: A Century of Fiction,
*   History, and Art*
Telling Western Stories: From Buffalo Bill to Larry McMurtry
Beyond the Missouri: The Story of the American West
Seeking First the Kingdom: Northwest Nazarene University,
*   A Centennial History*
Abraham Lincoln and Oregon Country Politics in the Civil
*   War Era*

COAUTHOR
Conversations with Wallace Stegner on Western History and
*   Literature*
The American West: A Twentieth-Century History

EDITOR
Writing Western History: Essays on Major Western Historians
Does the Frontier Experience Make America Exceptional?
César Chávez: A Brief Biography with Documents
New Mexican Lives: Profiles and Historical Stories
Western Lives: A Biographical History of the American West
Lincoln Looks West: From the Mississippi to the Pacific

COEDITOR
Basque Americans
Fifty Western Writers: A Bio-bibliographical Guide
A Bibliographical Guide to the Study of Western American
*   Literature*
The Twentieth-Century West: Historical Interpretations
Researching Western History: Topics in the Twentieth Century
By Grit and Grace: Eleven Women Who Shaped the American West
Portraits of Basques in the New World
With Badges and Bullets: Lawmen and Outlaws in the Old West
The Hollywood West
The American West in 2000: Essays in Honor of Gerald D. Nash
Wild Women of the Old West
Chiefs and Generals

The Life and Legends
of Calamity Jane

By Richard W. Etulain

University of Oklahoma Press : Norman

Library of Congress Cataloging-in-Publication Data

Etulain, Richard W.
   The life and legends of Calamity Jane / by Richard W. Etulain.
      pages cm. — (Oklahoma western biographies ; volume 29)
   Includes bibliographical references and index.
   ISBN 978-0-8061-4632-4 (hardcover : alk. paper)   1. Calamity
Jane, 1856–1903.   2. Women pioneers—West (U.S—Biography.
3. West (U.S—Biography.   4. Frontier and pioneer life—West (U.S.)
I. Title.
   F594.C2E88 2014
   978'.02092—dc23
   [B]
                                                    2014012696

The Life and Legends of Calamity Jane is Volume 29 in The Oklahoma Western Biographies.

The paper in this book meets the guidelines for permanence and durability of the Committee on Production Guidelines for Book Longevity of the Council on Library Resources, Inc. ∞

1 2 3 4 5 6 7 8 9 10

For Glenda Riley,
splendid western historian,
wonderful colleague

Contents

Illustrations

FIGURES

Illustrations

Illustrations

Series Editor's Preface

Stories of heroes and heroines have intrigued many generations of listeners and readers. Americans, like people everywhere, have been captivated by the lives of military, political, and religious figures as well as intrepid explorers, pioneers, and rebels. The Oklahoma Western Biographies build on this fascination with biography and link it with two other abiding interests of Americans: the frontier and the American West. Although volumes in the series carry no notes, they are prepared by leading scholars, are soundly researched, and include extended discussions of sources used. Each volume is a lively synthesis based on thorough examination of pertinent primary and secondary sources.

Above all, the Oklahoma Western Biographies aim at two goals: to provide readable life stories of significant westerners and to show how their lives illuminate a notable topic, an influential movement, or a series of important events in the history and cultures of the American West.

This compact biography by the series editor attempts to capture the life and legends of Calamity Jane, probably the most written-about woman of the nineteenth-century West. Born in 1856, Martha Canary, the daughter of a frustrated

Missouri farmer and his controversial wife, burst upon the western scene as Calamity Jane in the 1870s and remained on center stage until her death in 1903.

In the late nineteenth century, frontier male journalists, intrigued by Calamity's unorthodox actions, wrote hundreds of sensational stories about her in newspapers scattered across the northern West. The reporters trumpeted her incessant travels, excessive drinking, possible prostitution, and continual hobnobbing with groups of males. Once journalist-historian Horatio N. Maguire, dramatist Thomas M. Newson, and dime novelist Edward L. Wheeler published their biographical and fictional accounts of Calamity in the 1870s, she became a nationally known frontier figure. Later writers focused on her nonstop rambling, including traveling with the Kohl and Middleton Dime Museum tour group in 1896 and appearing at the Pan-American Exposition in Buffalo, New York, in 1901. Alcoholism and failing health led to her precipitous decline and demise.

Calamity's legendary notoriety rapidly expanded during the century and more after her death. The second half of this volume traces and evaluates this explosion of fame. These chapters examine the shifting images of Calamity Jane in biographies and histories, novels, movies, and retrospective newspaper and magazine accounts. Over time, beginning before the end of Calamity's life and expanding during the next five to six generations, three legends about her gradually coalesced: Calamity as a sensational Wild West woman; Calamity as an aspiring pioneer woman; and Calamity as kind, softhearted nurse, an angel of mercy. These legends of Calamity Jane, in existence since the 1870s and 1880s, remain in place—and are likely to continue.

Richard W. Etulain

Preface

It was the early 1990s. I was looking for an interest-grabbing subject for my next project. After twenty-five years as a professor of American history and literature with a specialty in the American West, I had gained job security and published more than a few essays and books. Now I was driven to write something that would appeal to general readers.

I was convinced that multitudes of readers would be interested in a stirring story about one of the Old West demigods. A quick search revealed that Wild West heroes such as George Custer, Wild Bill Hickok, Wyatt Earp, and Billy the Kid had all been subjects of several biographies. But not Calamity Jane. No one had done a thorough life story of her, even though she was often touted as the best-known woman of the Old West. Why was that? My curiosity whetted, I set out to find the answer.

A tentative conclusion was not long in coming. I discovered that the multitude of sources on Calamity Jane were narrow in focus, often at odds with one another, and frequently incestuous. It didn't help, either, that Calamity was illiterate, and what she did say about herself in a few interviews and in a ghostwritten autobiography was riddled with exaggerations, distortions, and blatant lies. I learned, too, that a half-dozen or so other eager writers had set out to produce a full-scale biography of Calamity but had given up because of the research difficulties they quickly encountered.

But I was foolish enough to enter where others had grown fearful to tread. I was stubbornly convinced that hard work would pay off; I had always believed in the truth of that cliché.

So the journey began in 1992. I spent parts of several summers researching by day and traveling by night, accumulating as many notes and copies of pertinent materials as a run-and-work, tightfisted academic could turn up. In a few years, after visiting probably more than one hundred archives and libraries, I had exhausted all Calamity collections. Although the research notes and ideas piled up, the newly written pages did not. After publishing several essays about Calamity Jane, I was delayed by other commitments and projects. Even during a decade of retirement, I could not get the Calamity project back on the road. Much later a chance trip to the attic renewed my interest in Calamity, helped reignite my energies, and in two years of additional research and intense writing, this book was drafted.

In twenty years of studying Calamity Jane off and on, my ideas about how to organize a book about her have frequently changed. At first I planned a brief, straightforward, and chronologically organized biography. Then I thought of doing a study of the mythic Calamity, tracing the step-by-step process by which she became a legendary figure. Finally, I concluded that I must do both: lay out the story of her life in the first section of the book and devote the second part to discussing the ever-shifting interpretations of Calamity from her own time to the present.

The following pages aim at that twofold purpose. Some of the biographical section treads familiar ground—but with a few tinkering differences. I do not provide extensive discussions of the competing views on controversial topics such as Calamity's birthplace and birth date, her "husbands" and children, and her ramblings. Instead, I put forth what I think to be the most defensible position on these contested subjects. These conclusions have come only after the most thorough research in pertinent manuscript and published sources. I have made this decision because I want to keep my book on Calamity concise and direct. For those who wish more discussion on other views, the essay on sources, the extensive bibliography, and a few textual comments add helpful details.

As I tell this story, I occasionally ask readers to ponder what Calamity, her family members, and her acquaintances *might* have thought about specific events or ideas. These are not wild speculations but educated guesses, pointing readers to the best evidence on these questions and moving carefully toward tentative, defensible answers. These ponderings are an attempt to broaden our understanding of Calamity, who, because she could not read or write, left us very few of her thoughts. Similar questions are raised about her family and friends, again because of such limited materials on several germane questions.

Another point about the content of the biographical section: readers will notice that I am hesitant in my comments on Calamity Jane as a prostitute. I use qualifiers such as a "possible prostitute," because there is no irrefutable, on-the-spot evidence that she sold sex. A few contemporaries say she did so in the "hog ranches" of Wyoming and the "joy houses" of South Dakota. No one, however, saw her in such a house; no one knew for certain she was a prostitute. So I hedge, not because I think she could not or would not have been one, but solely because satisfactory documentary support is not available.

Second, I tip the balance of the book's contents toward dealing with the interpretations that have sprung up around Calamity in the century and more since her death. Readers will encounter extensive comments on the first newspaper accounts, the dime novels, the pioneering historical biographies, and the memories of those acquainted with Calamity. The final four chapters trace at length the most significant novels, movies, and biographies about Calamity, as well as retrospective newspaper accounts. I furnish particularly thorough plot summaries of these sources so that readers can understand the complex, shifting images of Calamity— from those created during her own life to those of the early twenty-first century.

These pages advance no specific thesis, nor do they follow one theory. This book owes more to research in primary sources than to theoretical studies. I do not mean to denigrate those who are intrigued with thesis-driven or theoretical works; here I have simply not used those approaches.

This study, adhering to the guidelines of the Oklahoma Western Biographies series, carries no footnotes. But the essay on sources contains thorough comments about the major sources on which the volume is based. In addition, the bibliography lists all these as well as many other sources pertinent to study of Martha Canary/Calamity Jane. Further, for those wishing to pursue specific sources, I am depositing footnoted versions of the manuscript with the Montana Historical Society in Helena and the South Dakota Historical Society in Pierre, two archive-libraries with extensive collections on Calamity Jane.

In my two decades of sporadic work on Calamity Jane, I have piled up numerous debts to institutions and individuals. In the 1990s the University of New Mexico supported my research with several summer grants and release time in a sabbatical leave. I am grateful, too, to several publishers who have allowed me to use parts of previous essays in these pages. These include the Montana Historical Society, the University of New Mexico Press, Fulcrum Publishing, and the University of Arizona Press.

Several colleagues have also aided in the preparation of this book. My longtime western pard, Glenda Riley, read and commented on two of my earlier essays on Calamity Jane. David Holtby and Chuck Rankin, both outstanding editors, also sharpened the focus and content of two other pieces, a book chapter and a book epilogue. Dudley Gardner, Tom Bell, and Todd Guenther helped me with Wyoming details, as did Joyce Jensen with Billings, Montana, information. Virginia Scharff likewise encouraged my work on Calamity, and David Key and my daughter, Jackie Etulain Partch, helped with the research. Roberta Beed Sollid, author of an excellent study of Calamity Jane, provided valuable information. I also owe much to William R. Whiteside, nonpareil researcher in census, birth, marriage, and other obscure sources dealing with Calamity Jane, the Canary family, and friends and acquaintances of Calamity. His invaluable research lists are listed in the manuscript section of the bibliography. Finally, I am very grateful to dozens and dozens of librarians and archivists who have guided and helped me in my research and helped to select photographs and illustrations. In this regard I am much indebted to archivist Laurie Langland of Dakota Western University, Lory Morrow and Glenda Bradshaw of the Montana Historical Society, Judy Cox of the Mercer County (Missouri) Library, Paul Andrew Hutton, and Bob McCubbin for helping me secure the photographs I needed.

With the University of Oklahoma Press, Emmy Ezzell, Steven Baker, and Rowan Steineker, and freelance copy editor Jay Fultz, helped with manuscript, editorial, and photograph/illustration details. I am especially indebted to Chuck Rankin, colleague and friend, who took on this project and quickly and dependably pushed it into publication.

I owe most to James D. McLaird, professor emeritus of Dakota Wesleyan University. We first met through correspondence as Calamity researchers in the early 1990s. Throughout the next two decades, he answered my many questions, pointed me toward other valuable sources, and raised crucial questions for my work. He also read and commented on—and corrected—several of my writings on Calamity Jane. I am much indebted to him for his support, encouragement, and collegiality.

Finally, I want to thank two superb proofreading librarians, my wife, Joyce Oldenkamp Etulain, and my daughter Jackie Etulain Partch, for helping me catch and correct errors. Their help was invaluable.

The Life and Legends
of Calamity Jane

1

Foundations, Stable and Broken

In early July of 1876 several riders rode slowly into the new boomtown of Deadwood, Dakota Territory. Most of the group of miners, gamblers, and expectant entrepreneurs had begun their adventuresome trip in late June in eastern Wyoming. Stopping off near Fort Laramie, the riders had taken in new members and then continued traveling north toward the new mineral rush in the Black Hills. It would be a trip of destiny for two of the riders: Old West notables Wild Bill Hickok and Calamity Jane.

By early 1876, Hickok had already captured the imagination of many Americans. The starting point of Hickok's journey to stardom began with his appearance in a sensational and overblown article by George Ward Nichols in *Harper's New Monthly Magazine* (February 1867) lionizing Wild Bill as a demigod of the West. In the next decade Hickok became the best-known lawman and gunman of the Wild West, his reputation growing in a series of controversial events. He had recently married circus owner Agnes Lake and was headed to Deadwood, where he hoped to strike a rich lode of new income.

For Calamity Jane, most of her hyped reputation was still to come but barely beyond the horizon. Just twenty years old in summer 1876, she had been transformed in reputation in 1875 and early 1876 from a Missouri farmer's daughter named Martha Canary into a young woman without moorings, rumored to drink with abandon and cohabit with men. While Martha Canary was disappearing into the past, the controversial Calamity Jane was bouncing onstage.

When Hickok's riders took in Calamity near Fort Laramie about 1 July 1876, Wild Bill and Calamity met for the first time. They were not previously acquainted and did not become lovers, but from 1876 on, their names were conjoined in story and mythology. Indeed, when Calamity sauntered down the main street of Deadwood with Wild Bill, the ride was a coming-out party for her. After those early days in Deadwood, her life took off in new directions.

In the decade and a half after that memorable summer in Deadwood, Calamity became as well known as any woman in the frontier American West. The notoriety was decidedly melodramatic and sometimes lurid. She was frequently dubbed a "hellcat in red britches," a Lady Wildcat, and a female terror of the plains, becoming a favorite subject for journalistic hyperbole. But behind this adventuresome, gun-toting hellion was another person: Martha Canary, a young woman adrift in a pioneer man's world, without home, family, or occupation. When Martha was transformed into Calamity Jane in the pivotal years of 1875–78, her less dramatic side disappeared under a landside of purple prose. The young pioneer woman of the frontier lost out to the Wild Woman of the Old West. But behind the mythological figure of popular attire stands another woman who needs her story told.

Unfortunately, more than a century after Calamity's death, too much of her life remains uncovered. Since Calamity was illiterate, there are no signed records—not even a signature. But there are truckloads of lively stories ensuing from Calamity's wildness: Calamity came to town, went on a toot, and is currently in the cooler. The paucity of solid facts and the plethora of stylized stories forces Calamity's

biographers to sort through thousands of bits and fragments to stitch together a story, much of it at odds with
many of her previous life stories.

The story of Martha's ancestors remains short and blurry,
but it can be traced to the late eighteenth and early nineteenth centuries. The first of the Canary family known to
history is her paternal grandfather, James Canary, who was
born in Virginia in 1788. Only vague rumors of French
Huguenot and Irish heritage exist before Grandpa James.
Reared in the western section of Virginia that in 1863,
during the Civil War, hived off into a separate state, West
Virginia, James may have served in the War of 1812 and
received a military land grant in the West as a veteran's benefit. By 1820, as the U.S. census reveals, James was living in
eastern Ohio and now married (perhaps in 1812 or 1813)
to the former Sarah Wilson (Willson), who was born about
1794 in North Carolina. When the census taker arrived in
1820 at the Canary household, he encountered a rapidly
expanding family of four sons and four daughters, which
by 1825 had increased by one boy. The last of these children was Robert Wilson (or Willson) Canary, born in 1825,
and the father-to-be of Martha Canary, Calamity Jane. All
the children of James and Sarah Canary were born in Ohio
between 1813 and 1825.

James Canary was a lifetime farmer. Four consecutive census reports—1820, 1830, 1840, 1850—disclose the Canary
family residing in Monroe County, Ohio, a rural and agricultural region just west of the Virginia/West Virginia border. As adults, several of James's children farmed near him
and Sarah. Over time, through his diligence and careful purchases and exchanges, James gained valuable landholdings.

Out of the scattered and miniscule records, a few distin-
guishable patterns emerge about James and Sarah Canary.
They remained thirty years in Marion County in Ohio and
advanced economically as a farm family. Several of the Canary

children chose to remain near their parents even after they had established their own families. The census of 1830 indicated that an older man lived with James and Sarah, perhaps his own father, said to be another James or the father of Sarah. The census of 1850 also revealed that the Canarys now owned acreage estimated to be worth $2,500.

Then quick, dramatic changes transformed the lives of the Canary family. In the early 1850s, Grandpa James and Sarah began to sell off their land. In 1851 and 1852, three parcels were sold for $1,000, $700, and $900, for a total of $2,600. These unexpected actions engender questions. Why the quick sale of land after the long, diligent acquisition of these farmlands? Had incoming populations sealed off the possibility of land purchases for James's offspring or escalated prices beyond their reach, making it impossible to launch their own farming careers? Were the sons and married daughters urging their parents to move west so that the young families could all purchase land and ensure their futures?

No clear answers are forthcoming, but the chronology of the Canary family's move west can be partially traced. By 1852, James had sold all his land in eastern Ohio and was on his way west—with several of his children coming with him and Sarah. Soon after 1852, daughter Lana and her husband James Kilgore were in Iowa in Polk County, just north of Des Moines. Son James Thornton Canary also came to the same county in the mid-1850s. Most important for this story, the youngest Canary son, Robert, now thirty years of age, arrived in Iowa in the mid-1850s and married Charlotte Burge on 14 June 1855 in Polk County. She was fifteen, and her family had resided for some time in the area. Their residence there and the marriage license of June 1855 counter a decidedly negative rumor by a Canary family in-law that Robert "had been bedazzled by Charlotte's beauty in her early teens when he had found her in an Ohio bawdy house. On the spot he had married her to reform her." Nearly one year after the marriage, perhaps on 1 May 1856, Robert and Charlotte, now in Missouri, became the parents of their first child, a girl they named Martha.

Why the Canary stopover in Iowa? Had the Canary families hoped to find less expensive land there? Whatever the correct answer, very soon after arriving in Iowa, the Canarys were again on the move. This time they traveled south, just across the border into northern Missouri. James came too, and he may have come as a widower. Although his wife, Sarah, is listed in the census of 1850, she is missing from the enumeration ten years later. Eventually, daughters Lana and Mary and their husbands, along with James Thornton and Robert Wilson and their wives, arrived in Missouri, but evidence is strong that all were in Iowa—even if for a couple of years or even a few months in the mid-1850s. Whatever the reasons of push and pull factors, the stay in Iowa was brief. By 1852 James had sold all his land in Ohio, and four years later he was in Mercer County, Missouri, buying new parcels of land. For Grandpa James, and most of his children moving to Missouri, this would be the last stop in their journey west.

The Canary family and other families migrating west followed a familiar pattern. As agricultural areas east of the Mississippi filled up with newcomers, expanding families looked farther toward the prairies, plains, and beyond for more and less expensive lands. They wanted to find fertile lands for sons and sons-in-law who were looking for land of their own on which to establish families. Without saying so, Grandpa James seemed pulled west by these motivations.

When the Canary families entered Mercer County in the mid-to-late 1850s, they came to one of the last areas of Missouri to fill up with white settlers. Much like most other pioneers, the Canarys were tillers of the soil, looking for fresh opportunities in newly opened territories. They found in northern Missouri what they wanted, tillable land at modest prices. For two of James's married daughters, Mary

7

and her husband Robert Southers and Lana and husband James Kilgore, and for his son James Thornton, Missouri would be their final homes, or at least their domiciles for twenty-five years and more. Only for Robert and Charlotte Canary, the parents of Martha, would the stay be shorter and far less satisfying.

Mercer County and Princeton, its county seat, were barely more than a generation out of Indian control. Even though Missouri had become a state in August 1821 as a result of the famed Missouri Compromise, northern parts of the new state attracted far fewer settlers than lands along the eastern border near the Mississippi River and areas adjacent to the Missouri running diagonally across the state. Most of Mercer County lay in a land belt better for grasses, grazing, and small farms; it was clearly a much less fertile area than the richer farmlands to the north in Iowa.

In the late 1830s and early 1840s, the first groups of white immigrants came to Mercer County and the Princeton area. In 1845 Mercer was organized as a new county, carved out of Grundy County and named for the Revolutionary War general John F. Mercer. Approximately twenty-one miles square, the new county was marked by rolling hills, a few large water courses, isolation from other settlements, and distance from markets. Princeton, laid out in 1846 and incorporated in 1853, became the county seat, ideally located halfway between northern and southern boundaries and nearly so between eastern and western borders.

A land boom in the 1850s transformed the new, isolated county. The 1850 county population of 2,691 boomed to 9,300 ten years later. As the Canary families arrived in the mid-1850s, nearly all the available land was filling up with a fresh crop of incoming settlers. The Kansas-Nebraska controversies to the north, the disappearance of government lands in Iowa, and the "favorable conditions" in northern Missouri worked as molding push-and-pull forces. The newcomers spilled into the prairie lands that earlier immigrants had passed over as less fertile and productive. One of those areas a half-dozen miles east of Princeton became the Ravanna district, organized in 1857. To this area the Canary family came just as the floodtide of settlers washed over Mercer County. As one new immigrant of the time recalled later, when he came in 1856 "there were few houses on the prairie from the Iowa line to the southern part of the Medicine" township (the southwestern corner of Mercer County), but in the next year "there was a complete revolution." And, he added, "the immigrant from Ohio and Illinois was made welcome and given help to get his start." James Canary and the other Canary families fit that description.

Details in the U.S. Census of 1860 and local histories provide a capsule portrait of the area to which Grandpa James, Robert and Charlotte, and the other Canary households had moved. Among the 9,300 residents of Mercer County (another source lists 9,225) were 9,274 whites and 2 free blacks. Only 24 slaves resided in the county. The white population consisted of 4,831 males and 4,443 females. Surprisingly, the county seat of Princeton, with only 249 inhabitants, was the smallest of the county's ten largest townships.

The first appearance of the Canary family was in the Mercer County land records. On 28 April 1856, Grandpa James purchased 320 acres, paying $1,775 cash for the parcel of land. The price he paid—$5 or $6 per acre—for less-than-prime land suggests how much prices had escalated while newcomers were moving into the Mercer County area. Many in the previous generation in Missouri were able to purchase government land for $1–3 per acre. Still, the price James paid in Missouri was but half the amount, per acre, he had received when he sold his Ohio parcels four or five years earlier.

Then, quickly, James revealed his commitment to family by reselling his land to his children at greatly reduced prices. A few months after he purchased his half-section, he sold 40 acres to his son-in-law Robert Southers. Three years later, James sold an additional 100 acres to another son-in-law, James Kilgore. On the same day, 8 October 1859, he sold the remaining 180 acres of his original purchase to his son Robert for $500. (A second son, James Thornton, already owned his own land, which his father had helped him purchase.) In all, Martha's grandfather had parceled out 320 acres to his three children for $800, or less than half what he had paid for it in 1856. Perhaps declining health warned him he must sell, for he died less than three years later.

The census of 1860 also furnishes the first specific information about all members of Robert and Charlotte's family. These census records, a few other obscure notices, and vague reminiscences gathered more than a half century later tell us what we know of Martha Canary's first years in Missouri. When the census taker visited the log cabin farmhouse of Martha's family in Ravanna Township, he recorded the names and basic information about six inhabitants.

Martha's father Robert was thirty-five and married to twenty-year-old Charlotte. Three children were listed: M[artha], born in 1856; Cilas [Silas?], born in 1857; and Lana [or Lena], a year old. Robert was born in Ohio, Charlotte in Illinois, but all three children in Missouri. (Calamity Jane later wrote there were six children in all, but only Elijah [birth date uncertain] of those not listed in the 1860 census seems to have survived.) A farmer owning 180 acres of land worth $1,500 (he had bought this acreage the year before from his father for $500) and other personal property valued at $400, Robert could read and write, suggesting some earlier schooling. But his father James, his wife Charlotte, and his two sisters in the Princeton area were illiterate. Grandpa James may have lived with Robert and Charlotte; at least his name appears immediately after their family. James is also listed as being without property or personal wealth—a puzzling listing, as we shall see, because

U.S. Census of 1860, Mercer County, Missouri.

The U.S. census, taken in early summer 1860, revealed much about Robert and Charlotte Canary and their then-three children (listing no. 411). Martha, who became Calamity Jane, is listed first. Probably Grandpa James Canary was living with them. Courtesy Mercer County Library, Princeton, Missouri.

controversies over James's possessions, including some cash, would badly divide the Canary families in Mercer County two years later, leading to strong exchanges in court.

Martha's parents resided only six or seven years in Princeton before leaving in 1862 or 1863, but they and their family indelibly impressed themselves on the minds of their neighbors. Newspaper stories and remembrances forty to sixty years later recalled the Canarys. When Calamity died in 1903, a story in the *Princeton Post* noted that the news attracted "special interest by Mercer county citizens, a great many of whom remembered her father and mother

11

and a number of whom remembered the woman herself when she was a girl here." Some recalled that Robert and Charlotte—and perhaps James too—first lived in run-down buildings in the center of Princeton before moving to a farm a half-dozen miles to the east in what became the Collings neighborhood in the Ravanna Township. In these distant recollections, Robert was remembered as a rather nondescript and unenthusiastic farm worker. Most often, residents of Princeton recalled his lackadaisical attitudes, his lack of drive as an agriculturist, and his inability to control his lively, controversial wife.

It was Charlotte who remained fresh in the neighbors' minds. More memories about her surfaced than about all the other Canary family members together. Time and again Charlotte bruised the social expectations of neighborhood wives. Her brightly colored and eye-catching clothing, her cigar smoking, her public swearing, and her drinking (sometimes to drunkenness) negatively marked a woman when mothers were supposed to be more innocent.

When journalist Duncan Aikman came to Princeton in the mid-1920s to research his lively but exaggerated book *Calamity Jane and the Lady Wildcats* (1927), he found a handful of older residents who remembered the Canary family, particularly Charlotte. They reported more than a few incidents in which Charlotte, a bit tipsy, flirted with questionable men. One elderly informant recalled a never-to-be-forgotten incident when Charlotte galloped her mud-spattered and lathered horse into the yard of a new teenage mother and threw a swatch of calico cloth at her feet, yelling out "Hey . . . take that and make a dress for your damn bastard." The incident became an often-told story, de rigueur in speaking of Charlotte, and passed down for more than a century among families of the Princeton area.

Others recalled how Charlotte angered and alienated Princetonians. She frequently berated Bob as an ineffectual husband and worker, and she sometimes neglected her children. Her unorthodox behavior, including her uncouth public actions, stuck like a cocklebur in their minds.

Still, kind actions and energetic actions were recalled too. The same young woman who had the calico cloth flung at her called Charlotte "a crazy, show-off, harum-scarum woman, drunk or sober," but remembered that Martha's mother was "good-hearted to the core." Some neighbor wives were upset—perhaps a bit jealous—that the young, vivacious Charlotte could whip through her domestic duties, leaving plenty of time for dashes to Princeton they could never wrestle out of their tiring list of labors. Someplace and sometime, Charlotte also alienated her sister-in-law, Delilah, the wife of James Thornton Canary, who spread vicious and unsupported rumors about her. Indeed, the Thornton Canary family, unlike the Kilgore and Southers married daughters, chose to buy a farm in the Brantley district five miles distant from all the other Canary families clustered together in the Ravanna area. The Thornton and Delilah Canary household seemed always a bit removed from the other Canary families.

One wonders how Grandpa James got along with the frisky—maybe risqué—teenager his youngest son had married. A few guesses, based on bits of information, may be hazarded. Since the census taker suggested that James lived with Robert and Charlotte, he may have resided with them up to his death in 1862. (There is the slight possibility that he may have been living with his son-in-law James Kilgore and his wife Lana [James's daughter], since their household listing immediately follows the name of Grandpa James.) But since the administrator for James's estate pursued Robert and Charlotte for money, livestock, and farm implements that they refused to share with other inheritors, the guess that Grandpa lived with them seems defensible. After the death of Sarah sometime in the 1850s, he may have moved into the Robert and Charlotte household, which included the three grandchildren in 1860.

13

The Canary Farm.

This sign located about five to six miles east of Princeton indicates the site where Robert and Charlotte's family resided in the late 1850s and early 1860s. It may also have been their daughter Martha's birthplace. But the text is incorrect in stating Martha was born in 1852 and that she was a "comrade" of Buffalo Bill. Etulain collection.

Did Charlotte get along with her hardworking, dependable, and loyal father-in-law? There is no evidence she did not. One wonders, then, if the rumors about Charlotte's untoward behavior, including her drunkenness and flirtations, occurred after James was gone. What seems abundantly clear is that after his death any balance in Robert and Charlotte's home disappeared, replaced with an increasing alienation from the rest of the Canary relatives in the Princeton area.

Martha was but six or seven when her family left Missouri, but she too was recalled three generations later.

Although Aikman pictures her as a profane, almost risqué pre-pubescent tomboy, one neighbor woman "remembered Jane as a nice child who played with . . . [her] children." Another recollected Martha as a lively little girl who relished frolicking with community children. Two or three schoolmates distinctly called to mind that Martha attended a "subscription school" on a nearby farm, later known as the Keith School. If she learned to read and write in the year or two she attended that log cabin school, she seems to have forgotten those lessons. (There is not a single sample of Martha/Calamity's writing as an adult.) However, if Martha's family left in 1862, she may not have attended school before leaving Princeton.

In 1862–63 a series of quick happenings pushed Martha's family out of Mercer County and sent them careening toward an increasingly desperate future in the next four or five years. A key occurrence was the death of Grandpa James in spring 1862. He had been the center pivot of determination and dependability for decades—from Ohio, to Iowa, to Missouri. The following December, Robert and Charlotte sold their farm to a neighbor. Some contemporaries recalled Robert telling them he hoped to find better land to the west.

Martha's parents, especially Charlotte, may also have felt increasingly anxious about the fiery debates surrounding the erupting Civil War in 1861–62. The political sympathies of Grandpa James and his children are not clear. James, of course, came to adulthood in Virginia, although in the area that became a free state, West Virginia, in 1863. Martha's uncle, James Thornton Canary, briefly joined local Missouri forces sympathetic to the Confederacy, but when the state moved clearly into the Union camp, he dropped out, and nothing further is evident about his involvement in the fractious war. A few vague rumors surfaced about Charlotte expressing proslavery sentiments (some called her a "secesh [secessionist] spitfire"). If those stories are true,

15

her position on slavery made her increasingly unwelcome in northern Missouri, where Republican and Union sentiments rapidly surfaced and dominated from 1862 onward. In fact, two years later President Abraham Lincoln wrote to engineer Grenville M. Dodge about the "irregular violence in Northern Missouri . . . [that was] driving away people and almost depopulating it."

Proslavery sentiments, itchy feet, and discontent with farming aside, the major reason for Robert and Charlotte's departure from Princeton lies buried in the Mercer County court records. Significantly, biographers of Calamity Jane overlooked these records until the 1990s, meaning the major reason for Martha's family abandoning Missouri remained untold. The controversies surfaced quickly after the death of Grandpa James and decisively divided his family heirs in Mercer County.

The reasons for conflict first became evident in Grandpa James's probate records, which reveal much about James's family as well as his holdings. In filing the first installments of the probate hearings, administrator Hannibal Armstrong listed the names and locations of James's children. They were Joseph, a resident of Washington or Belmont County, Ohio; Joshua, of unknown residence; Levina Canary Jones, Wheeling, Virginia; Abner, near Parkersburgh, Virginia; Lanny Canary Kilgore, Mercer County, Missouri; Rachel Ann Canary, married name unknown, residing near McConellsville, Ohio; Mary Canary Southers, Mercer County; and Robert Willson Canary, Mercer County. Revealingly, the name of James Thornton Canary is not listed. Of note, too, is that most of the older children remained in Ohio or Virginia, and most of the younger offspring moved with James to Missouri. As biographer Duncan Aikman correctly observed, "the whole situation suggests that the Canarys conducted their emigrations as a family group until Grandfather Canary died"—at least those who moved west to Iowa and then Missouri.

Even though the census of 1860 indicated that Grandpa James was without personal wealth, the probate records of Mercer County revealed otherwise. An extensive listing of James's possessions, with their estimated values listed alongside, showed that he owned livestock, farm implements, household goods, a "Family Bible" (worth $3), and "one large Testament" (50 cents). These possessions totaled $490.50. In addition, the executor claimed, before James's death in April 1861 he had loaned his son Robert about $600, over time. Moreover, James also owned $417.68 of "Specie bank notes checks etc." In all, James's personal property was estimated to be worth about $1,500 at his death.

By late 1862 but particularly in early 1863, Armstrong as executor of James's estate began pursuing Martha's parents in the courts of Mercer County. In November 1862, Armstrong leveled strong charges against Robert and Charlotte in preparation for his case in the Circuit Court proceedings of March 1863. Martha's parents were, he asserted, withholding some of James's assets. In addition to refusing to part with James's property, including farm implements, livestock, and personal effects, they refused to distribute the cash James had on hand at his death. In some way the defendant Robert Canary "got possession of the same [James's effects], and refused to deliver the same or any part thereof, to [the] plaintiff [Armstrong] though requested to do so." Since these personal assets and borrowed funds were part of James's legacy, Armstrong implied, they too should be restored to James's inheritance and be used to pay off his debts, dividing the remainder among his heirs. Approximately two months later, following up on the court's charges, Sheriff W. B. Rogers delivered in person to Robert a copy of the charges and the court's command to appear in the March 1863 session.

Robert was hailed into court on these matters several times in 1862, 1863, and 1864. But, as the proceedings revealed, the defendant "comes not." When Robert failed to appear, the court rendered its verdict against him and gave permission to Armstrong to restore funds held by him to James's estate. It was a pyrrhic victory, however; Robert and Charlotte were nowhere to be found.

Probably early in 1863, Martha's parents left Princeton for a less threatening place. After selling their farm in the previous December and receiving the sheriff's writ a few days later, Robert and Charlotte seem to have left Missouri. Had a string of bad decisions on their part led to the need to get out of town? Had they grown tired of the drudgery of farming? Were they dreaming of some kind of new and more adventurous life in the West? Or had these circumstances combined to bring on the move?

No strong evidence answers the questions. Nor is it clear if Robert, Charlotte, or both wanted to make the move. But when they decided to pull up stakes and leave, they were abandoning the Canary family's practice, going back thirty or forty years of traveling with and residing near one another. Now, they were leaving Robert's two married sisters and his brother to go west. One suspects, from a few bits of scattered evidence, that the antsy, assertive Charlotte may have voted more for the life-changing separation than Robert, who was breaking off his lifelong connections to other members of the Canary clan.

Local traditions include two stories about the Canarys' departure. One posits that she immediately headed west. The other (more likely) version says they moved north to Iowa, just across the border to Appanoose County, before venturing west the next year. Whenever the long journey began, with such high hopes, it soon turned downward into disappointment and within three or four years ended in tragedy.

The next decade of Martha's life is a virtual tabula rasa of documentation, with but a half-dozen or so verifiable footprints. What route the Canarys took west and how long the journey lasted remains a mystery. Perhaps they immediately joined a wagon train for Montana as many other Missourians and midwesterners were doing. Or, perhaps they traveled up the Oregon Trail to Utah and then embarked north. More Missourians went out on the Oregon Trail than on any other route, and there were several notable jumping-off places for the Oregon country in Missouri. Maybe they heard of the new gold strikes in the Alder Gulch boom in western Montana and headed in that direction, dreaming of a more satisfying life than they had experienced as a frustrated and rather unsuccessful farm family.

For the Canary family trip from Missouri or Iowa to Montana there are but two sources, both suspect in their dependability. One was Calamity's ghostwritten autobiography *Life and Adventures of Calamity Jane* (1896), which was undoubtedly prepared as a come-on for her appearances in a Wild West show. That eight-page pamphlet plays up the lively, arduous, and even frenetic events of her life. It also includes an armload or two of other impossible happenings. What Calamity says in this pamphlet about the western trip must be viewed in light of its publicity purposes.

She says the family spent five difficult and challenging months traveling from Missouri to Virginia City. Some times when the trails were so primitive and difficult travelers "had to lower wagons over ledges by hand with ropes" because the paths "were so rough and rugged that horses were of no use." During the trip, Martha says, she became a "remarkable good shot and fearless rider for a girl of my age." Although the details for the trip itself seem designed to exaggerate the drama and dangers of Martha/Calamity's girlhood, there is no reason to disbelieve the general if rather skimpy outline of her story about the overland trip to Montana.

Another little-known source provides the human side of the difficulties the Canarys faced in a trip for which, by experience and funding, they were patently unprepared. Boney

Earnest, a friend of Buffalo Bill Cody, recalled many years later that he encountered the Canary family near Fort Steele in Wyoming. He remembered them as pressed for cash, trying to get to the gold fields, where they could "make some money." Earnest's memories, although probably partially correct, nonetheless incorrectly date the meeting as not in 1863 or 1864 but in 1872. He also thought Martha was in her mid-teens. Since he claimed to know her later, perhaps he was mixing up the chronology of the two meetings. At any rate, it is the only glimpse of the Canary family on their way west.

In the early 1860s, miners and would-be miners were rushing to western Montana. Initial findings and expansive rumors of the new strikes were stampeding men with picks and shovels to the northern Rockies. From 1860 to 1863, hard-rock miners worked promising lodes in modern-day Idaho; from 1862 to 1865, new strikes sprang up on the eastern slopes of the Rockies. The latter discoveries, in what is now Montana, led to rushes to Bannock (July 1862), Alder Gulch/Virginia City (May 1863), Last Chance Gulch/Helena (July 1864), and Confederate Gulch/Diamond City (January 1865). Many of the new miners to Montana came from the West—from California, Colorado, and Idaho. But even more arrived from the Midwest, with Missouri furnishing more newcomers than any another state. Did the Canary family accompany one of these groups? Perhaps, although no immigrant train listed their names. The incoming Missourians gave a decided pro-Confederate cast to the Montana camps and often opposed the partisan politics of Abraham Lincoln's Republican appointees after Montana became a new territory in May 1864.

The isolation of these boomtowns and the lack of established law and order often led to violent illegal actions and equally shocking extralegal vigilante responses. Such was the case in Montana when notorious highwayman Henry Plummer, disguised as a sheriff, plundered Idaho and Mon-

Virginia City, Montana.
Virginia City was a western mining boomtown when the Canary family
arrived in this area in the mid-1860s. It became a setting of frustration and
ultimate tragedy for the Canarys. Courtesy Montana Historical Society,
MHS 956-061.

tana camps, killing those who opposed his secret and strong-
armed deeds. Wasting no time, vigilantes, after discovering
those nefarious deeds, quickly strung up Plummer and his
henchmen. About the same time as the Canary family was
arriving in Virginia City, acts of violence were roiling the
region.

The overnight and confusing appearance of ten thousand
or more newcomers in western Montana placed extraordinary pressures on the mining communities. An excess of five
thousand immigrants crowded into the Alder Gulch area
of Virginia City and its neighbor Nevada City. In 1864,
from the central or Platte route, came nearly one thousand
wagons with miners and families descending on the Virginia
City region. When Robert, Charlotte, and their children
arrived in Montana, perhaps as early as 1863 but more likely

in 1864, the mining camps were already caught up in a red-hot bonanza.

A single revealing document, startling for what it discloses, records the sudden downward spiral and quick disintegration of Martha's family in Montana. On the last day of 1864, the *Montana Post* in Virginia City carried a brief story headlined "Provision for the Destitute Poor." It highlighted the difficulties of "three little girls, who state their names to be Canary." Almost certainly Martha, her sister, and an infant in their arms, had appeared at the home of James Fergus asking for aid. As one of the three commissioners of Madison County, Fergus was in charge of aiding the poor. There was a good deal for him to do in a boom-town immersed in its own self-interests. Nor was it unusual for miners, without stable income or as the result of injuries, to find themselves in the need of help from others.

The winter of 1864–65 had turned vicious. When huge accumulations of snow blocked routes into Alder Gulch, little or no food made its way into the region. The price of flour, for example, shot up to the extravagant price of $100 per 150 pounds. As a result, the Canary family, like so many others, was in extreme need. The hungry Canary children went begging.

But the newspaper reporter boldly added much more about Martha's parents. "The father, it seems, is a gambler in Nevada [City]. The mother is a woman of the lowest grade." Then the journalists added, "A *calico slip* without any additional clothing, was all that defended the poor children from the inclemency of the weather. . . . We understand that the little ones returned to Nevada [City], where they have existed for some time." For the writer, this was "a most flagrant and wanton instance of unnatural conduct on the part of parents to their children."

What had happened? Had Robert and Charlotte, removed from the agricultural pursuits they knew but detested and now pressed by unexpected consequences, turned to dangerously different occupations? Perhaps, the riches-to-rags nightmare so typical of idealistic gold-seekers forced them into work different from what they planned. Could one imagine the phlegmatic Robert as a successful card shark? Was the reporter indicating that Charlotte had turned to prostitution? If so, what was happening to the three—or as many as six—Canary children while Dad was gambling and Mom was selling sex? Tragedy already crouched at the door of the Canary family.

One might speculate a bit about Robert and Charlotte's marriage. Neighbors and perhaps relatives in Missouri thought Robert rather ineffectual and controlled—possibly even driven—by his vivacious and assertive wife. Yet, if Calamity is right in her counting, six children were born to Robert and Charlotte in about ten years of marriage, maybe three between 1860 and 1866. Things must have been frisky—and fertile—in the Canary household.

Only Calamity's suspect autobiography of thirty years later relates what happened next. Evidently some time after the earlier newspaper story in December 1864, the Canarys, at least Charlotte, moved to Blackfoot City, Montana. There in the Ophir Gulch, north of Alder Gulch and west of Helena, a new strike in May 1865 drew boomers like a powerful magnet from other areas for full-bore labors in fresh diggings. The wild scramble for pay dirt brought hangers-on, those who mined the miners, and swelled the population to two thousand inhabitants. Calamity's 1896 account is the only solid evidence of what happened to the Canarys there. Charlotte died and was buried in Blackfoot City in 1866. No notice of Charlotte's death has surfaced in Montana's archival records, and the nearby lonely cemetery, high on a hillside overlooking the now vanished boomtown, contains no marker for Charlotte, despite other tombstones for those who expired in the 1860s.

What could Robert do with his motherless brood of young children? Vague rumors suggested he had heard that the Mormons to the south looked after their families and might take in other needy ones such as the Canarys. So, after Charlotte's death, south he went. How the financially hard-pressed Robert managed to fund the jaunt south is not clear. But tragedy, like a venomous serpent, struck again, with Robert's death in 1867 in the Salt Lake City area. Ironically, even at the world's richest center of genealogical information, there is no record of Robert or the Canary children in 1867–68.

Now Martha faced huge new challenges, without parents or a home and with the pressing responsibility of younger children. Unstable and uncertain as it was, life with Robert and Charlotte had given her a semblance of a home. Even that was gone. What could she do? How could she find a home and provide food and clothing for herself and for younger siblings?

Years later Martha/Calamity's nephew, Tobe Borner, furnished a few details about the possible actions of his aunt in the next few years. When Tobe pressed his mother Lena (Lana), Calamity's younger sister, for the story of the sisters' early life, she told him that Calamity turned to prostitution to provide for her and brother Elijah (Lige), who was probably born on the way west or in Montana. On another occasion, Tobe mentioned that the children were farmed out to Mormon families in Salt Lake City.

Ponder what Martha had experienced in her young life. First, there were the undoubted conflictive and divisive years of her parents in Missouri. Next, the exhilarating, eye-opening trip to Montana but also the growing uncertainties of a full-throttle boomtown existence. Then the twin tragedies of the deaths of her mother and father. Now, even larger challenges. What kinds of role models had Robert and Charlotte provided their oldest daughter? How had the financial and perhaps moral decline of her father impacted her? Even more important, what was the molding force of Charlotte on her daughter? If observers were right in suggesting that Charlotte was the stronger, more assertive parent, how did Martha react seeing her mother bruise and often break so many expected gender roles for nineteenth-century women? Surely Martha had seen her mother's flirtatious relations with men and perhaps knew if she marketed sex.

Before she became a teenager, Martha Canary was an orphan, without family, home, or a supporting community of friends and relatives. She had no one. Her only obvious legacies on which to rely and build were the uncertain ones of her father and mother, now gone.

At the end of 1867, Martha was only eleven—but also a survivor.

2

Finding Her Way

In the summer of 1869, a census taker discovered Martha
Canary in the out-of-the-way railroad hamlet of Piedmont,
Wyoming. His listing of her in that special census in Carter
County in western Wyoming provides one of the few solid
facts about Martha after the death of her parents in 1866–
67 and before her emergence in the Black Hills of South
Dakota in 1875–76. Indeed, in these nearly blank years of
Martha's life she had to find herself, moving from orphan to
adult, but in this arduous journey of self-definition she left
few footprints for others to follow.

Calamity's later autobiography furnishes a few helpful hints about her little-known actions. After her father's
death, she tells us, she "went to Fort Bridger during 1868,
then to Piedmont, Wyoming, with the U. P. Railroad."
Fortunately, the census taker caught up with Martha and
recorded her as living in Piedmont. It was the second census, and the only one in addition to that of 1860, in which
Martha's name was listed.

The physical and social settings of Piedmont shed illuminating light on one brief period of Martha Canary's early
life. Her lifelong tendency to be scurrying about, her frequent domiciles in half-formed and male-dominated settlements, and her repeated brash, unsettling behavior—all
these signs and symbols of Martha's later life appear early

on in Piedmont. Here, in an isolated frontier setting, at the onset of her teen years, she was beginning to make her way in an unorthodox life.

Piedmont both resembled and broke from other overnight, "hell-on-wheels" towns that sprang up along the Union Pacific Railroad in the late 1860s. The first of the transcontinental railroads was snaking across Wyoming in 1868 and 1869. Eighteen miles west and south of Fort Bridger, Piedmont, at first an out-of-touch stage station, soon became a water—and wood—refueling stop along the tracks as trains faced a steep climb up the slopes to the west. To supply the expanding charcoal needs of the railroad and nearby smelters in Wyoming and Utah, Piedmont resident Moses Byrne constructed five bee-hive shaped kilns. They remain to this day as silent emblems of Piedmont's earlier importance. In the late 1860s, a tent town leaped into existence, quickly replaced by homes of woodsmen, railroad laborers, other workers, and members of two or three large Mormon farm and ranch families. When the census enumerator arrived in summer 1869, he encountered a jerry-built small town of nearly twenty houses and more than ninety residents.

The social makeup of Piedmont reveals much about one of Martha's early homes after the death of her parents. Of the town's residents, seventy-seven were male, mostly single laborers, and of the sixteen women, nine were married, with six of the other females as younger members of families. Only "Martha Canary," as the census records, was unmarried and without an immediate family.

The census provides a few more details about Martha. It confirms that she was born in Missouri, and that by summer of 1869, she had been in Piedmont for five months and intended to remain as a resident. Revealingly, Martha's age is given as fifteen, not thirteen. She probably added the two years because no one would know her real age, and, more importantly, her lifestyle undoubtedly badly bruised

Wyoming Census, Carter County, 1869.

The census taker caught up with Martha Canary (sixth name down) in the small railroad town of Piedmont in western Wyoming in the summer of 1869. She was working for Emma Alton. Her age is falsely given as fifteen, probably Martha's exaggeration in order to pass as an older young woman. Courtesy Wyoming State Archives.

society's expectations for a new female teenager. Although the census does not list another member of the Canary family, a false local tradition circulated that Joseph [*sic*] Canary, Martha's father, had been killed in a Piedmont saloon and buried in an unmarked grave just outside town.

Much later, in the 1940s and 1950s, two elderly gentlemen recalled Martha at Fort Bridger and Piedmont. Both remembered that in Piedmont she lived in a boardinghouse operated by Mrs. Emma Alton. A thirty-one-year-old immigrant from England whose full name was Saria Neeley Andrews, Emma was the mother of two sons from a previous marriage. She is listed in the census as Emma Alton and her husband, Edward Alton, as a laborer in Piedmont. Although the Altons appear to be man and wife in the census, her great-grandson says they did not marry until 1873. Emma Alton is listed immediately after Martha in the census report.

One of the elderly men, Charles Andrews of Scottsbluff, Nebraska, recalled Martha as his babysitter in Piedmont. His mother, Emma Andrews Alton, had "hired her [Martha] to tend me." But Martha's actions were upsetting. "She spent most evenings dancing with soldiers and finally a neighbor told of seeing her dressed in a soldier's uniform at some party. Mother blew up and fired her," Andrews reminisced. Since Ed Alton served at Fort Bridger before he moved to Piedmont, he and Emma may have been instrumental in finding a home for the new teenager. The other man, James Regan, knew Martha in both Fort Bridger and Piedmont. He remembered that Mrs. Alton had "mothered" Martha in Piedmont.

The months—or perhaps nearly a year—at Piedmont reveal an emerging pattern in Martha's formative years. Alone, barely in her teens, and without any education or training, she was like a modernday homeless waif. She had to rely on the kindness and generosity of others. Although Martha evidently tended children and worked in the Alton boardinghouse, she was unable to adopt the family. Her unorthodox and unruly behavior had alienated Emma Alton. In fact, in later years, despite strong evidence to the contrary, Mrs. Alton asserted that she had had nothing to do with Martha Canary-cum–Calamity Jane. Quite possibly, Calamity's even more notorious actions later on were embarrassing to a woman who had tried, unsuccessfully, to rein in an unruly teenager. Martha's untoward actions were equally alienating to other women and men who attempted to befriend her. Early on as a young adult, she was already following her mother's independent model, but without a family or an occupation for support.

While at Piedmont, Martha may well have witnessed a memorable event that transpired on the Union Pacific Railroad. It happened in early May 1869. U.P. railroad leaders, including vice president Thomas Clark Durant, were on their way to celebrate the completion of the transcontinental line at Promontory Summit in northern Utah. Durant and others were riding in the luxurious car built for Abraham Lincoln (he never rode in it, but it was used in his funeral train) when the special was forced to an unexpected stop in Piedmont. An angry crowd of three hundred unpaid tie cutters and wood haulers waylaid the train to gain their back wages. A quick, worried telegram to the U.P. headquarters in the East brought partial funding, and the railroad moguls were released to go on to the festivities. It was a dramatic happening in little Piedmont that Martha probably observed.

After the Piedmont interlude, Martha disappeared, for the most part, from the scene for several months. She is not listed in the 1870 census, and no contemporary newspaper records her doings. There are persisting rumors, however, that after Piedmont—or even just before—Martha landed in the mining boomtowns springing up in western Wyoming. Continuing rumors of gold discoveries brought as many as two thousand people to such areas as South Pass City, Atlantic City, and Miner's Delight (also known as Hamilton City).

Martha Canary may have been among those dashing to the newly opening mines and towns. Local historians posit that Major Patrick A. Gallagher, who had served earlier at Fort Bridger, came to the mines in 1868 with his young wife Frances (Fannie). It is said that the Gallaghers found Martha alone at "the overland forts," "adopted" her, and brought her to South Pass City. But when *Chicago Tribune* reporter James Chisholm visited South Pass City and met with the Gallaghers in the summer of 1868, he referred to the few women in the area but did not mention Martha, leading some to doubt that she was there. One longtime resident of South Pass City, interviewed fifty years later, had a different view, recalling that Martha was with the Gallaghers. Martha "was quite a nice and likeable looking young woman even while she was in South Pass," the woman remembered, "but she finally ran away from them [the Gallaghers]." During her stay with the couple, Martha did not attend the school Fannie Gallagher was leading. Martha, the interviewee continued, "was not exactly wild for she was only a young girl at this time."

Still, Martha's actions were sufficiently alienating to cause problems. As local historian Nolie Mumey concluded, Fannie Gallagher "wanted to give . . . [Martha] a home and train her to become a member of the family," but she "did not like the discipline. One day Mrs. Gallagher gave her a thrashing, and she objected so strenuously that a miner's committee investigated the incident. As a consequence Mrs. Gallagher refused to have any more to do with her." After hearing of these problems, "the miners took up a collection and sent . . . [Martha] to the railroad." Perhaps the brief stay in South Pass City and Miner's Delight came between Martha's days at Fort Bridger and her months at Piedmont, but no contemporary newspapers mention her. Indeed, no dependable chronology of her life is available in the years between 1867 and the early 1870s.

For the most part, Martha was off-scene from 1869 to 1874. These silent spaces in her biography in the early 1870s, nonetheless, illuminate aspects of her life and times. As a teenager she had achieved little that was newsworthy. Frontier journalists rarely paid much attention to young people—unless their deeds led to a crime or a spectacular achievement. A gender bias also dampened down stories about young girls and women. Men's actions dominated western newspapers. True, as more than a few biographers and historians suggest, Martha was already battering social mores by dressing as a man (illegal in many communities), drinking, and maybe selling sex. But these untoward actions, however repugnant to many contemporaries, did not produce headlines. Not until Martha was transformed into Calamity Jane in 1875 and thereafter did her aberrant conduct play across frontier newspaper pages.

Off scene, however, Martha's life was unfolding, particularly through her links to her sister, Lena (Lana), and her brother, Elijah (Lige). Most of this little-known story comes from Tobe Borner, Martha's nephew and the son of Lena and John Borner. Unfortunately, his narrative of the Canary family and Martha and Lena is a mish-mash of facts and errors. In later years, Tobe wrote to several inquirers wanting information about Martha/Calamity Jane, the Canary family, and his mother Lena. Because no one else had said much about the Canary family and their coming west, his writings in the 1940s became a major source of misinformation about the pre-1867 years of the Canary family.

The Canarys came from Ohio, as part of a Mormon train, Tobe told several questioners. The father, Elijah [sic], was a Methodist minister but had studied the Mormons and become a member of their faith. The family, consisting of father, mother, and children (Martha, Lena, and Lige), were on their way west when an Indian attack led to the death of the parents. Martha helped rescue the family and drove their wagon into Salt Lake City, sold it, arranged for homes for Lena and Lige, and began working there in a boardinghouse.

Nearly all this information diverged markedly from what census and other more reliable sources had to say about these matters. Tobe told others that his mother gave him this information before she died when he was eleven years old. Assuming that the information Tobe relayed was what Lena told him, several questions emerge. Why had Lena misinformed her son and the rest of the family? She was about seven when her mother died in Montana, and one year older when Robert died in Utah. She was old enough to recall the lives of those parents and their fate, so far removed from the story Tobe told. Even if she did not know or recall that Robert gambled and that Charlotte might have turned to prostitution, she would have remembered, surely, that her father was not a Methodist minister or a Mormon, and that he and Charlotte had not died in an Indian attack. Had Lena, as a married woman in a stable marriage trying to raise respectable children, embelished a story that made her parents more acceptable to her and her children? That would seem to be the case. More than a century later, that story misled her descendants away from the facts of Robert and Charlotte and the true story of the earliest years of Martha and Lena.

Other parts of Tobe's story seem more believable. When the Canary children arrived in Salt Lake City, Martha arranged for homes for Lena and Lige to stay. She then went to work in a boardinghouse. A bit later, perhaps about 1871 or 1872 (Tobe does not give exact dates), Martha moved to the mining towns of South Pass City and Miner's Delight, where she worked in a hotel for merchant James Kime.

While in the Wyoming mineral boomtowns, Martha met John Borner. An immigrant from Germany, Borner had worked in the railroad towns before moving to the mining camps, where he served as a transporter, carrying goods back and forth between the mines and Salt Lake City. After Borner broke his leg in an accident, Martha helped set it and nursed him back to health. When he told her he had been asked to bring a woman back to Fort Washakie as a worker and companion for the wife of Indian agent James I. Patten, Martha urged him to take Lena to fill that need. She also asked Borner to bring Lige back from Salt Lake. While Lena would go up to Fort Washakie, Lige would stay with Martha in South Pass City or Miner's Delight. The agreement was made for Lena, but it was decided that Lige would stay at the farm/ranch that Borner was establishing near the new town of Lander. After becoming acquainted with Lena, John maintained a well-traveled road between his farm and Fort Washakie. Romance had blossomed, and Lena and John were married in August 1875. Eventually, they had seven children before Lena died from a farm accident in 1888, at just twenty-nine years of age.

Meanwhile, Lige worked for John Borner, but that did not go smoothly. Still a teenager (his birth is given as 1860, 1862, or 1868—the last date obviously wrong since his mother died in 1866), Lige was a half-wild boy-man. Already, he rode like a skilled cowboy and knew how to handle a gun. As Tobe Borner put it, "Lige would jump onto . . . [a] horse's back from the top rail of the fence and stay on as long as he could." He and his friends would frenzy the range stock by driving them up "against the corral fence." After only three months with John Borner, Lige "had taught all the horses to buck, and since Borner was no bronco buster, he didn't appreciate it."

Truth to tell, Martha and Lige's lives were running in different directions from Lena's. If Lena married a respectable immigrant businessman and farmer and began a large family, Martha and her younger brother never found such stability in their lives. As we shall see, Martha became a wanderer, rarely able to stay in one place for more than a few weeks or months. The same peripatetic pattern defined Lige's life, although he seems to have stayed with John and Lena Borner "for two or three years." Without an education or occupational training, Lige worked as an itinerant farmworker, but before long got himself into trouble in western

Wyoming, spending several years in prison in Wyoming and later another stint in Idaho for a crime there. Even though Tobe Borner claimed that "when Lige was about 17 years old he left for the Klondyke . . . and we never heard of him again," the Borner family may well have been sprucing up another story to make it more palatable for the family, as they had done for the early Canary narrative. The story of Lige's arrest appeared in the Evanston, Wyoming, newspaper, and surely the family would have heard that Lige was in trouble.

In her autobiography, prepared about twenty-five years later, Calamity summarized her life between 1870 and 1875 in a few sentences. As usual, the details are a variegated mix of the improbable, unadulterated stretchers, and helpful information. Her claims of having served as George Custer's scout in Arizona in 1870 and 1871, at the age of fourteen and fifteen, are a bald falsehood since Custer was not in the Southwest during this period. One must also quickly dismiss her brags of being with Generals Custer, Nelson Miles, and Alfred Terry because they were not involved in the "Muscle Shell or Nursey Pursey [*sic*] Indian outbreak" at this time. A pattern gradually emerges in the autobiography that lessens its value: as Calamity prepared to travel with a dime museum show in 1896, she needed stories that ostensibly documented her life as a sensational woman of the Old West. Her autobiography wilded up her life by placing her in events in which she did not participate and stationed her next to military leaders and Indian fighters she did not know, let alone accompany.

But one should not dismiss everything in Calamity's very brief life story. We know she was in Piedmont, credible family stories place her in the Wyoming mining boomtowns, and her mentions of other places have credibility. Her references to stays, even if brief ones, in Fort Bridger and Fort Steele, and her allusions to Fort Russell and Fort Sanders add entirely believable—if not entirely provable—information.

In fact, stories exist about Martha visiting some of these places. Boney Earnest, who had asserted that he met the Canary family on its way to Montana, claimed he also saw Martha later in the Rawlins–Fort Steele area of Wyoming. Martha was looking for employment, Earnest reported, and he helped her land a place for a few months. She soon left, only to return a bit later. Martha "knocked around there for a little while and got pretty tough and some old woman was there and she stayed with her . . . and finally fell from grace altogether."

Another early Wyoming resident recalled seeing Martha in the early 1870s. Young farmer-rancher John Hunton, in his journal published a half century later, reported that Martha, as well as several other youthful prostitutes, came to a "hog ranch" near Fort Laramie to serve the soldiers. Not surprisingly, that and other similar activities went unrecorded in Calamity's autobiography and her later newspaper interviews.

A pattern was emerging in Martha's travels in the late 1860s and early 1870s. She had begun in Salt Lake City and then proceeded northeast to western Wyoming and Fort Bridger, Piedmont, and the mining boomtowns. The next stops were farther east in Rawlins and Fort Steele. Stories surfaced decades later that she traveled on to Kansas cowtowns and met Wild Bill there, but they are yarns without much substance and often depict Martha, incorrectly, as already twenty or older.

Stronger evidence for Martha's presence in Cheyenne in the early 1870s is manifest. Her brief stays there signaled a change in directions in Martha's unfolding journey. Thus far in the 1870s she had moved east, backtrailing along the Union Pacific line and visiting nearby forts and towns. Cheyenne was a natural stopping-off place. Less than a decade old by the mid-1870s, Cheyenne still betrayed its nascent origins as a railroad town. In the 1870s it became Wyoming's territorial capital and largest city, wobbling between

Early Cheyenne.

Martha Canary, becoming known as Calamity Jane, was in and out of Cheyenne, perhaps as early as the late 1860s and certainly by the early 1870s. Besides living and working there for short periods, it was her launching point for the Deadwood Stage route and her eventual arrival in Deadwood in 1876. Courtesy Wyoming State Archives (8784).

two and three thousand in population. But it retained its reputation as a wide-open frontier community, struggling to retain social and economic balance and to survive. Later, Martha herself added a revealing description of early Cheyenne in telling a reporter: "When I first came to Cheyenne there was not a respectable shelter in the place . . . and the proprietor of tent was a lucky person indeed." Then, unexpectedly, rumors of dramatic gold discovery in Dakota's Black Hills rippled through Cheyenne in the mid-1870s, redirecting attentions to the north.

Martha was already in the area before the news of the possible Black Hills strikes invaded Cheyenne. Once in Cheyenne, perhaps as early as 1868 and surely by the early 1870s, Martha followed a life's pattern gradually coming into focus: after temporary jobs in dance halls in Cheyenne, she headed out for new sites, new towns, new adventures. Already, Martha was living out the first stages of a lifetime journey of campfollowing. In the early 1870s, the new adventures were north to the forts above Cheyenne, particularly the sites at Fort Russell (1867) and Fort Laramie (1834). Soldiers were stationed there for protection against Indians.

Martha migrated, it is thought, to these areas in 1873 and 1874. John Hunton, the frontier entrepreneur noted above, reported Martha's presence at "hog ranches" near the forts. Hunton, who disliked the mythic Calamity Jane who emerged later in popular mediums, spoke of Martha as an entertainer and part-time prostitute. Two or three observers placed her specifically at the Coffey and Cuny Three Mile road or hog ranch near Fort Laramie. Hunton's assertions, from a close-at-hand observer, were the first explicit but nonetheless distant evidence that Martha was selling sex while still a teenager. But that could have happened earlier. As we have seen, Lena had reportedly berated Martha for her antisocial behavior, and the older sister (by then known as Calamity Jane) had fired back that she had turned to prostitution to support Lena and Lige after their parents' deaths. If true, that meant Martha might have been engaging in sexual relations about the time she became a teenager.

Whatever the truth about those accusations and defenses, Martha's life was at an unexpected crossroads in 1875. Even before the name-changing events that took her to the Black Hills in 1875–76, Martha had left off her west-to-east rambling and was now looking and stumbling north, physically and metaphorically.

In spring 1875, Martha made her first trip to the Black Hills. Her excursion there was part of a series of historical events stretching back to 1868 and beyond. In that year the U.S. government made a treaty with the Sioux, allowing the Indians a large reservation in what became western South Dakota. Six years later in the summer of 1874, George Custer marched through the region scouting the terrain and gathering information. When his troops reported scattered traces of pay dirt, gold-hungry prospectors urged the government to throw open the Black Hills for prospecting. More than a few prospectors rushed, illegally, into the Hills to search for gold. In 1874–76, the federal government, under President U. S. Grant's indecisive leadership, seemed puzzled about what to do with the Black Hills. Even though most prospectors in the area (there may have been as many as fifteen hundred in the Hills by August 1875) were hustled out of the region as interlopers, the army, following the wobbly guidance of the Grant administration, failed to protect Indians from the mining invaders. Behind the scenes, the Washington politicos, under pressures from ambitious and hungry westerners, seemed bent on changing the terms of the 1868 treaty rather than holding to its stipulations.

The Newton-Jenney Expedition to the Black Hills in 1875 resulted from the inconsistent and reversed decisions in the nation's capital. Sponsored by the Office of Indian Affairs and the Department of War, the expedition was to provide a scientific study of the Black Hills region and, particularly, examine its rumored mineral deposits. Inadvertently, the expedition also supplied the vehicle to bring Martha Canary-cum–Calamity Jane to the Black Hills in summer 1875.

The expedition left Fort Laramie on 25 May and returned to the fort in mid-October. Under the leadership of geologist Walter P. Jenney and his assistant Henry Newton, the scientists and their support staff, numbering seventeen, were escorted by Lieutenant Colonel R. I. Dodge and his more than four hundred soldiers. Among the scientists was Dr. Valentine T. McGillycuddy, serving as topographer for the expedition. One of the teamsters was Harry (Sam) Young, later a bartender in Deadwood at the time of Wild Bill Hickok's assassination. "Mac," a reporter with the *Chicago Inter-Ocean*, was one of the five journalists traveling with the expedition. All three—McGillycuddy, Young, and Mac—wrote about Martha/Calamity Jane and avowed that she tailed along with the expedition through much of the summer.

The three writers referred to Martha as "Calamity" or "Calamity Jane," suggesting that she became thus identified just before or during the first days of the trip. In her autobiography, Calamity made the bogus assertion that she became Calamity Jane as a result of her heroic actions in saving a "Capt Egan" after he was badly wounded in a fight with "Nursey Pursey" (Nez Perce) Indians. After she lifted the injured Egan onto her horse—"in front of me"—and rode to safety, he "laughingly said: 'I name you Calamity Jane, the heroine of the plains.'" Obviously not, since Calamity gets the dates and details wrong, and Egan later responded that there was not an iota of truth in Calamity's tale. It is more likely that Martha's unorthodox, even alienating behavior resulted in the new nickname. Truth to tell, no one knows when and exactly why she became Calamity Jane. But once christened with the new name, Martha Canary disappeared. Few in the following century knew her real name or her early life story.

Harry Young in his book *Hard Knocks* (1915), published forty years later, and McGillycuddy's account, *McGillycuddy, Agent* (1941), pieced together from the doctor's notes by his second wife, also deal with Calamity's participation in the Black Hills Expedition. Indeed, McGillycuddy's story so resembles Young's that some scholars think the doctor— or his wife—followed too closely the teamster-bartender's narrative. But both books provide solid evidence about Calamity in the summer of 1875.

The two accounts go awry, however, in their handling of Calamity's early years. McGillycuddy virtually repeats what Young wrote about Calamity's beginning life in 1860 at Fort Laramie as Jane Dalton, the infant daughter of soldier Dalton and his wife Jane. After his discharge, Dalton took his wife and infant daughter to his hay ranch about 120 miles from the fort. Tragically, an Indian attack ended the lives of the parents and left little Jane an orphan. A Sergeant Bassett and his wife adopted the child, and she grew up a "child of the regiment" at the fort. McGillycuddy closely followed Young's story in a letter to the *Rapid City Journal* on 1 October 1924. The doctor's good word was so valued that his version of Calamity's origins became gospel in and around the fort. Repeating this version in her biography in 1941, McGillycuddy's second wife, in a revealing footnote, indicated that her husband had heard this story about Calamity from Colonel Dodge and members of the Fourteenth Infantry. And fending off attacks on this version, Mrs. Gillycuddy added, "Whatever evidence has appeared to prove this story untrue, the Doctor said she was known to everyone in 1875 as Jane Dalton." Perhaps the doctor fully and correctly followed local folklore in the Fort Laramie area, but, as we have seen, the Dalton origins story is wide of the factual information in censuses and other more dependable sources. Unfortunately, the Dalton story stayed in front of many biographers dealing with Wyoming–South Dakota areas and kept them from finding out the more reliable information in the census and Princeton, Missouri, records.

McGillycuddy rehearses Calamity's attempts to join the expedition. She first asked Dodge if she could go along, but he refused. Then she came to the doctor to see if he would aid in her mission. When he begged off, she sauntered off, evidently with an alternative plan in mind.

Calamity then dressed as a soldier and surreptitiously became part of Dodge's command. Enamored with a Sergeant Shaw, she traveled with the troops. At first, she seemed safe in her subterfuge. The soldiers protected her anonymity. But one day while crossing the camp grounds she met an officer of German heritage, a martinet of the first order, and promptly saluted him. The salute was quickly returned. When soldiers witnessing the exchange chuckled too loudly, the officer demanded an explanation. They told him he had just saluted Calamity Jane, a woman. Angry, he quickly reported the embarrassing incident, and Calamity was tossed out.

But what could be done? The expedition was now sixty miles from the fort. Calamity could not be left adrift; Indians threatened nearby. Two versions of the story follow. McGillycuddy says Calamity would reappear several times, be thrown out, and then sneak back. It became a repeated game. Keep soldierly order but look the other way. Young counters with another version. Calamity, having been tossed from the soldiers, approached the teamsters and asked if she could not join them. The wagonmaster agreed, and she often rode with Young in his wagon. She helped with the cooking for the teamsters. McGillycuddy adds that it "was useless to order her out of any one camp, since she easily slipped into another. She was not quarrelsome. She cared for sick soldiers, mended their clothes, and continued to be a valuable though unauthorized addition to the expedition." The doctor was dead center in observing that Calamity "was crazy for adventure." He might have been right too in stating that "as for morals, she didn't know the meaning of the word."

Two other sources on the expedition merit mention. Revealingly, Calamity did not specifically note the Black Hills Expedition in her autobiography. She was with soldiers in the Black Hills in 1874 and 1875, writes Calamity, because the federal government had sent them there "to

First photograph of Calamity Jane.
This photo of Calamity, by photographer A.
Guerin, was taken in 1875 at French Creek (Dakota
Territory) near Camp Harney. Guerin was a photo-
grapher with the Newton-Jenney expedition to the
Black Hills, which Calamity surreptitiously joined
in late spring 1875. It is the first known photograph
of Martha Canary just as she was becoming known
as Calamity Jane. Courtesy J. Leonard Jennewein
Collection, McGovern Library, Dakota Wesleyan
University.

protect the lives of the miners and settlers in that section,"
and she "remained there until fall of 1875." This assertion
is incorrect, of course, since the soldiers in 1875 were sent
to protect the scientists on the Jenney-Newton Expedition,
but that, evidently, was too mundane for the Wild West
purposes of her autobiography. Nor does Calamity mention
Col. Dodge, Dr. McGillycuddy, or teamster Harry Young.
Or that a photographer took her picture in July 1875 near
Lower French Creek, the first extant picture of Martha just
becoming Calamity Jane.

Thomas C. MacMillan, or "Mac," the journalist from the *Chicago Inter-Ocean*, was more specific. In early July he wrote that a young woman with the "high latitude nomenclature" of "Calamity" had "followed the expedition from the first till now." She had the reputation, he continued, "of being a better horse-back rider, [and] mule and bullwhacker (driver) and a more unctious coiner of English, and not the Queen's pure either, than any (other) man in the command." Mac had to "confess," too, that Calamity's "costume . . . is remarkably similar to that worn by Uncle Sam's boys, and it does not appear to be the custom here for ladies to ride as they do further east."

J. R. Lane, officially acting assistant surgeon of the expedition, provided another glimpse of Calamity's character. On the Newton-Jenney journey, she was taking along "her brother, a lad of 16, whom she supports," Lane wrote. That meant Calamity was probably looking after Elijah, who was likely a bit younger than sixteen since he did not appear in the 1860 census. More revealingly, Lane's article for a Chicago newspaper in June 1875 made clear that Calamity was trying to shepherd her younger brother even as she was traipsing along with the Black Hills expedition.

Accounts differ about whether Calamity completed the trip with the group. McGillycuddy thought so, but others reported that she was sent back to Fort Laramie in July. Whatever the truth of the matter, Calamity was now appearing on a wider stage. For example, Captain Jack Crawford, another correspondent traveling with the expedition, wrote a few months later that "a woman . . . accompanied the soldiers last summer. They called her Calamity Jane." He mentioned also that a mining claim close to Custer City was named "Calamity Bar" but failed to note that a nearby small mountain had become "Calamity Peak."

The increasing attention being paid to the Black Hills and northern plains and conflicts between miners and Indians there opened the door for more Calamity Jane escapades to the north. Even though the Fort Laramie Treaty of 1868 had set aside the Black Hills and surrounding areas as Sioux Country, more than a few groups of whites coveted the area. Legally and morally, the Hills belonged to the Indians, but that did not keep the crescendo of white expansionism and military-Indian competitions from continually mounting in the seven years from 1868 to 1875. Caving in to these increasing pressures, the Grant administration in November 1875, encouraged by cabinet officials and military leaders, came to direction-changing decisions about the Black Hills and adjacent areas. Washington sent out a proclamation that all Indians must come to reservations or government agencies by 31 January 1876; unless they did so, they were to be considered hostiles and hunted down. Not surprisingly, many Indians did not follow these commands, so military forces were ordered to round up Natives outside the agencies and bring them, by force, onto the reservations. Among those sent out was Gen. George Crook.

A veteran of the Civil War and frontier conflicts with Indians in the Pacific Northwest and Southwest, Crook came to the Department of the Platte in the winter and spring of 1876 and became part of the pincher movement launched against the Sioux and their allies. In February Crook gathered nearly nine hundred officers, enlistees, scouts, and civilians at Fort Fetterman, eighty miles to the north and west of Fort Laramie. On 1 March the command, known as the Big Horn and Yellowstone Expedition, set forth up the Bozeman Trail, with eighty wagons of supplies. They were headed north toward southeastern Montana, the Powder River country, just west of the Black Hills. Murderous weather, with disastrous blizzards and temperatures well below zero, was perhaps a more dangerous enemy than the Indians. On 17 March, Crook's forces under the command of Col. Joseph J. Reynolds engaged the Indians. The fight was a disaster for the troops. Even though the Indian village was destroyed, the army succeeded in alienating the Cheyenne there and drove them into the arms of the Sioux. Even the Indians' ponies, captured early in the conflict, were lost in an Indian counter raid. Disgusted with what he considered Reynolds's inept leadership, Crook retreated to Fort Fetterman and later filed charges against Reynolds.

Calamity Jane was with the expedition in March 1876. It was the second installment of her several appearances in 1875–76 that further catapulted her from obscurity as Martha Canary to national notoriety as Calamity Jane. She was as busy as a barnstorming performer from March to August of 1876.

Calamity's specific roles in these adventures are hazy. In her autobiography, she provided useful general details but also made wild, unsubstantiated claims about her actions. "In spring of 1876, we were ordered north with General Crook to join Gen'ls Miles, Terry and Custer at Big Horn River." Those comments ring partially true, although Calamity was not part of any "orders." Then come the dramatic stretchers: "During this march I swam the Platte river at Fort Fetterman as I was the bearer of important dispatches. I had a ninety mile ride to make, wet and cold. I contracted a severe illness and was sent back in Gen. Crook's ambulance to Fort Fetterman where I laid in the hospital for fourteen days." Most of the account is exaggerated; no evidence exists that Calamity carried important messages, that she was any kind of central figure in the march, or that she was in the hospital for two weeks. Yet she was with Crook, traveling through the terrible weather.

Other observers provide less sensational, more mundane information about Calamity's part in the Crook expedition. Just before Crook's command left on its march north, a man at the Chugwater Ranch, about fifty miles above Cheyenne, wrote in his diary: "Calamity Jane is hear going up with the troops. I think there is trouble ahead." "Moccasin Joe"

Howard, an officer with Crook, also remembered Calamity among the teamsters. One must conclude, although with limited evidence, that Calamity secretly joined the expedition, not as a scout as she claimed, but perhaps as a teamster or bullwhacker, or even as a campfollower or prostitute. It was a quick trip since the Crook campaigners had retreated back to Fort Fetterman in about a month.

Calamity's visitation schedule roared into high gear in the next four months, up and down the Black Hills–Cheyenne axis. She evidently traveled back to the Black Hills shortly after Crook's unsuccessful mission in March. At least, the diary of David Montgomery Holmes, a traveler between Deadwood and Rapid City, contains the following entry for 5 May: "We met a party today coming in from Cheyenne, one of the party was 'Calamity Jane,' and camped for the night." Another source, in some ways more distant and less satisfactory, places Calamity in Custer City in late April, headed toward Rapid City and eventually Deadwood early the next month. Teamster Jesse Brown recalled many years later that, while stopping over in Custer, he observed "a government mule outfit [come] in and Calamity was driving one of the teams." She was "dressed in a buckskin suit with two Colts six shooters on a belt." Brown remembered her as "about the toughest looking human that I ever saw." And then Brown provided one of the earliest and then-rare descriptions of Calamity's excessive drinking: "The first place that attracted her attention was a saloon, where she was soon made blind as a bat from looking through the bottom of a glass." Also in April, Calamity may have seen—or more likely heard about—the horrendous outcome of an Indian attack on and the mutilations of the Metz family and their black servant near Custer City. Some think Calamity's pronounced anti-Indian views may have been sharply augmented as a result of these vicious killings.

By the end of May, the fast-traveling Calamity was back in Cheyenne. Although she claimed in her autobiography that she remained out of action because of a protracted illness, the District Court records of Laramie County in Wyoming tell a much different story. On 24 May 1876, Maggie Smith (alias Calamity Jane) was indicted for stealing a bundle of clothes and other personal effects three months earlier. A bench warrant, charging Calamity with "grand larceny . . . against the peace and dignity of the Territory of Wyoming," was issued the next day. Arrested but pleading not guilty, Calamity was jailed in Cheyenne. After several days of proceedings, including testimonies from the alleged victims, the jury on 8 June declared "the Defendant. Not. Guilty," and she was discharged.

Calamity immediately and joyfully celebrated her release. She paraded down Cheyenne's streets in a gown loaned to her by the wife of one of the sheriff's staff, flourishing her freedom. Two days later, off she went on a new adventure to the north. "Greatly rejoiced over her release from durance vile," the *Cheyenne Daily Leader* reported, Calamity gained access to a horse and buggy and headed for Fort Russell. But, in a story published on 20 June and entitled "Jane's Jamboree," the newspaper divulged that Calamity had overindulged in "frequent and liberal potations" that were "completely befogging her not very clear brain." She pushed the horse on to Chug, fifty miles away, without stopping. Then, "continuing to imbibe the bug juice at close intervals and in large quantities," Calamity trotted on to Fort Laramie, ninety miles farther up the trail.

Calamity's autobiography vaguely refers to accompanying military expeditions in "the spring of 1876," but she does not specifically mention Gen. Crook's second expedition north in June 1876. In late May, Crook pulled together another force and again headed up the Bozeman Trail. He was part of a larger but not tightly knit pincher strategy attempting to corral the Sioux, with Gens. John Gibbon from the west and Terry and Custer from the east providing the other forces to squeeze the Indians into submission.

Calamity Jane as General Crook's Scout.

This photograph, probably taken in 1876 or 1877, sometimes appeared with the caption "Gen. Crook's Scout." Another version of the photograph has Calamity seated and holding her rifle. This was the second photograph taken of Calamity. Courtesy J. Leonard Jennewein Collection, McGovern Library, Dakota Wesleyan University.

By 14 June, Crook was at Goose Creek, near present-day Sheridan, Wyoming, poised to push north.

About this time in mid-June, as the best evidence attests, Calamity joined the Crook forces. Capt. Anson Mills reported that "in organizing the wagon train at Fort Fetterman, the wagonwaster had unintentionally employed a female teamster, but she was not discovered until we neared Fort Reno, when she was suddenly arrested, and placed in improvised female attire under guard." Mills also admits that Calamity greatly embarrassed him when, the day she was taken in, Calamity blurted out "There is Colonel Mills, he knows me!" Perhaps the connotation of "knows" upset Mills most, since he was a married man. Although Mills's chronology seems wrong, he clearly places Calamity with Crook's command.

So does Capt. John Bourke, then a lieutenant with Crook. "It was whispered that one of our teamsters was a woman," Bourke wrote in his book *On the Border with Crook*. It was "no other than 'Calamity Jane,' a character famed in border history; she had donned raiment of the alleged rougher sex, and was skinning mules with the best of them." But, he added, Calamity was eventually discovered because "she didn't cuss her mules with the enthusiasm to be expected." Station master John Hunton, an often reliable source, also recalled that Calamity and "other women of the same character . . . smuggled out with . . . [Crook's] command and remained with it until found out and ordered back."

None of these sources substantiates Calamity's claim to have served as a scout for Crook, a claim that became a central support for the mythologized Calamity emerging in the late 1870s. But Frank Grouard, in charge of some of Crook's scouts, did allege that he hired Calamity to scout when several other scouts had to leave the command. Although no official record confirms Grouard's remembrance and others point to errors in his account, his assertion cannot be easily and entirely dismissed.

Whatever Calamity's exact role with the Crook troops, she was not long with them. Her social schedule for June was tight and full. Making good time north after her release in Cheyenne, she moved on quickly to Fort Laramie and to Fort Fetterman. Calamity probably arrived at Crook's camp shortly before or after his unsuccessful Battle of Rosebud on 17 June. If she served as a scout, strong evidence suggests she was sent back with wounded soldiers on 21 June.

Some on-the-ground participants largely discounted Calamity's role with Crook in June 1876. Captain Jack Crawford, who joined Crook's troops after the Rosebud, and after interviewing scouts and other participants, countered rumors of Calamity as a scout as well as later heroic stories about her actions. He claimed writers had not wanted to criticize Calamity while she lived, but one year after her death in 1903, he wanted to clear out the romantic and sensational underbrush that had grown up around her. His convictions about the events of June 1876 were brief and direct: Calamity "was never employed as a scout by General Crook, who gave her no recognition whatever, except to order her out of camp when he discovered she was a camp follower."

Despite the reservations of Capt. Jack and other naysayers, legends about Calamity as "the female scout" quickly took off and expanded in the next few years. A widely circulated book by journalist Horatio N. Maguire, *The Black Hills and American Wonderland* (1877), was already hailing Calamity as a well-known scout for Crook and other frontier military leaders.

But Calamity's participations in expeditions to the north earlier in 1875–76 were as sideshow affairs compared to the big tent appearance that awaited her in midsummer 1876. Wild Bill Hickok was soon to appear, and he accompanied, albeit reluctantly, Calamity onto a much larger stage.

3

Negotiating Deadwood

They were on their way to the new booming Eldorado of Deadwood in the fabled Black Hills. Composed of about a half-dozen stout wagons packed with supplies, and containing enthusiastic men overflowing with hoped-for possibilities, the pack train headed north out of Cheyenne in late June 1876.

During the late spring, James Butler "Wild Bill" Hickok, his partner Charles "Colorado Charlie" Utter, Charlie's brother Steve, and brothers Joseph "White Eye" and Charley Anderson had been planning their two-week trip of 290 miles to the Black Hills. Charlie and Steve Utter were hoping to launch a transportation line between Cheyenne and Deadwood, and the newly married Hickok dreamed of making a strike in Deadwood that would help him support his new wife, Agnes Lake Thatcher, a circus owner and performer of some note.

For Calamity Jane, the Hickok-Utter caravan became the vehicle that carried her to the center stage of a romantic, sensationalized Old West. The rhythm of her life, already in uncertain high gear in June 1876, whirled into overdrive in the coming months. Although meeting the Hickok-Utter group in early July as a result of entirely unexpected circumstances, Calamity's encounter led to a more public and dramatic life. Her reputation as a notorious young woman of the Old West zipped to the forefront in July and August 1876. By fall of 1877, she had become a nationally known character.

The Hickok-Utter party moved ahead with minimal troubles or delays. The steady, untroubled beginnings probably resulted from the earlier good planning and preparation of Charlie and Steve Utter. Even though Hickok had been in and out of Cheyenne since summer 1874, he had been unable to gain much of a livelihood there (in fact, he was charged with vagrancy in 1875) nor to make much headway in planning a Deadwood expedition. But after his marriage to Mrs. Lake (she preferred Lake to Thatcher as her last name) on 5 March, he seemed more motivated to prove he could make a living for himself and his new bride.

The expedition was facing uncertain physical, cultural, and military terrain. Although the Fort Laramie Treaty of 1868 promised the Black Hills to the Sioux, the discoveries of gold by George Custer's expedition to the Hills in 1874, and by others then and in the next year, had greatly complicated matters. More than a few miners pushed illegally into the Indian territory of the Black Hills environs. They were along French Creek in December 1874, and by October 1875 prospectors were in the Deadwood area. At first, the U.S. military half-heartedly chased out the trespassing miners. But when the Washington government, under strong pressure from expansionists, called for Indians to come to reservations in late 1875 and they did not come, lands to the north were flung open in February 1876. The following April, the town of Deadwood was laid out, and at month's end the first jerry-built buildings had sprung up.

When the Hickok-Utter train left Cheyenne on 27 June, they were not certain what they would find to the north. Progress was steady, however. Four days later they passed John Hunton's ranch, serving as stage stop. Early in July they were just north of the Fort Laramie area, where thirty wagons and perhaps more than a hundred persons joined them. The military encouraged such expanded numbers so that Indians might be less inclined to attack. A small group of prostitutes, expecting to ply their trade in Deadwood, also joined the train at Government Farm, a few miles above Fort Laramie.

Calamity Jane was among the women who joined the Hickok-Utter group. She may have been among the prostitutes. It is not clear where she had been staying in the days after being sent back from Crook's command about 21 June. Perhaps she had quickly moved on from Fort Fetterman to Fort Laramie, where she could benefit from the soldiers' payday at the end of the month, or perhaps she had been selling sex at one of the nearby hog ranches.

When the Hickok-Utter train stopped at Government Farm, close to Fort Laramie, the officer of the day asked if they couldn't take Calamity with them to Deadwood. Partying and bundling excessively with John Barleycorn, Calamity was being detained, in drunken and nearly naked circumstances. Even if Hickok and Colorado Charlie might have hesitated about taking Calamity on board, Steve Utter did not. He knew Calamity, he said, and would look after her.

Fortunately, a very helpful firsthand account exists of the Hickok-Utter trip, their encounter with Calamity and her traveling with them, and their first weeks together in Deadwood. About a half century after these events, White Eye Anderson carefully reconstructed those dramatic days as part of his memoir, published in 1980 as *I Buried Hickok: The Memoirs of White Eye Anderson*. (Anderson's nickname, "White Eye," came from his white eyebrow, the product of a cinder burn earlier in his career.) Nearly everything Anderson recalled compares well with the relatively few known facts of the first encounter between Wild Bill and Calamity.

White Eye provides a partial portrait of Calamity's life just after she turned twenty, from the end of June until the end of August 1876. When the travelers met Calamity near the first of July, she "had been having a hell of a time of it." Celebrating excessively with the soldiers at payday time, she had been tossed into the guardhouse in a "very drunk and near naked condition." The officer of the day provided Calamity with soldiers' underwear, and the travelers furnished her a buckskin shirt and pants and a hat. "When she got cleaned up and sober," White Eye recalled, Calamity "looked quite attractive."

Anderson believed that Wild Bill and Calamity were meeting for the first time. He added, too, that Hickok "surely did not have any use for her." Although Calamity was traveling *alongside* but not *with* Hickok, she often tapped his keg of whiskey for a generous quaff—so much so, in fact, he cautioned her to save some for other thirsty pilgrims. On occasion, around the campfire, Calamity spun yarns; Wild Bill said very little, but Calamity's tales were "some of the toughest stories" White Eye had ever heard. When Calamity began her tellings, "there would always be a big crowd

James Butler "Wild Bill" Hickok. Calamity Jane knew Wild Bill for only about five weeks, but biographers and popularizers have made them a couple in dozens of biographies, novels, and movies. Wild Bill was assassinated by Jack McCall, a drifter, in the Nuttall and Mann Saloon No. 10, on 2 August 1876. Courtesy J. Leonard Jennewein Collection, McGovern Library, Dakota Wesleyan University.

come over to the campfire to hear her talk." "We all liked her," Anderson added, "even though she was rough." During the travel, Calamity often helped with camp duties. She pitched in to aid White Eye with the cooking, sometimes telling him "Here, White Eye, let me show you how to do it." In addition, she packed up the grub and helped the travelers move on. Overall, Anderson thought of Calamity as a "big-hearted woman," revealing that he and she "got very well-acquainted" and "became good friends." Even though "thirteen or fourteen ladies of easy virtue" traveled with the group, Calamity seemed to spend more time with the men than with Madam Moustache, Tid Bit, Dirty Em, and the others. She also proved her skills with a rifle and pistol, on one occasion killing a coyote others had missed with rifles but she brought down with a six-shooter at the questionable range of "over one hundred yards." White Eye especially remembered Calamity's "wonderful command of profanity; . . . she could cuss to beat the band."

About 12 July, Wild Bill and Colorado Charlie, their companions, and Calamity made a "spectacular entry" into Deadwood. So memorable was the grand entrance that many years later old-timers recalled the carnivalesque invasion. Dressed in resplendent buckskins, some of them brand new, the entrants paraded to the end of Main Street, greeting old acquaintances and gathering attention from those who wished to make their acquaintance. "They were mounted on good horses," pioneer journalist Richard B. Hughes recalled, "and clad in complete suits of buckskin, every suit of which carried sufficient fringe to make a considerable buckskin rope."

Calamity never expressed what the entrance and first weeks in roiling Deadwood meant to her. But, surely, the frenetic, full-throttle life in the boomtown must have reminded Calamity of her nonstop days in the gold rush towns of Montana nearly a decade earlier. Speculation based on some evidence suggests that the months from summer 1876 onward must have given Calamity some sense of déjà vu.

Halfway through 1876, Deadwood was bubbling with round-the-clock action as the West's latest instant city. The frenzy came quickly. After the first Black Hills discoveries in 1874–75, the rushes spread northward into what became the Deadwood area. Some prospectors struck pay dirt in the fall-into-winter days of 1875, and others in pell-mell fashion tumbled into strike claims in early 1876. By March more than six hundred prospectors were working Deadwood and other nearby areas. As the weather turned warmer, hundreds—even thousands—flooded in. A few prospectors, fortunate Alkali Ikes, panned hundreds of dollars and often more in the coming weeks and months. And, if one chose to labor for others, he could readily find work for $4–6 per day, not including room and board. Prospectors stampeded to Deadwood and surrounding discoveries. Rough estimates of the booming tornado of incoming population in midsummer 1876 zoomed up as high as ten thousand, overflowing the Deadwood environs.

Not all the rushers got rich, of course. In fact, most seemed to break even or gained barely more than living wages. One source estimated an average income for miners in the Black Hills in the late 1870s as $330 per year, or "less than a dollar a day for each pilgrim." By 1878, placer mining was already falling away as miners had panned out much of the surface or stream-bed dust or nuggets. The hardrock or shaft mining, demanding many fewer miners and yet much more capital, began to take over the Deadwood area.

Calamity arrived in Deadwood just as the boomtown hit an early raucous peak. A few jerry-built log cabins and other buildings had been thrown up, but many of Deadwood's three to four thousand residents lived in tents. By mid-fall businesses, including banks, a drugstore, a grocery, doctor and lawyer offices, and a general store, were available and open for trade. Churches and schools were less evident.

Newspapers soon sprouted, with the *Black Hills Pioneer* launched in 1876 and the *Black Hills Times* the next year. Even the telegraph, speeding north from Denver, connected Deadwood to the wider world in December 1876.

Not surprisingly, other elements of Deadwood were more standard fare for Calamity in 1876. Places and activities that attracted Calamity in the Black Hills were much like those that captured her before Deadwood and that became apparent soon after her appearance. On 13 July, the *Black Hills Pioneer* announced: "'Calamity Jane' has arrived." A few days after the group came to Deadwood, Calamity strode into the camp of Wild Bill, Colorado Charlie, and the Anderson brothers. "Boys," she told them, "I wish you would loan me twenty dollars." She explained: "I can't do business in these old buckskins. I ain't got the show the other girls have." The men loaned her the money. Wild Bill also told her to wash up. "After she made her purchases she took a bath in the creek and Steve [Utter] washed her body thoroughly with perfumed soap," reported one writer.

The transformation worked. Calamity became an in-demand worker, hostess, and dancer in Deadwood's roaring saloons and lively theaters. A few days later, she returned to Wild Bill's camp dressed attractively as a woman. "She pulled up her dress," one eye witness recalled, "rolled down her stocking and took out a roll of greenbacks and give us the twenty she had borrowed." Obviously, her work was going well, although she "didn't express it in just that way," the author reported, hinting at the pungency of Calamity's earthy vocabulary.

Calamity also proved to be a supportive companion. One unusual incident displayed, early on, the individualistic and assertive person she was becoming. "Tid Bit," a diminutive redhead who also accompanied the Hickok-Utter group to Deadwood, had agreed to sexually serve Laughing Sam, a rascally gambler who tried to pass off a counterfeit payment to her of filings and sand rather than gold dust. When

Calamity heard what had happened to her friend, she borrowed a brace of six-guns from Charlie Utter and strode into a saloon to face down Sam. Explaining to bystanders what the dishonest Sam had done, Calamity let him have it verbally. "I never heard a man get such a cussing as she gave him," one observer reported. Cowed, Sam no longer "laughed"; he yielded to Calamity's demand that he hand over two $20 gold coins to Tid Bit. Calamity's courageous—and pugnacious—behavior in the saloon generated much admiration.

Wild Bill appeared less inclined than Calamity to move expeditiously toward finding a job and earning an income. His morning regimen included, according to eastern journalist Leander Richardson, crawling out of bed already clothed, shoving "his big revolver down inside the waistband of his trousers, and run[ning] like a sprinter down the gulch to the nearest saloon." After downing a shot or two, he returned to camp for his daily bath in the creek, an unusual act for the times, one that often generated wonderment in the gathered onlookers. Although making a few half-serious gestures toward prospecting, Hickok spent most of his time practice shooting and, chiefly, gambling. Several writers have written extensively about Wild Bill's activities in Deadwood, without reminding readers he was there a maximum of twenty days. Clearly, Hickok had not yet found himself in Deadwood, was floating, and perhaps worried about his safety and future. He may even have been depressed. But the two letters he wrote to his new wife—"Agnes Darling"—were positive and forward-looking, promising that he was planning ahead to work and save for her.

Calamity and Wild Bill did not stay together in Deadwood. She lived elsewhere, but on occasion came to Bill and Colorado Charlie's camp when she was hungry. Deadwood pioneer John McClintock, who witnessed the arrival of Calamity and Wild Bill in mid-July, wrote that afterwards Calamity "was seen frequently in his [Wild Bill's] company, and following him about the streets, during the few weeks he lived after their arrival in Deadwood." But most others in the Dakota boomtown at that time thought Wild Bill and Calamity were rarely together.

Calamity was most assuredly not with Hickok on the fateful day of 2 August 1876. Wild Bill was gambling again. The previous night he had played cards with and won heavily from Jack McCall, whom bartender Sam Young decried as "a worthless character and decidedly repulsive." The next afternoon McCall entered the front door of the No. 10 Saloon, where Wild Bill was gambling with three others. Coming to the bar and then furtively moving down it to locate behind Wild Bill's chair, McCall quickly pushed forward and fired his pistol into the back of Hickok's head, shouting "Damn you, take that." Hickok slumped forward, probably instantly dead. McCall, after misfiring his pistol at bartender Young and at least one other, fled to a nearby butcher shop, where, cornered, he surrendered.

Calamity, although not in the saloon at the time of the murder, claimed in her autobiography that she was in Deadwood at the time and hurried to the assassination scene. "I at once started to look for the assassian [*sic*] and found him at Shurdy's butcher shop and grabbed a meat cleaver and made him throw up his hands; through the excitement on hearing of Bill's death, having left my weapons on the post of my bed." Most biographers correctly dismiss these outrageous claims as part and parcel of the exaggerations that marked her undependable life story.

But Calamity was involved in events following Wild Bill's death, even if not in the way she or other writers presented them. Some assert, on shaky grounds, that Calamity came into the saloon and cradled Hickok's head. Contemporary journalist Richard Hughes wrote that Calamity was "one sincere female mourner" and her "grief for a time seemed uncontrollable." White Eye Anderson, also present at the time, added that Calamity and several other dance-hall girls placed wildflowers on Hickok's grave. Later writers and filmmakers, trying to turn the Wild Bill–Calamity story into torrid romance, overemphasized Calamity as totally distraught and unhinged in her reactions to Hickok's death.

Calamity resided in or near Deadwood for most of the next two or three years. It was a reasonably stable period in her life, although "stable" connotes something unique for Calamity. She found work in the boomtown, made acquaintances, and her nursing efforts gained newspaper attention. But before long, adventures in other areas of South Dakota and nearby Montana beckoned, and the indefatigable Calamity was on the road again.

Most of all, Calamity had become a dance hall girl in Deadwood. In the female-starved, miner-driven boomtown, saloons and all-night dance halls, theaters, and the ubiquitous, undefinable "hurdy gurdies" offered numerous positions for women hostesses, entertainers, and "dance hall girls." Leander P. Richardson, a nomadic journalist who visited and stayed in the Deadwood area for five days in midsummer 1876, described the new mining camp as a madhouse of rough citizens and their thrown-together houses and businesses. "Every alternate house was a gambling saloon," he wrote in *Scribner's Monthly*, "and each of them was carrying a brisk business." The townsmen were an equally mangy bunch. Richardson said of them, "Taken as a whole, I never in my life saw so many hardened and brutal-looking men together. . . ." Or, as another writer put it, "Deadwood liked its people with the hair on."

These entertainment establishments provided employment for a variety of female occupations, often depending on the reputation of the emporium. Residents of Deadwood recognized the hierarchy of the establishments, descending from the most prestigious to the unacceptable. At the top, as the "most respectable and notable of all" the Deadwood drama venues, was the theater of Jack Langrishe. A gifted

Booming Deadwood, 1876–77.

When Calamity Jane arrived in Deadwood, South Dakota, in 1876 with Wild Bill Hickok and his entourage, the boomtown was boiling over with activity. She quickly participated in the entertainment activities of the instant town. Courtesy Nebraska State Historical Society.

actor and the skillful manager of an acting troupe, Langrishe arrived in midsummer 1876, leased a flimsy building of canvas and rough boards, and began featuring high-class drama presentations for a year or two. Other theaters, such as the Deadwood Theater, Park Theater, and Wertheimer Hall, offered drama productions and added alcohol and "lady entertainers," without, it is said, losing all their respectability. At the bottom of the theater scale, as so-called dens of iniquity and places of ill-repute, were the Gem, Bella

Union, Melodeon, and Green Front. In the latter four theaters the permeable boundaries separating theater, saloon,
and bawdy house got lost. Drunkenness, fistfights, and,
perhaps, prostitution were not unusual activities.

For Calamity and other female "waitresses and performers," these places of entertainment could be threatening—
if not dangerous. The boisterous men expected a good time
in the theaters, dance halls, and saloons, often fueled by
an overabundance of high-octane spirits. The patrons also
expected the hostesses to dance with them, take drinks, and
pay attention to their stories. If these expectations were
not met, disruptions, fights, and a gamut of violent actions
often broke out, with the women frequently caught up in
the melees.

Calamity more than survived these demanding challenges. Newspaper reporters and other Deadwood contemporaries provided numerous stories of her dancing—and
drinking. As Deadwood pioneer John McClintock put it,
Calamity figured "conspicuously in the many dance halls,
and was ever on the move." Unfortunately, she seemed
most drawn to the Gem Variety Theater, more of a dance
hall than a theater. Al Swearingen, the Gem's unsavory
manager, turned the Gem into what McClintock labeled
a "notorious den of iniquity." A more recent authority on
Deadwood calls the Gem the worst, the most disreputable
of the dance halls, a hangout for prostitutes, supported by
"dissolute and degraded" patrons. But some of the boomtown's leading citizens also visited the Gem, making it one
of the liveliest places in town.

Swearingen was an energetic entrepreneur, not above
pressuring his family and friends to support his controversial establishment. Kitty Arnold, a well-known "waiter girl,"
Swearingen's own wife, and Calamity served as dancers and
hostesses at the Gem, the place where Calamity was most
often seen. As a reporter from the *Cheyenne Daily Leader*

Gem Theater, Deadwood.

Calamity Jane became a dance hall entertainer in several Deadwood saloons but especially in the Gem Theater, operated by Al Swearingen. It was a wide-open, full-throttle place of dancing, gambling, and entertainment. Courtesy South Dakota State Historical Society.

put it, she was "tripping the light fantastic toe" in several hurdy-gurdies, including the Gem.

Bartender Sam Young related a revealing story about Swearingen, the Gem, and Calamity that most biographers have repeated. Needing more girls to tend to his voracious customers, Swearingen outfitted Calamity with "a team, wagon and cooking utensils . . . and sent her to Nebraska to get a new supply of girls. At this business she was a huge success, the result of her first trip being ten girls." Not only did Calamity carry off her assignment with dispatch, she returned to the Gem and proceeded to take charge of the new recruits, initiating them into the dubious demands of taskmaster Swearingen.

After examining these actions of Calamity and similar ones later, one historian concludes: "That Jane was a prostitute is generally well-established." Perhaps, but unproven. Indeed, no irrefutable evidence exists to prove that Calamity sold sex in Deadwood. That she worked at houses of prostitution and hog ranches and that she had numerous "husbands" without benefit of clergy are readily provable. But no source from a "lady of the night" or a patron of these "joy palaces" ever testified to Calamity as an out-and-out prostitute. The best conclusion: she might have been. Calamity biographer James McLaird is dead-on when he warns readers, "It is misleading to portray young Martha as a regular occupant in a house of prostitution." The same warning holds for Calamity Jane in the following decade or two.

The feminine side of Calamity also emerged in her early years in Deadwood. This subject proved difficult for many journalists and some of her early biographers. After bringing her on scene as "one of the boys" who chewed tobacco, swore like the troopers and bull whackers she accompanied, drank in excess, and was involved in numerous masculine activities, reporters, pioneer memoirists, and biographers were puzzled about how to treat her work as a dancer and hostess, her interest in children, and also her maternal instincts. Frequently, after lengthy descriptions of Calamity's gender-bruising actions, storytellers countered with brief almost defensive descriptions of her willingness to help the needy, especially those who had been injured or were sick.

The evidence is clear and rather extensive: Calamity identified with the challenged, particularly those who were sick, destitute, or defenseless. The pattern of siding with and aiding the needy surfaced during Calamity's years in Deadwood. Still, there is the remaining problem: too many biographers and other writers about Calamity, having criticized her antisocial, untoward, and sometimes shocking activities, try to balance their accounts by overemphasizing or exaggerating her acts of mercy. In these ambivalent stories she becomes the whore with a social conscience, the harlot with a heart of gold.

Consider one of the most revealing examples of such attempts to balance the Calamity-as-prostitute with the Calamity-as-ministering angel. Two early arrivals in Deadwood, Jesse Brown and A. M. Willard, tried a half century later to correct the "fantastic yarns" that had grown up around Calamity. Instead, they concluded, she "was nothing more than a common prostitute, drunken, disorderly and wholly devoid of any element or conception of morality." Perhaps that starkly negative description bothered these muckrakers, for they also proceeded to lionize Calamity's efforts as a nurse—particularly during the devastating smallpox epidemic of 1878. Overly wrought words like those of Brown and Willard became, as James McLaird rightly observes, the "cornerstone of the Calamity Jane myth."

At the height of the smallpox attack, Brown and Willard wrote, "Hundreds were prostrated upon their rude beds and most people were afraid to go near them. Women were few to be had and they too were in terror of their lives." But one heroine braved the challenge. "In the hour of terror and death, there came to the front, a willing volunteer, the mule-skinning, bull-whacking, and rough, roving woman from the depths, Calamity Jane. Day and night she went among the sick and dying, and for week after week ministered to their wants or smoothed the pillow for the dying youth whose mother or sweetheart perhaps, was watching and waiting for the one never to return." And then the clincher: "It made no difference to her, that she knew them not, or that no gold would be there to repay her for the labor, the sacrifice, the danger."

Hyperbolic, melodramatic descriptions such as these made it difficult for later writers to accept accounts of Calamity's aid and nursing. But the evidence is available. White Eye Anderson provided a succinct summary of Calamity's actions for the brief time he knew her in Deadwood. "Calamity was a great friend in time of trouble. If anyone got sick or hurt, she nursed them until they got well. She knew how to be rough, but could also be kind and good."

The most talked-about of Calamity's humanitarian efforts was her nursing or help for those in dire circumstances. In fly-by-night, untethered mining towns, violent acts, accidents, and infectious diseases often invaded and took over the flotsam, jetsam of violent, careless, and unsanitary residents. Deadwood was no exception.

In more than a few instances, persons who needed Calamity's help received it. One of the best remembered of her nursing examples involved the Henry Robinson family. When the six Robinson children came down with "black diphtheria," Calamity came, uninvited, to the Robinson home to care for the children she loved, especially one of the little girls. Although three of the children died, including Calamity's favorite family daughter, she had ministered to the Robinsons in a time of great need. They did not forget that help. (Nearly twenty-five years later, a surviving Robinson brother took charge of Calamity's funeral in Deadwood.) In another instance, an elderly shopkeeper, George Simon, recalled how Calamity "saved his life when he was sick." Charles Fales, an old pioneer in the Deadwood and Ft. Pierre areas, remembered how Calamity nursed his sister (or his aunt, in another version); she was warned as she began her labors that Miss Fales was an upright, prim woman, so Calamity would have to wear a dress and refrain from smoking, drinking, or swearing, which she did while nursing for several weeks. Once freed from her demanding duties, Calamity headed for the nearest saloon and was quickly sauced.

The stories of Calamity's nursing during the smallpox scourge were especially numerous. Even if one makes allowance for the bloated rhetoric of Brown and Willard and like-minded fabulists, Calamity's aid to the smallpox victims is clearly documented. George Hoshier, an early comer to Deadwood and later a pallbearer at her funeral, testified that Calamity went to Elizabethtown, a part of Deadwood, to care for a man, "a stranger to her . . . [who] had the smallpox. Nobody else would go near him, and she went and took care of him and brought him through all right." Deadwood madam Dora Du Fran, writing under the pen name of D. Dee, testified to Calamity's willingness to aid smallpox victims. She stayed with them, Du Fran wrote, serving as "cook, doctor, chambermaid, water boy, and undertaker, with the duties of a sexton thrown in."

Estelline Bennett, part of an early family in Deadwood, told a similar story. When a group of Deadwood pioneers met Calamity on her return to the Hills in the mid-1890s, they all recalled her heroic, dangerous work with smallpox victims in a pest house established for their care. Dr. Babcock, an early Deadwood physician, warned Calamity about nursing the very sick patients, but she waved aside his warnings and proceeded to tend the victims no one else would care for. Bennett cited Dr. Babcock's belief that "without her [Calamity's] care not one of them could have pulled through." Much later, in the mid-twentieth century, several elderly residents of Deadwood "remembered well and definitely the specific details of some of Calamity's nursing exploits."

The well-balanced views of journalist J. Leonard Jennewein are helpful in evaluating Calamity's role as a nurse. At first Jennewein believed all the stories about Calamity as a second Florence Nightingale; then, he came to disbelieve them. But, after additional study and reflection, he kept to "a skeptical middle course." In his view, there were "too many persons who relate[d] the good deeds of Calamity, with specific names and places, to do any high-handed debunking." Even though naysayers have attempted to dismiss or downsize these stories of Calamity's valiant efforts, the eyewitness accounts of dozens of recipients or participants in her ministrations make it difficult to discard these stories simply as attempts to balance her questionable behavior with a list of good deeds.

Calamity's life in Deadwood encompassed other activities besides her work in theaters and saloon and dance halls and her nursing. A few glimpses of these, however fleeting, add fragments to the mosaic of Calamity's life and character.

On one occasion Calamity had a momentary brush with religion, even if on her own unorthodox terms. Bartender Sam Young and socially elite Estelle Bennett tell similar stories about Calamity and Henry Weston Smith, an evangelical itinerant preacher in the Hills. One day in August 1876 as Smith was preaching on a street corner, Calamity, a bit shaky with drink, grabbed a hat and reportedly told the listeners: "You sinners, dig down in your pokes, now; this old fellow looks as though he were broke and I want to collect about two hundred dollars for him. So limber up, boys." Circulating through the crowd, Calamity quickly gathered more than the needed amount, but when she tried to break into Smith's sermon and give him the collection, he waved her aside. Upset, Calamity fired back "You d old fool, take the money first and then proceed with your preaching." Finishing his sermon, Smith headed south to Crook City. Hours later two travelers found Smith dead and scalped. When the preacher's body was returned to Deadwood, Calamity, it is said, told a friend, "Ain't it too bad . . . that the Indians killed the only man that came into the Hills to tell us how to live. And we sure need the telling."

Calamity called Deadwood home for most of much of 1876 through 1879 and as late as 1881. It was rumored that, for a short time, she ran her own bagnio, that she bossed the girls at the Gem Theater, and that she even rented a home for a few months. Newspapers in 1876 and early 1877 began to trace her whereabouts and broadcast her doings, especially if activities could be dramatized—or

CALAMITY IN MALE ATTIRE.

Calamity Jane in portrait.

Writer Thomas N. Newson, in his book *Drama of Life in the Black Hills* (1878), included, above, a photograph now lost. Newson also provided, on the right, two rather amateurish illustrations of Calamity as masculine figure (top) and a more feminine one (bottom). Newson's illustrations and text provided a fuller, more diverse pictorial and word description of Calamity than appeared in most other written sources. Etulain collection.

CALAMITY IN FEMALE ATTIRE.

even sensationalized. The *Black Hills Daily News* reported, for example, that Calamity was among the crowd frenzied with the alarming news of Wild Bill's assassination, when it nearly exploded as "a Mexican" on horseback cantered into town with a grotesque trophy of a severed head. Calamity was said to be present again when, a few days later, another raider raced into Deadwood with a decapitated Indian head. These events were all the more charged in light of the fact that Custer and his troops had been annihilated to the west and north of Deadwood six weeks earlier.

Calamity also spent a good deal of time outside Deadwood during those years. Several times she traveled east, back and forth to the Missouri River at Fort Pierre, where she camped out for days at a time. For a brief duration she worked in a dance hall in nearby Sturgis and also as a laundress. According to the *Cheyenne Daily Leader*, Calamity was in Custer City in November 1876 "eschew[ing] the wine-cup" and "sling[ing] hash as a waiter" at a Custer City hotel.

Not surprisingly, Calamity added exaggerated and false information in her 1896 autobiography about her Deadwood days—in an attempt to enliven her reputation while on the traveling circuit with a dime museum. She claimed to have rescued a mail coach after Indians killed the driver John Slaughter, to have served with the Seventh Cavalry in building Fort Meade, and to have driven ox trains back and forth between Fort Pierre, Rapid City, and Sturgis. None of these claims can be proven, with careful scholars dismissing them as stretchers promoting her Wild West shows. She may have traveled on stagecoaches and with bullwhackers and freighters, but no record substantiates that she had full-time employment with any of these firms. A decade later Calamity asserted in similar fashion that she was a woman road agent with Bill Bevans (Bevins), Reddy McKemma (McKimie), and their gang in a string of stagecoach robberies. She furthered tantalized newspaper readers with her yarn that in the late 1870s she "embarked in a business that you nor no one else will ever learn anything about from me; but I will say that I became well acquainted with every road agent who helped to hold up a Black Hills coach." Already nationally known through her appearance in regional histories and widely read dime novels, Calamity seemed to relish her notoriety, adding new stories to sustain and expand her sensational reputation.

But a much less spectacular story, a friendship that reveals the human side of Calamity and her life in Deadwood, was gradually spinning out. It displays more of her real life than the hyped stories she and reporters were peddling. The friendship began and evolved in unexpected and unusual ways. The other key figure in this revealing subplot was William ("Billy") A. Lull.

The son and grandson of Methodist ministers, Lull had set out from New York in 1875 for the West. Planning to work in St. Louis, Lull was waylaid in Chicago by news of the Black Hills gold rush. By summer he was on his way to western Dakota. Chased out of the Black Hills by the military, he was back in the Deadwood area early in 1876 when the area opened to prospectors. Before long, Lull secured a good position managing a small hotel for a Mr. Porter, a Creole man from New Orleans. At Porter's Hotel, Lull met Calamity.

Several decades after his two to three years in Deadwood, Lull told of his growing friendship in a brief piece entitled "Calamity Jane, Deadwood City in Early Pioneer Days." Calling himself "New York Billie" or "Billy," in what later would be termed a work of creative nonfiction, Lull provided abbreviated but illuminating glimpses of Calamity and her character. Calamity was, Lull wrote, "a lone Wolf. She had neither Partner nor Paramour." And when Billie tried to befriend her, she "did not take kindly to [his] friendly advances. Probably she had never been treated as a Lady before." Calamity stiff-armed Billie's offered friendship, telling him, "Go to H—— baby face."

But Billie did not give up. Something about Calamity attracted him more to her than to the other dance hall girls staying in Porter's Hotel. "She had a Personality of her own," Lull wrote, and Billie "felt that her surliness was a cloak to hide something that she was ashamed to let appear on the surface." Lull has Calamity working at the Bella Union Theater (rather than the Gem), a "born gambler," and "bucking the Tiger" in the game of faro at several places.

The relationship between Billie and Calamity changed markedly when she came down with a severe case of mountain fever. When Billie tried to help Calamity, he was rebuffed with a "burst of profanity." The same reaction followed

Mapping Calamity Jane's Deadwood.

New Yorker William B. ("Billie") Lull befriended Calamity at Porter's hotel in Deadwood, where he worked and she stayed. His sketch of the "badlands district" shows the hotel where she stayed as the second building on the left, and the Bella Union dancehall, where she worked, across Main Street. Courtesy South Dakota State Historical Society.

when a doctor attempted to look after Calamity and provide needed medicine. The doctor also told Billie that Calamity needed "some things that only a woman can do for her." The other dance hall girls refused to help Billie minister to Calamity until he threatened them with eviction from the hotel. They, too, were "cussed out" by Calamity. But Billie "had faith that deep down in Jane's heart was a tender spark, and that the cuss words were only a cloak to hide any display of Gratitude that she may have felt."

Once Calamity had recovered sufficiently to return to work, her attitude toward Billie changed. Although she avoided any conversations, Calamity demonstrated her thankfulness for what he had done to move her through to recovery. Thinking about the change, Billie concluded that Calamity "was not all hard and calloused, as she would have People think." But she "was able to fight her own battles, never asking aide, or help, from others."

In the next few weeks Calamity demonstrated, rather obliquely and wordlessly, her gratitude for Billie's aid. She quietly paid off her hotel debt, and then in a revealing symbolic gesture gave Billie a tintype of herself, as she told him, to "remember Calamity Jane by." When Billie prepared to leave after more than two years in the Hills, Calamity, at the last minute, appeared at his stage, wishing him well and predicting he would never return to Deadwood. If Lull remembered correctly many years later and avoided loading up his creative history with excessive sentiment, he recalled that when he "boarded the Stage for home . . . for the first time in her life there was a Tear in her Eyes as she bid me good bye."

The Lull-Calamity friendship, even after one sifts out the created conversations after many years and the factual errors, provides intimate glimpses of Calamity missing in most accounts. Lull, in writing in 1941 to a woman self-proclaimed as Calamity's daughter, stated that "I knew your mother probably better than anyone." Perhaps he did, but even more certainly since Calamity could not herself write about her feelings and attitudes, Lull opens the window ever so slightly in understanding her character. Behind the Hellcat of the West façade, behind the masculine bravado, was a young woman who, although fending for herself and others, nonetheless felt gratitude for a baby-faced minister's son from New York who helped her through a crisis.

If William Lull's story adds appealing complexity to Calamity's character and broadens her experience in Deadwood, other events and people sometimes obscured rather than clarified her life in the Hills. In 1877, Dr. A. R. Hendricks insisted that he knew Calamity well before she arrived in Deadwood. She was, the doctor told a reporter, the daughter of a Baptist minister, B. W. Coombs, in Des Moines, Iowa. The last in a family of four, she had been born in 1847. None of these assertions proved true—then or later—but they complicated the already vague stories about Calamity's formative years. Another story from Sidney, Nebraska, indicated that Calamity was from that area, and when the storyteller was pushed for details, he declared that she was "Calamity Jane No. 2." In Denver, still another young woman of controversial actions was called Calamity Jane. So persuasive were her credentials that a leading historian on the Cheyenne to Deadwood stage wrongly identified her photo as that of the original, authentic Calamity Jane. Later, she proved to be Mattie Young, who died in Denver after a carriage accident due to her drunkenness.

The most widespread alternative theory about Calamity's early years is the one we have already encountered. It is the Jane Dalton story, which asserted that Calamity was born in Fort Laramie, lost her parents in an Indian attack, was adopted, and grew up "a daughter of the regiment." This story was particularly strong in the eastern Wyoming and the Deadwood areas. Dr. McGillycuddy, teamster and bartender Sam Young, Estelline Bennett of Deadwood, and

Dora Du Fran, the Hills madam, all subscribed to this misleading story of Calamity's girlhood. The storyline became gospel truth through the later writings of Doane Robinson, well-known historian of South Dakota.

When these stories about several Calamity Janes spread into the Black Hills, some took root and flowered. So much so that even denials in Deadwood newspapers could not kill off the noxious weeds of misinformation. "These are not our Calamity," the local journalists wrote, but the wrong stories continued—even into the twentieth-first century.

There were even confusions within the Black Hills as to whether the untoward actions of some dance hall women, drunks, and prostitutes were those of Calamity. The most widely noted of these notorious women was denominated the "Heroine of the Hills" by the *Deadwood Black Hills Daily Pioneer*. Some thought this woman, arrested for drunkenness and controversial behavior, was certainly Calamity. But she was, instead, a Mrs. Bloxsom. The *Pioneer*'s rival, the *Deadwood Black Hills Daily Times*, castigated its journalistic competitor in the Hills and denounced Bloxsom as "a low down idiotic sort of a prostitute who has been herding with Indians, negroes and soldiers." On another occasion, the *Deadwood Daily Champion* denounced Calamity as a "fraud," with its editor criticizing her as unworthy to be named with western worthies like Buffalo Bill Cody and Wild Bill Hickok. One source states that after the story criticizing Calamity appeared, she invaded the *Champion* office, stirred up a "fearful racket," and later returned to steal the editor's picture from the office wall so as to make fun of him in several bars. The editor claimed to have retreated to a nearby "uninhabited gulch" and remained there until Calamity's "rage had cooled."

These sensational stories confused readers—then and later. Was Calamity Jane a notorious dance hall woman, guilty of drunkenness, and perhaps a prostitute? Or, was she a kind-hearted young woman who nursed the afflicted and stood up for other badgered women and the marginalized? In truth, she was undoubtedly both, but that verity was difficult for either-or thinkers to sort out. Already, alcohol had captured Calamity, leading frequently to boisterous and embarrassing actions. But she also, obviously, wanted to help others, particularly those who seemed rather powerless in a male-dominated, inchoate society. And the friendship with William Lull revealed that behind the façade of stoical and imperturbable masculinity was a young woman of feeling and thankfulness.

Further changes seemed on the horizon. At the end of 1877, Calamity told a reporter she was no longer Calamity Jane but Maggie Cosgrove. She told one group that she had married George Cosgrove, who had come to the Hills in the Wild Bill–Charlie Utter train of 1876. From 1877 to 1879, Calamity was seen with Cosgrove in several Dakota and Wyoming locations. She put it succinctly on one occasion: "Boys, . . . I am married to George now and am living straight and don't do any business on the outside." But the relationship with Cosgrove was off and on, as such relationships were with most men Calamity labeled "husbands."

Beginning in 1876 and until at least 1881, Calamity was in and out of Deadwood. She also popped up in Fort Pierre, Rapid City, Sturgis, Cheyenne, and several other sites. Calamity Jane, part Wild Woman, part pioneer woman, part ministering angel, had negotiated Deadwood and emerged as a complex, on-the-move protagonist.

4

Overnight Fame

A Dime Novel Heroine

Information about Calamity's life and career exploded onto the national scene in the years from 1876 to 1878. In 1875–76 she had first appeared in regional newspapers as Calamity Jane; then her notoriety spread in 1876–77 through much of the northern West but particularly in the northern Rockies and upper Great Plains. In 1877–78, her name and stories about her fanned out from the West and onto the national media. Journalist Horatio N. Maguire profiled Calamity in his two books *The Black Hills and American Wonderland* (1877) and *The Coming Empire: A Complete and Reliable Treatise on the Black Hills, Yellowstone and Big Horn Regions* (1878), information from which was picked up and printed in New York newspapers. Another journalist, T. M. Newson, furnished an even more extensive treatment of Calamity in his play, *Drama of Life in the Black Hills* (1878). Most important of all was Calamity's appearance in dozens of dime novels, beginning with *Deadwood Dick, the Prince of the Road; or, The Black Rider of the Black Hills* (15 October 1877). The first of author Edward L. Wheeler's more than thirty dime novels, the work featured Calamity as a rambunctious, devil-may-care heroine who could outride and outshoot many of her male companions. The immensely popular Deadwood Dick series made Calamity an overnight sensation. In less than three years, Martha Canary had been transformed into a national heroine.

Her life would never again be the same.

Calamity was raised to mythic status during an emotional high point of interest in the American Wild West. In a five-year period stretching from the killing of Gen. George Custer and the assassination of Wild Bill Hickok in 1876 to Billy the Kid's demise and the OK Corral shootout in 1881, the entire country was awash in a frenzy over a fascinating frontier. The apotheosis of Calamity, in the pages of western newspapers, in a widely read history, in a pioneering western drama, and in a flock of florid western dime novels, made her a suitable companion to male figures finding their way into a Wild West pantheon.

Horatio N. Maguire's two books were notably important works of nonfiction that established early conclusions about Calamity. He set the scene, authoring the first images of Calamity. His journalistic background helps elucidate the manner in which he portrayed her in his historical/promotional works about the northern interior West, books published in 1877–78. Born in Kentucky in 1837 but leaving home quickly during his early teens, Maguire turned to typesetting and then newspapering. By the early 1860s he had traveled across the continent, working in Portland, Oregon, as an editor and publisher. Turning back, he stopped off briefly in Idaho Territory and arrived in Montana Territory and began writing for the *Montana Post* in summer 1865. Calamity's family probably was still in the Virginia City area at this time. In the late 1860s and the 1870s, Maguire turned to positions in law and politics.

But wanderlust stuck again. By 1876 Maguire was in Deadwood, practicing law. Evidently the legal business could not hold him; Maguire was soon back as an editor and

Horatio N. Maguire, journalist and historian.

In 1877, Maguire authored *The Black Hills and American Wonderland* and the next year *The Coming Empire*. Both books included valuable information on the newly christened Calamity Jane. Courtesy J. Leonard Jennewein Collection, McGovern Library, Dakota Wesleyan University.

publisher of several Dakota Territory newspapers. While in the Deadwood area he met the youthful and newly minted Calamity Jane. He remained in Dakota until the death of his wife in 1880 and then, after brief stops in the East and back in Montana, he moved to Oregon and afterwards to Spokane, Washington, where he died on 13 March 1903. In his closing years, Maguire was an ardent Populist and spiritualist.

On a few occasions Maguire seemed a reformer. He attacked bloated capitalists and monopolists. He also decried the "wholesale slaughter" of the disappearing buffalo herds and harpooned Montana despoilers polluting the air and blocking out the "cherished hopes and highest human aspirations" of the hoi polloi. But these were the exceptions.

For the most part, Maguire served as an unrepentant booster. He also had a keen eye for the unusual—both people and events. Because he was part promoter and part scene-setter, Maguire had no trouble boosting the humanness of Calamity in his books. First he had to describe her eccentricities, as he did in two packed paragraphs in *The Black Hills and American Wonderland*. He opens these brief comments in a small town, where the author is speaking to a Montana acquaintance and asking him how far it is to Deadwood. The Montana friend replies, "Only a mile and a half; that girl on the horse is going there now."

Maguire, questioning whether the rider is a woman, goes on to describe the lithesome Calamity and adds a capsule biography. The rider is "a "dare-devil boy"; she cannot be a young woman. But she is. "That's Calamity Jane," the man from Montana tells him. The author has apparently heard of her, but he's still uncertain: "There was nothing in her attire to distinguish her sex, as she sat astride the fiery horse she was managing . . . save for her small neat-fitting gaiters, and sweeping raven locks." Her bravado, her man-like actions were also eye-catching: "Throwing herself from side to side in the saddle with . . . daring self-confidence . . . she spurred her horse on up the gulch, over ditches and through reservoirs and mudholes, at each leap of the fractious animal giving as good an imitation of a Sioux war-whoop as a feminine voice is capable of."

No one before Maguire provided much of a description of Calamity, instead usually tallying up her untoward actions or attitudes in a sentence or two. Whether Maguire overly dramatized the scenes is not clear. But one must note—and emphasize—that dozens of later reports, and particularly dime novelist Edward L. Wheeler, religiously followed much of Maguire's detailed description.

Still, Maguire did not know as much about Calamity's personal history as he let on. His biographical portrait of her was riddled with errors. He had her origins all wrong: she did not come from Virginia City, Nevada (a common error in early accounts of Calamity; perhaps hearing of her being in Virginia City as a young girl, writers assumed, erroneously, that the older and better-known Nevada boomtown was her home); and she was not from a "family of respectability and intelligence." Nor did she don "male attire in the mining regions of Nevada." There was good evidence, however, that by 1877 Calamity had had experience as a bull-whacker, driving a variety of wheeled vehicles.

Maguire also stumbled into the tangled thickets of Calamity's personal life. After a "first step of ruin [was] taken," he wrote, "she had not the moral courage to seek retrievement." Instead, she would accept the reputation of "a woman of the world" and be the "mistress of her own destiny." What specific "step of ruin" Calamity had taken and when and how Maguire did not reveal. Nor did any other source. Most probably, Maguire was guessing, as would other journalists and dime novelists.

Finally, Maguire came to ambiguous conclusions. He might speak of Calamity's "most remarkable career of ruin, disgrace and recklessness," but he also noted that she had "redeeming qualities." She had not asked for the sympathies of others, choosing instead to stand by herself, "in brave defense of a frowning world." And, in the end, even though critics might condemn her controversial actions, she was "still in early womanhood, and her rough and dissipated career [had] not yet altogether 'swept away the lines where beauty lingers.'" Here Maguire slightly misquoted Lord Byron's poem "The Shores of Greece," which stated, "Before Decay's effacing fingers / Have swept the lines where beauty lingers. . . ." These words from Byron soon tumbled out in numerous newspapers in stories about Calamity in 1877–78, and thereafter.

Maguire's depiction of Calamity, though brief (consisting of only two paragraphs from a thirty-five-page pamphlet), nonetheless spread like a racy rumor. As we have seen, Calamity's name first appeared in print in 1875 and regularly in bits and pieces in 1876–77 in the Black Hills and Cheyenne areas and as far east as Chicago. Maguire's pen portrait of Calamity traveled on to New York City. Some have speculated that portions of his promotional pamphlet may have appeared serially in New York and other north-eastern papers, but no one has turned up such printings.

Journalists in the northern West quickly snapped up Maguire's descriptions of Calamity and paraded them in their own papers. The exact words and descriptions Maguire used in late winter or spring of 1877 quickly reappeared in periodicals of the region. On 10 June, the *Rocky Mountain News*, citing the "Nebraska Press," spoke of Calamity's "small neat fitting gaiters and sweeping raven locks," her origins in Virginia City, Nevada, and her "family of respectability and intelligence." Four days later a similar story appeared in the *Cheyenne Daily Leader*. And then in July the *Salt Lake Tribune* also described Calamity as "strangely like one of Bret Harte's heroines." It too depicted Calamity in the exact terms Maguire used. All these journalists ended their stories in June and July with the purloined poetry of Lord Byron, that Calamity's "rough and dissipated career [had] not yet altogether 'swept away the lines where beauty begins.'" The rapid, wide circulation of these stereotyped images of Calamity meant that she had gained regional renown by the end of summer 1877.

But that notoriety in the northern West was as a side-show affair compared to the big-tent publicity Calamity had showered on her by the end of the year. Some way or another, Maguire's flamboyant portrait of Calamity surfaced in New York. Probably sometime during summer 1877, dime novelist Edward L. Wheeler learned of Calamity Jane and set out to make her the heroine of the first installment of his multivolume Deadwood Dick series. On 15 October 1877, that dime novel appeared as *Deadwood Dick, The Prince of the Road; or, The Black Rider of the Black Hills*. It was a splash best seller, launching a series of thirty-three dime novels under the imprint of Beadle and Adams, a leading publisher of the dimes and other popular fiction. Once the Deadwood Dick series, featuring Calamity Jane as leading woman, captured millions of readers, Calamity could no longer hide her story under a far-western bushel basket—even if she had so wanted. She had become—and would remain for the remainder of her life—a dime novel heroine, a young woman of "yellowback" fiction fame.

Dime novels zipped onto the American popular literary scene at the beginning of the Civil War. These popular novels by Edward L. Wheeler and hundreds of other authors proved to be literary links between the earlier captivity narratives and James Fenimore Cooper's Leatherstocking Tales and the later Westerns of the twentieth century. The linkages were particularly apparent in fiction set in the West and featuring frontier characters such as hunters, scouts, and, later, cowboys. From 1860 to the turn of the century, the American reading public was awash in dime novels. Fiction set on the frontier or on lands west of the Mississippi was the most popular type. One survey of fifteen hundred novels issued by Beadle and Adams, the most successful of the early publishers, revealed that approximately 75 percent dealt with frontier or western subjects. So popular were western dime novels that several other companies launched their own series. It was rumored that huge supplies of dime novels, most with western settings, were sent by the boxcar loads to soldiers hungry for reading material during the Civil War years.

Two dime novels published in 1860, the first year such works appeared, illustrate the themes and emphases that writers abandoned and adopted in the next two generations. In the 1860s and 1870s, the dime novel clearly shifted from the ethnic feminine focus of Ann S. Stephens's *Maleska: The Indian Wife of the White Man* to the white, masculine, heroic, and triumphalist frontier in Edward S. Ellis's *Seth Jones; or, The Capture of the Frontier.* Ellis's dime novel sold more than a half-million copies and quickly became the most powerful model for hundreds of others.

The dime novelists followed on Ellis's heels by featuring strong masculine heroes who retained both an appealing gentility and a western democratic bearing. Many of the more than five hundred dime novels starring Buffalo Bill portrayed such a hero—one of courage, tenacity, and inner resources but also one free from frontier boorishness and social inadequacies. Early in the twentieth century, the cowboy hero of Owen Wister's classic Western, *The Virginian* (1902), charismatically combined characteristics of gentility and western go-ahead.

Building on the traditions of Cooper and other romantic writers, dime novelists gradually realized they must find fictional mates for their heroes. That was not an easy task because the virginal, upper-society women of Cooper and the sentimental novelists would not work smoothly in a new Wild West literature. Experiments followed. As American Studies scholar Henry Nash Smith pointed out in his extraordinary study *Virgin Land: The American West as Symbol and Myth* (1950), writers first used Indian women and later women disguised as men to introduce less socially constricted and more independent heroines in their dime novels. Such experimentation prepared the stage for Calamity Jane and such literary cousins as Hurricane Nell and Wild Edna (both also Edward Wheeler heroines) and Phantom Moll. The frenetic frontier settings and scenes dominating western dime novels demanded Wild West heroines. Wheeler's Calamity Jane partially filled that need.

Wheeler's *Deadwood Dick, the Prince of the Road*, the initial dime novel in the Deadwood Dick series, clearly displayed his talent and revealed his gift for depicting a Calamity Jane figure who would capture the imagination of millions of readers. In addition, the opening novel in the series provided much of the imagined background of Calamity that would dominate many of the more than thirty installments in the series.

Deadwood Dick dime novel series.

Like most of the thirty-three installments in the Deadwood Dick dime novel series, *Deadwood Dick on Deck* (1878) features Calamity Jane as a devil-may-care sidekick of the highwayman Deadwood Dick. She is portrayed as a fearless rider, skilled with a gun, and bent on bringing justice in a lawless West. The series sold quickly and widely, turning Calamity into a nationally known figure in the late 1870s.

Edward L. Wheeler (1854?–1885?), an enigmatic chap, seemed satisfied with plying his writing trade out of the publicity limelight. And hard-peddle it he did. From 1877 to 1885, he churned out thirty-three Deadwood Dick installments in the Half-Dime Library, but maybe wrote as many as one hundred dime novels, total, in this brief period. Working at a red hot pace, he may have completed a dime novel every two or three months. Although his letterhead stationary touted Wheeler as a "Sensational Novelist," he kept out of sight. Almost nothing is known about him.

But his writings reveal his innovative style, even if boxed-in within the restrictive limits of dime novel expectations. Wheeler's writing tricks and his very limited knowledge of the American West and Calamity Jane also much influenced the kinds of stories he told about her and her male and female companions.

Deadwood Dick, the Prince of the Road; or, The Black Rider of the Black Hills clearly epitomized the kinds of dime novels Wheeler would write in the Deadwood Dick series and the essential nature of the Calamity Jane figure he would use repeatedly. His characterizations and plotlines demonstrated Wheeler's willingness to break from the western hero who had evolved from Cooper forward into the first dime novels. Wheeler's hero, easterner Ned Harris (Deadwood Dick) living disguised in the Black Hills as a highwayman, in no way represented the genteel, moral, and emulative qualities of traditional western heroes. Similar to some leading men in other road agent or outlaw dime novels, Deadwood Dick is forced outside the law to gain revenge on malefactors because the law, the courts, and society itself have failed to indict evildoers.

In *Deadwood Dick, the Prince of the Road*, the hero represents the eastern worker who has fled west and become an outlaw to gain freedom from crooked eastern capitalists. Living in the guise of a highwayman, Deadwood Dick attempts to gain revenge on his chief persecutors, Alexander and Clarence Filmore, who have robbed him and his sister, chased Dick from his adoptive home, and abused him. In turn, Dick has purloined money rightfully his and now, once in the West, he calls for the hanging of these murderous brothers because an uncaring society fails to pass and uphold laws protecting good people from such evil men. At the end of the novel, Dick discloses that his real name is Edward Harris and cries out "Now, I am inclined to only those who have been merciful to me. . . . Boys, *string 'em up!*"

The role of Wheeler's heroine as a sidekick and possible mate for the hero is somewhat circumscribed once he places the road agent Deadwood Dick at the center of his novel. Wheeler's Calamity, although based tangentially on the specific and general information Maguire provided about her in his 1877 book, is largely a fictional character, a creation of the author's fertile mind.

Still, even though Wheeler's characterization of Calamity is nearly a continent away from the facts, it deserves extended discussion because it became one of the most widespread descriptions of her in the nineteenth century. Wheeler's Calamity repeatedly reveals how little he knew about her, how innocent he was of western history and geography, and how unfettered his imagination. There is strong, clear evidence, too, that he was acquainted with Maguire's comments about Calamity, which had surfaced just a few months earlier.

The first dime novel about Calamity owed much to Wheeler's predilections. As with all of the author's major characters, Calamity's backgrounds are hazy at best. One character tells another he doesn't know "her real name . . . few in Deadwood do." But, he adds, she is a sensational figure, "an odd one" at that. She can "ride like the wind, shoot like a sharp-shooter, and swears like a trooper." And she has done well financially, owning "two or three . . . lots in Deadwood; a herding ranch at Laramie" and part of a successful mine. None of these entrepreneurial achievements was true, of course, of the historical Calamity.

Comments about Calamity's actions spark a contentious exchange between the same two characters. Hearing of her early controversial deeds, one listener blurts out: "God forbid that a child of mine should ever become so debased and—." The other speaker fires back: "Hold! There are yet a few redeeming qualities about her. She was *ruined* . . . and set adrift upon the world, homeless and friendless; yet she has bravely fought her way through the storm, without asking anyone's assistance."

These echoes from H. N. Maguire's portrait of Calamity become even more explicit when two mistaken notions are repeated. Calamity "comes of a Virginia City, Nevada, family of respectability and intelligence." Descriptions from Maguire are also repeated. Calamity wears a "jaunty Spanish sombrero" and boots, with "tops reaching to the knees." Then the widely quoted clincher from Byron, via Maguire: a "slightly sunburned" face "yet showing the traces of beauty that even excessive dissipation could not obliterate."

Calamity is off-scene for long stretches in *Deadwood Dick, the Prince of the Road*. Still, not surprisingly, she gallops on stage in time to right wrongs, aid Deadwood Dick, and stand off the villains. Indeed, many of her actions— especially her riding and handling of guns—are so adept that she seems more man than woman. Her gender identity is blurred, as were the identities of so many western heroines in dime novels. These fuzzy woman/man and man/ woman characters are central figures in many of Wheeler's dime novels. The heroines similar in character to Calamity are much more likely to ride with Deadwood Dick and other men; they are rarely companions to the fair, fainting females in dime novels, who are usually from the effete East.

Other aspects of Wheeler's Calamity deserve attention. Although she is clearly of lower middle class or even lower class origins, she does not speak, most of the time, in the backwoods vernacular of so many fictional working- or lower-class men. In fact, his women rarely speak in a rural or backwoods idiom. But in this opening installment of the Deadwood Dick series, class divisions do play an obvious role. Toward the end of the novel, the hero proposes to one of the polished eastern women; she rejects him to marry a man closer to her social status and free from the road-agent activities of Deadwood Dick. Then, he tries to land Calamity as a wife, but she too refuses, telling him, "No . . . I have had all the *man* I care for. We can be friends, Dick; more we can never be!" When his two proposals come to nothing, Deadwood Dick returns to being "Prince of the Road," and "Calamity Jane is still in the Hills."

In centering on the characterizations in Wheeler's first Deadwood Dick novel, readers often forget that he was bringing on scene the latest sensation of an attention-catching Wild West. As Wheeler puts it, Deadwood in the Black Hiils was the "magic city of the West." Just as the many boomtowns of the California Gold Rush, Mother Lode, and the recent Denver stampede had captured the attention of eastern Americans from 1848 to 1860, and just as the Yukon rush to the Klondike would at the end of the century, Deadwood and the Black Hills grabbed center scene in the late 1870s. Readers were entranced with these magical settings as much as they were with the larger-than-life characters.

Just two months later, the second installment of the series, *The Double Daggers; or, Deadwood Dick's Defiance. A Tale of the Regulators and Road-Agents of the Black Hills,* rolled off the Beadle and Adams presses. It also featured Calamity Jane as a central character. She's portrayed as the "girl dare devil" who dashes through canyons and gulches and hides out in mysterious caves, but also gambles in Deadwood. If she gets involved in a heated card game, she may stay at the tables for nearly a week. Calamity befriends Deadwood

Dick/Ned Harris, but, showing no love interest, remains aloof. In fact, she tells a new acquaintance, she has "very few friends—for the simple reason I don't want many."

Wheeler's details about Calamity remain scanty, suggesting how few valuable nuggets of information he had turned up in the biographical lodes he was working. There is the correct information that she is "clad in male attire" and handy with guns and horses. Wheeler also trots out again Maguire's description, via Lord Byron, of Calamity: her face is "not really handsome; yet a rough and dissipated career had not altogether 'Swept away the lines where beauty lingers.'"

The author elaborates on the theme that a rapacious man had "ruined" Calamity early on, leading her to a life of wandering. Her "relatives in Nevada" would never get her hoarded riches of gold. "Curse them!" she exclaims, "they'll never get any o' my tin—bet your pile on *that*. When they kicked me out of doors, it was forever." That remembered act and other "rankling recollection[s]," when they are recalled, "make her almost despise and curse the race of men." On one occasion she comes close to disclosing "the whole bitter, terrible story of her life."

Wheeler lards his narrative with manufactured, sensational misinformation about Calamity. He depicts her as immensely wealthy, owing property in Deadwood, silver mines in the nearby mountains, and part ownership in the Metropolitan saloon in Deadwood. "Besides all this," the author adds, "she has ten thousand dollars' worth o' greenbacks on her person, all the time." None of these assertions is true, but dime novel readers probably were not worried about such dubious exaggerations.

Calamity as a dime novel heroine, like the flesh and blood woman, is a whirling machine of nonstop action. Wheeler employs the familiar literary tricks of popular fiction to heighten Calamity's on-the-move character: fortuitous chances and circumstances allow her to arrive on a scene at the right time, and chapters end with a threatened assault or unfinished dramatic action, a cliff-hanger.

But Wheeler may have come closer to the truth about his fictional heroine at the close of the novel. In updating and foreshadowing the lives of the novel's major characters, he says: "Calamity Jane I don't think will ever marry; her life will continue that of a dare-devil and reckless adventurer that she is, until the end." In spite of his wrong-headed predictions about a husbandless life for Calamity, the novelist had caught the rambling, devil-may-care actions of her early years.

Wheeler rarely took a break from writing. His most productive year for the Deadwood Dick series came in 1878, when he churned out six volumes in the series. In these works, Calamity continued to be a central or strong supporting character. The final volume published in 1878, and the eighth installment in the Deadwood Dick Library, was *Deadwood Dick on Deck; or, Calamity Jane, The Heroine of Whoop-Up*. It was one of the two in the entire series of thirty-three that carried Calamity's name in the title. *Deadwood Dick on Deck* and the first in the set, discussed above, are the most widely cited of the Deadwood Dick volumes.

Deadwood Dick on Deck provides the fullest description, thus far, of Calamity. Wheeler not only details her young life, her physical appearance, her loves, her morals, her actions, but also her own observations about herself, as well as the opinions of several others about her. As a result, Calamity is a central character throughout the dime novel, rarely off-scene. Indeed, Deadwood Dick is more often absent from the plot than Calamity.

The novel's opening uses the same technique Maguire did in *The Black Hills and American Wonderland*. Two characters see Calamity, and the older, more experienced man describes Calamity to the younger, new immigrant to the Hills. Around a campfire, Colonel Joe Tubbs, a garrulous old miner, tells his eastern pard Sandy, newly in from Washington, about Calamity. It is rumored, he begins in his heavy vernacular, that "she war deserted up at Virginny City, an' tuk ter thes rovin' life ter hunt down her false lover; another [rumor says] that she hed bin married ter a Nevada brute, an' kim over inter thes deestrict ter escape him." And there were other bad stories about Calamity, most which the old-timer disbelieved, because they came from "a gang o' toughs who hed a grudge agin' her."

But when Sandy replies that Calamity must be a "hard case" woman, Tubbs quickly and strongly demurs. No, he replies, "tho' thar's many who lay claim ter that name who ar' below par, I don't reckon Janie ar' quite thet fur gone." Although a dare-devil, a drinker of whiskey, a gunman of the first order, an avid swearer, and "the most reckless buckario in ther Hills," he concedes that "ther gal's got honor left wi' her grit, out o' ther wreck o' ther young life." Besides, Tubbs adds, "Janie's not as bad as ther world would have her; . . . [and] out hayr in ther Hills, Sandy—ef a female ken't stand up an' fight for her rights et's durned little aid she'll git."

Having introduced Calamity through this fireside conversation, the narrator then takes the reins of his story. He devotes more than ten paragraphs to describing Calamity, as if he himself had been in Deadwood to see her in person. The description of her dress replicates the cover of the novel, which features an artist's rendition of Wheeler's words. Calamity is described as both "graceful and womanly," and in age "anywhere between seventeen and twenty-three." (Calamity turned twenty-two in 1878.) Her face was "peculiarly handsome and attractive, though upon it were lines drawn by the unmistakable hand of dissipation and hard usage, lines never to be erased from a face that in innocent childhood had been a pretty one." Her dark eyes were piercing, the long, raven hair attention-catching. She wore "buckskin trowsers" and "a boiled shirt, open at the throat, partially revealing a breast of alabaster purity."

If much of this physical description was stolen from Maguire's two-paragraph portrait of Calamity, so were the dime novel's details about Calamity's actions. In one scene she spurs her lively horse Trick down a canyon, rocking "not ungracefully from side to side with the reckless freedom peculiar to the California buchario." Calamity fearlessly dashes from gulch to gulch, and in an especially dramatic tableau, stands on the back of her horse as it runs "at the top of its speed." Added to the nonstop actions is Calamity's tendency to give out "a ringing whoop, which was creditable in imitation if not in volume and force to that of a full-blown Comanche warrior." To top off everything, Calamity lights a cigar "at full motion" while riding her "flying steed." These frenetic descriptions alone were enough to turn readers breathless and to cause Wheeler to label her an "eccentric girl" throughout the novel.

The ups and downs of Calamity's love life and moral journey also get full play. We hear that Calamity, as a teenager, was named Jennie (or Jane) Forrest. At sixteen she was betrothed to Charley Davis and promised to wait for his return, which never happened. After Charley left, Calamity says that "terrible changes have come since then." She once "was a maiden, and as modest as they make 'em." Now she dresses and acts differently.

At first Calamity refuses to tell the story of her lost virtue. Rather, she first must kill the man—"one of the basest, vilest wretches upon God's fair earth." The assaulter, if indeed rape is what happened (we are not told), proves to be Arkansas Alf Kennedy, the Danite Ghoul, who is depicted in Wheeler's anti-Mormon phrases as a henchman of Brigham Young. When a resident of Whoop-Up, a mining boomtown exploding into existence overnight, says of Calamity "yer character don't consist altergether o' truth and—," she shoots him, and heatedly replies: "If I was dishonored once, by one such as you, no man's defiling touch has reached me since. That villain still lives who foully robbed Jane Forrest of her maiden name, but *never* of her honor; . . . as there is a God to hear my oath, he shall never live to ruin any others." Calamity is unable to dispatch the lecherous Alf, but another citizen does.

Calamity also reveals considerable gender ambiguity, both dismissing her feminine identity and disclosing her womanly need for love. Asked why she dresses as a man rather than a woman, she answers, "Ye see, they kind o' got matters discomfuddled w'en I was created, an' I turned out to be a gal instead of a man, which I ought to hev been." But she also falls in love with the masculine, protective, and warm-hearted Sandy. When he disappoints her, declaring his love for another woman from the East, Calamity admits to her attraction for Sandy but also tries to hide and protect her feelings. "I got some very foolish notions into my head about you but a lettle bit ago, while I war a witness ter thet scene. I crushed out them thoughts—ground 'em under my heel." The attractions are not gone, however; they reemerge even though Sandy does not reciprocate.

In some ways, Calamity illustrates the moral geography of Wheeler's fictional landscapes. As one distraught woman tells a thieving rascal from the East, "In Washington [read, the East] you have well-clothed, gold-enamored dummies; here, in the mines, though ofttimes rudely dressed, you can find *men*. The difference is, Washington is a refined hell, with nothing but imps and devils for inhabitants; Whoop-Up is a rough Paradise, with now and then a sprinkling of angels." Wheeler depicts Calamity as one of those independent, free westerners, a rough angel with a heart of gold in a warm breast.

As in most dime novels with prescribed lengths, the brief, frantic conclusions tie up—or try to tie up—several plot lines. The good guys, Sandy and Calamity among them, are exonerated and lionized. But there's no future for them. Sandy takes a sophisticated eastern woman in the Hills for his wife. Gossip has it that Calamity and her old beau "will soon start East on a bridal tour." The narrator has strong doubts. "As to the truth of this [gossip]," he says, "I cannot say; I doubt much if Calamity will ever marry, especially since Sandy is gone." Wheeler, of course, would redirect the narrator's course and later bring Calamity and Deadwood Dick in and out of marriage.

Although many volumes in the Deadwood Dick Library, especially those early in the series, were set in the Black Hills, Wheeler took his plots to other new sections of the West. Novels were set in Durango, Colorado; Tombstone, Arizona; in Oregon; in Nevada; and in several other locations. One of his favorite sites outside the Black Hills was Leadville, Colorado. An example was *Deadwood Dick in Leadville; or, A Strange Stroke for Liberty. A Wild, Exciting Story of the Leadville Region* (1879). A two-gun Calamity is featured on the cover, dressed exactly as in Maguire's account, ready to do in the villains.

One shouldn't expect too much, however, from Wheeler's shift of scene to the Rockies in Colorado. True, Leadville had become a new mining boomtown in the late 1870s, but the author's treatment of the site is generic; he does not refer to specific mountains, rivers, or other local areas proximate to Leadville. His characters live in untamed areas, ride through valleys, canyons, and gulches similar to those in the Black Hills area. On occasion, too, Wheeler's notions of western geography get him in trouble when he speaks of Nevada and Virginia City as north of the Black Hills.

Calamity, the "Girl Sport," plays something of a minor role in *Deadwood Dick in Leadville*. She does not appear until page eight of the thirty-one-page version of the novel, and is off-scene fully three-quarters of the time. But on page ten Calamity precipitously pulls her revolvers to keep villain Ralph Gardner from decapitating a foolish gambler who has

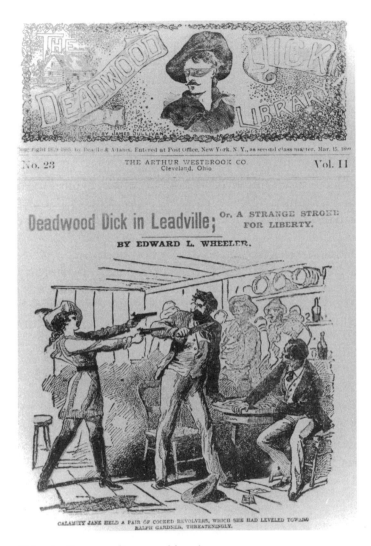

Calamity Jane as a dime novel heroine.

Author Edward L. Wheeler depicts Calamity as a "girl sport" and handy with her guns in *Deadwood Dick in Leadville* (1879). This dime novel cover, one of two in the series to feature Calamity, illustrates a scene in the novel where Calamity stands off the villain, saving the life of a man.

offered his head as a stake in a card game. That dramatic scene is replicated on the front cover of the novel, one of the two covers in the series to feature Calamity. But following that central scene Calamity disappears for ten pages.

Generally, this novel, one of the weakest of the entire series, does little with Calamity. Part of the problem is Wheeler's failure to achieve his intended mysterious settings, and the dark and threatening tone is also contrived. The extended scenes of violence and killing also greatly mar the novel. Only two or three occurrences tell us much about Calamity. One is when she tells others, "I enjoy a free fight, when it is for the right." And the final scene, in which Deadwood Dick allows himself to be hanged, despite Calamity's pleas for him to flee, is beyond belief.

Wheeler seemed unable to decide on the possible marriage of Deadwood Dick and Calamity Jane. As we have seen, in *Deadwood Dick on Deck* Calamity came close to marrying her old beau Davis. Deadwood Dick marries other women, with Calamity being his fourth wife. But later even that union is reversed. In *Deadwood Dick of Deadwood; or The Picked Party* (July 1880), the couple are married in the final scene. That narrator tells us: "A week later, in a quiet town miles northward, they [Deadwood Dick and Calamity] were united in matrimony." The marriage is repeated less than a year later when they are united again in *Deadwood Dick's Doom* (June 1881).

In several volumes in the series, Calamity had been at best a sporadic supporting or almost nonessential character. But in *Deadwood Dick's Doom; or, Calamity Jane's Last Adventure. A Tale of Death Notch* she is back on center stage. Set in an imagined, out-of-the way stage stop and supposed mining town of Death Notch somewhere between Pioche, Nevada, and Helena, Montana, the novel presents Calamity in usual-unusual roles. She first enters the action on page thirteen in familiar terms: as "the notorious free-and-easy, reckless waif of the rocky Western country." But she has come to Death

Notch for unusual reasons. Deadwood Dick, her friend of a few years, has invited her down to the "lower mining districts" because he is "going to settle down for good, in some lonely spot" where he can enjoy more "peace and quiet." Dick promises Calamity that "the hand you have so long sought shall be yours. We will go hence down the avenue of life, hand and hand together as man and wife." In responding to Dick's call to come to Death Notch, she looks "forward eagerly for the appointed time to come when she should go to claim the love and protection of the only man she has ever worshipped." The beckoning to matrimony was particularly satisfying to Calamity because "she had never quite given up the hope that Dick would at some distant day, recognize her devotion to him, and take her as a wife. When he urged her to come to Death Notch to become his wife, all the bitterness of her strange, young life had seemingly melted into glorious sunshine, and she was happy."

But, of course, no dime novel plot could allow these steps to matrimony without a good deal of stumbling and danger. A vicious "Mormon devil" (Wheeler often fingered a Mormon as Calamity's defiler) complicates the plot, and so does a disguised Deadwood Dick, whom Calamity and everyone else are surprisingly unable to recognize. Indeed, Calamity becomes largely the tool of Wheeler's thematic and organizational predispositions. A revenge motif powers much of the novel, involving Calamity. She is taken in by masks and disguises; she is sucked into the overnight mining boomtown; and she is caught in West-versus-East conflicts. And, as in nearly all dime novels, women like Calamity are taken captive and threatened with violent deaths, but there is never a hint of sexual abuse or rape. Calamity is on the scene in the second half of the novel but is "used" more than characterized.

Wheeler also exhibits here his often changing—sometimes erratic—depictions of Calamity. Early on, he speaks of her as an individualistic, independent woman little interested in men. She is introduced here as freedom-loving and as "the same graceful, pretty-girl-in-breeches she had always been," but when Deadwood Dick speaks of marriage, she dashes down to Death Notch, primed for matrimony. In the closing paragraph of the novel Calamity and Dick are married in a ceremony, with "the two wild spirits who had learned each other's faults and each other's worth in lives, bonded with commingled shame and honor." Wheeler, as narrator, "joins in the wishes of his readers that they [Calamity and Dick] may 'live long and prosper.'" So, in less than one year, Wheeler has his Black Hills hero and heroine married—and married again.

Recently, a scholar viewing the entirety of the Deadwood Dick Library from 1877 to 1885 describes the series as "sequential." Perhaps, but that description suggests a straightforward, beginning-to-end sequenced series. Instead, another pattern presents itself. Wasn't the cavalcade of Wheeler dime novels more like H. N. Maguire's description of Calamity's riding—fast-forward but also swinging back and forth and sometimes including a gallop up a diverging path? Discernible trends mark the Deadwood Dick series, certainly; but also evident is a good deal of plot, subject matter, and characterization wobbling as Wheeler moves on.

In several of the initial novels in the Library, Deadwood Dick and Calamity gained almost equal billing, as they did in *Deadwood Dick, The Prince of the Road* and *Deadwood Dick on Deck; or, Calamity Jane*. Gradually, however, Calamity's roles diminished; sometimes she did not appear in the first ten pages of one of the minibooks. Occasionally, as in *Deadwood Dick's Ward; or, The Black Hills Jezebel* (May 1881) she is entirely off scene, never making an appearance. After Wheeler decided to marry Dick and Calamity, he seemed uncertain about what to do next, perhaps under the pressure of having to churn out another installment of the series every two or three months.

Another trajectory in Wheeler's Deadwood Dick series sidelined Calamity even further. As the scenes of violence increased in the dime novels, Calamity is less involved. Dick can be at the center of the mounting mayhem of fierce fights, saloon brawls, and communal civil wars; but Calamity is not a central protagonist in the expanding violence. For example, in *Captain Crack-Shot, The Girl Brigand* (1881), a young woman heads up a band of cutthroat killers, and, along with Deadwood Dick and his superdog Skip, is a central actor in the pell-mell uproars and riots, but not Calamity.

Truth to tell, Wheeler's Deadwood Dick's dime novels were sloughing off into mediocrity. They were becoming more frenetic, violence-driven, and less believable. Some were little more than a series of fistfights, gun battles, knife gougings, or homicidal uprisings. Quite possibly readers demanded nonstop action; at least Wheeler was writing such frantic fiction. His racial and ethnic aspersions were also increasingly widespread and vitriolic. His African Americans ("niggers") are stereotypes, slow and dense; his Asians, sinister and nonhuman; his Indians, "red savages"; his Jews grasping; and his Mormons, vicious abusers (including attacking Calamity sexually), with nary a Latter-day Saint among them.

The final five novels in the Deadwood Dick series betray these mounting problems. Several signs in the last handful of Deadwood Dicks foreshadow the final demise of the series. They are much less revealing, too, about the character of Calamity Jane.

Obviously, Wheeler had trouble deciding where he wanted to take the Deadwood Dick–Calamity Jane relationship. In *Deadwood Dick's Claim* (July 1884), Calamity is rumored dead but returns to viciously oppose Dick. "We were husband and wife," she states, but "we now hate each other as cordially as we once loved." At the end of the novel, Dick, finding Calamity dead, buries her, but, not surprisingly, she reappears in the next novel, *Deadwood Dick in Dead City* (April 1885), saying she was not the person Dick had interred. The hero and heroine mend fences, work together, and Calamity adopts Rex, a little boy recently orphaned. In *Deadwood Dick's Diamonds* (June 1885), they are the best of pards, rescuing one another, working side by side against several rascals. But in *Deadwood Dick in New York* (August 1885) Calamity never appears on-scene, and is referred to only once as a wise wife helping her husband. In the final novel, Dick and Calamity are together once more as a supportive husband-and-wife team, but they meet their demise at the end, Calamity by lynching at the hands of an angry mob, and Dick in a bitter shootout with the same rabble.

The organization and content of the last two novels in the Deadwood Dick series are so at odds with the previous installments that one wonders if Wheeler was their creator. The subject matter is somewhat unusual, the creaking plots wobble along, the different diction and syntax stand out. Perhaps the series and author Wheeler were "played out," as his miners often said in their dying boomtown. The individual volumes were also systematically spaced out, appearing much less frequently than in previous years. About the same time, the final, or thirty-third installment, was published, Wheeler disappeared, with his death date never exactly stated. One could surmise that a ghostwriter might have written or at least finished the final series novels.

Over the years, biographers and historians have often pointed to the exaggerations, at best, or the totally imagined characterizations, at worst, of Calamity Jane in the Deadwood Dick series. Conversely, students of popular culture take a different tack in examining more closely what Wheeler wrote about Calamity, whether factual or not. Both approaches have validity. The fact finders, hoping to locate as many exact details about Martha Canary/Calamity Jane as possible, zero in on the distortions that make the Deadwood Dick novels a nearly worthless source for a Calamity biography. On the other hand, those interested in examining the legends that flowered around Calamity find much to comment on in the dime novels. A bifurcated conclusion about the sources is possible: while largely dismissible as dependable historical sources, the Deadwood Dick novels are the most extensive source for understanding some of the legends launched about Calamity Jane during her own lifetime.

As Wheeler's Deadwood Dick series were transforming Calamity into a nationally known figure, other writers were adding to her notoriety in divergent ways. The most significant of three accounts was by T. M. (Thomas McLean) Newson. He provided a unique source, the only dramatic work written about Calamity before her death. Born in New England in 1827, Newson moved to frontier Minnesota in 1853 before serving in the Civil War. There he became a pioneering newspaperman. After exploring remote parts of Minnesota, he accepted the invitation of Dakota journalist Clement A. Lounsberry to visit Deadwood and its environs while the Black Hills vibrated with gold frenzy. Recognizing the hunger of readers for information on the Hills, Newson quickly wrote *Drama of Life in the Black Hills* (1878). The ninety-two-page dramatic work, subtitled *3 Acts, 26 Scenes, 10 Characters and Illustrated with 40 Engravings,* was the first of various works Newson authored, most of them about St. Paul, Minnesota, but also about Indians and General Custer. Newson admitted that he was not writing "a history of the Black Hills," but, he claimed, his portraits were "drawn from living realities." He would stress "every day occurrences which are truthful." He would also include a brief "historical sketch" of the Hills and a bit about his trip to this new wonderland.

Of the historical and imagined and composite characters, other than the wandering nameless "Professor," Calamity Jane receives the most attention. Newson devotes nearly eight pages of text to Calamity, including the paragraphs that H. N. Maguire wrote about her in *The Black Hills and American Wonderland*, and a valuable, brief pen portrait. In addition, three amateurish illustrations of Calamity appear in Newson's pages, as well as another illustration/photograph evidently made from an early head-and-shoulders view of her that has never surfaced. Although some of Newson's descriptions of Calamity seem contrived and far-fetched, he added new information and reinforced other authentic details. He evidently was able to speak directly to her and interview others who knew her well in the Hills.

Newson reiterated information about Calamity that surfaced in 1875 to 1877, primarily in regional newspaper stories. She was a cross-dressing, saloon-inhabiting, tradition-breaking young woman. In two illustrations, Newson depicted her once in men's and then women's clothes, and his text included more than a few tidbits about her roles as saloon dancer and card player. He also noted how viewers were first struck by—and then accepted—Calamity's masculine ways, including her dressing in buckskins, smoking cigars, and drinking wine with the miners while they imbibed stronger stuff. Newson also provided descriptions of Calamity missing from other contemporary accounts. Whether these delineations resulted from his direct conversations with Calamity (which he claimed to have) is not clear, but they merit consideration.

Calamity enters Newson's drama in Act 1, Scene 8. She is described, in the views of one newcomer, as "a nicely dressed young man, about 20 years of age, with small cane, cigar in his mouth, leaning on his elbow on the counter." He urges the bartender to "set 'em up" for the whiskey-thirsty miners gathered in the saloon. Once Calamity's correct gender is clarified, a "gentleman" provides a capsule

DRAMA

—OF LIFE IN THE—

BLACK HILLS.

3 Acts,
26 Scenes,
30 Charac-
ters.

Illustrated
with 40
Engrav-
ings.

To which is added a brief narrative of the trip, a Historical Sketch of the
Hills, and notices of many of the prominent actors in that mining
camp, accompanied by an original poem, entitled

GOLDEN NUGGETS,

—BY—

THOMAS McLEAN NEWSON.

SAINT PAUL.
DODGE & LARPENTEUR,
1878.

Thomas N. Newson's dramatic Calamity Jane.

Journalist Thomas Newson wrote and produced *Drama of Life in the Black Hills*, the first play about Calamity in 1878. The published version of the drama sold widely in the northern West, greatly expanding that region's knowledge of Calamity. The drama included unique but amateurish sketches of Calamity. See figures on page 70.

biography. "Dressing in male attire for years, Calamity Jane has acted the scout of Gen. Crook's army, has scaled the mountains, fought Indians, rode horse-back, a la male; has drank whiskey, panned out gold, and, changing her clothing, has acted the woman in the dance, around the social board, and even at the bed of death."

As usual in the early descriptions of Calamity, Newson's vignette combined fact and fiction. A bit later in the play, Calamity returns dressed as a woman, drinks with customers, and wins a card game before leaving by herself. No surprises here; Newson and his mouthpieces repeat what others were saying at the time about Calamity.

But descriptions of Calamity that followed in the drama also included infrequent or little-known facts about her life and career. In Scene 3 of Act 2, our Black Hills heroine reappears: "Calamity Jane, dressed in a plain black silk dress—comely figure." Whereas some of the other saloon dancers are noisy or drunk, "Calamity is quiet, with an occasional remark; dances modestly. . . ."

The scene shifts to the Recorder's office, where he and the wandering Professor ask her a series of questions. When the Professor queries Calamity about the origins of her name, she responds, "Because of the calamity of my birth—I ought never to have been born. . . ." (E. L. Wheeler used these words of explanation in one of his dime novels.) Calamity continues, "I was born in the army after my father's death. Never went to school; can neither read nor write. My mother was a laundress in the army; my father was a soldier. Have brothers and sisters." If these are Calamity's words or close paraphrases of them—and there's no reason to suspect their authenticity—she was already scrambling together an autobiography, part facts and part stretchers.

Calamity tells the questioners she is twenty-one and had "led this rough mode of life" "ever since I was a baby. In fact, I'm a bold soldier boy." When asked if she isn't tired of such a life, she tells them yes, but hesitates when a follow-up question is put to her: would she like to return to a life as "an innocent, guileless, thoughtless child?" Soon, still without responding, Calamity breaks into tears and is crying when the curtain falls.

In the next scene Calamity reveals a bit about her domestic arrangements. She comes on scene with her husband Jim, who tells her they are headed the next day to a nearby ranch, stocked with cattle and horses, "and everything necessary to make us comfortable." She hesitates only in not wanting to leave friends in town. She asks Jim what would he suggest she do "if there comes another Indian war, and Crooks [sic] wants me to go as a scout?" By all means go, he encourages her.

At this stage in his text, Newson reprints the two paragraphs that appeared the previous year in H. N. Maguire's *The Black Hills and American Wonderland*. Then follows Newson's own pen portrait of Calamity. Headnoted with the photography of Calamity and packed with descriptions and conclusions, this one-page vignette is the most significant part of Newson's account.

Newson's minibiography contains biographical information as well as descriptive and interpretive comments. He asserts that she was "born in the midst of a wild whirlwind of dissolute life—thrown when a mere child upon the cold world of sustenance—uneducated, uncared for—with a mother incapacitated to love her . . . father dead. . . . surrounded with sadness." Calamity "grew up among the rough and tumble of the world, and is to-day what a delicate society would denominate, a strong-minded woman."

Newson then describes Calamity physically. "She is about 22 years old" and "has a dark complexion," "high cheek bones," "receding brow," dark black hair. She has a "rather pleasant eye, but when in passion, [it emits] . . . a greenish glare." Her walk is "awkward," but "her movements are all free and unstudied, yet in no sense unbecoming."

Newson also asks readers to recognize—and remember—the positive side of Calamity. "Her conversation is

107

animated, her language good, and her heart warm and generous." She is sui generis—imitating "no one—an original in herself," who "despises hypocrisy, and is easily melted to tears." She was also "forgiving, kind-hearted, sociable, and yet when aroused, has all the daring and courage of the lion or of the devil himself."

Newson ended his portrait with an avalanche of mistaken and sometimes repetitive statements, but ones accepted as gospel by many of Calamity's supporters in the Deadwood and Custer areas. "She has long been in the Hills," he stated, although in reality, a bit more than a year at that time. But her run-up to Deadwood in 1876 was very impressive: she had been a "scout in the army," had "traveled all over," had "fought Indians," had "scaled the mountains . . . [and] rode horseback." Still, "when dressed in her own garments she looked comely; when equipped as a man she has all the characteristics of the sterner sex, with her pistols, bowie knives, and other weapons of death."

Judging from scattered newspaper reports, Newson's book sold very well. Undoubtedly, there was a hungering for accounts of the latest frontier boomtown, as there had been and would be for such extravaganzas as the California Gold Rush, the rush to Denver, and later Tombstone and Leadville, for example. Newson's drama played in Deadwood, and he lectured about the play in the Hills and perhaps in other places as well.

Some residents of the Black Hills were not entirely happy with Newson's work, however. They thought his featured portraits of Calamity, Nellie the coquettish singer and gambler, Aunt Sally the black cook with Custer, Wild Bill Hickok and his friend Charlie Utter, Kitty Leroy (a much-married theatrical performer), and nameless miners left out more representative good folks at the Hills. Even Newson's treatments of so-called Capitalists made them out to be more greedy Robber Barons in the making than solid, stable community citizens. Of course, there might have been, too, the very human and longtime resentment haunting residents about a foreigner from Minnesota trying to tell Dakotans about themselves. They wanted to tell their own story in their own way, much as other Americans preferred their home country views to those of Frenchman Alexis de Tocqueville and Englishman Lord James Bryce, two first-rate interpreters of the nineteenth-century United States. To the Black Hills questioners, Newson had already given his stance: "The scenes in the Drama," he told them, "where Calamity appears are, in every essential particular, true, and are presented, as they occurred under the observation of the author." So there!

In the same year Newson's play appeared, H. N. Maguire published his second book about the northern West, *The Coming Empire: A Complete and Reliable Treatise on the Black Hills, Yellowstone and Big Horn Regions* (1878). The 177-page tome promised to be a history, a survey of possible mineral deposits, and a "comprehensive and reliable exhibit of the natural resources" of the region. Maguire wanted to showcase the "undeveloped wealth" of the upper interior West as an available safety valve for "unemployed men and women" of the nation. The rich valleys, the abundant resources, the promising future—here they were in abundance.

Writing first about the Louisiana Purchase and the Lewis and Clark Expedition, Maguire quickly skips through the exploration and first settlement of the Northern Rockies and Plains to the Black Hills gold rush in the 1870s. He briefly addresses conflicts with Indians and the appearances of the Custer and Jenney expeditions in the mid-1870s as prologues to his emphases on life in Deadwood and Black Hills.

Maguire notes that, to catch the attention of general readers, he will introduce "many well-authenticated adventures and anecdotes characteristic of the Far West." After a good deal of prefatory discussion of mining techniques and

"Miss Martha Canary ('Calamity Jane'), The Female Scout."

This early illustration of Calamity as a young woman of electric, daredevil actions appeared in Horatio N. Maguire's book *The Coming Empire* (1878). It reflected the initial stories and illustrations of Calamity as a Wild Woman of a Wild West.

sites, the author turns in Chapter 5 to a lively treatment of Deadwood, the nearby gulches, and the assassination of Wild Bill Hickok.

Maguire's very brief consideration of Calamity Jane appears in this chapter on Deadwood. But the immediate context and content of this discussion differ markedly from his treatment of her in the previous year in *The Black Hills and American Wonderland*. The second account places Calamity with the "sporting men" and "sporting women" who rushed to the Hills. Among these "soiled doves" were "Kitty the Schemer," "Tricks," and Calamity.

Maguire's tone in his treatment of Calamity is largely jocular, tinged with a bit of sympathy. He begins by stating that Calamity thinks she has been "shamefully abused" by newspapers from coast to coast. These "sensation mongers" have portrayed her as a "horse thief," "highwaywoman," "three-card monte sharp," and "minister's daughter." These are all lies, she retorts—"the last especially." After Calamity makes a case for dressing and working like men, she asks "Hasn't a poor woman as good a right to make a living as a man?" And the author agrees ("probably with much truth") with Calamity's personal defense: if she was guilty of any wrong kind of work, society, not she, was "to blame"—because "she always came near starving to death when she tried to support herself in a more womanly way."

The most valuable contribution of Maguire's volume was not his one-paragraph sketch of Calamity. That treatment was too brief and rather flat. Instead, the remarkable illustration of Calamity galloping through a forested and high rocky mountain landscape grabbed readers then—and through subsequent decades. Captioned "Miss Martha Canary, ('Calamity Jane'), The Female Scout," the illustration wonderfully captured the electric eccentricity that set Calamity apart from her contemporaries and helped launch her reputation as a Wild Woman of the Old West.

The third of the important works published contemporaneously with Wheeler's dime novels was the nine-part serialized dime novel, *Calamity Jane: The Queen of the Plains.* Appearing in early1882 in *Street and Smith's New York Weekly* and with the dramatic subtitle "A Tale of Daring Deeds by a Brave Woman's Hands," this work of popular fiction provided still another stylized view of Calamity. Said to be the work of "Reckless Ralph," the frenetically paced narrative galloped even past Wheeler's nearly breathless plots.

The Street and Smith dime novel included several of the, by now, familiar ingredients of the genre. In the opening scene of furious firing, more than twenty renegades mow down bandit "Mountain Jim." Before he dies from his grievous wounds, however, the outlaw tells a young woman whom he has protected that he is not her real father and that she should find her father and clear up the mystery surrounding her now-gone mother. The plot, for the most part, follows the young woman's dangerous mission of gaining revenge on the killers and uncovering the true identity of her parents.

The weaknesses in this dime novel are even more abundant than in Wheeler's works. The characters are poorly drawn, the action creaks and groans with implausible actions and disguises, and the omniscient author plays God in determining the moral regions of right and wrong. Sites lack any power of place, history is rearranged or forgotten, and the vicious racial prejudices of the day are exhibited in numerous anti-Chinese, Indian, and African-American statements.

The Street and Smith Calamity Jane is even less believable than Wheeler's heroine. As a disguised young man, Calamity wins the heart of a smitten hotel keeper; and then in the next scene, where she has flitted like a genie escaped from a magic bottle, she, as a rough-hewn, sturdy young woman handy with a gun, ramrods a saloon and gambling den in Deadwood. Her growing reputation as a frontier hardcase so scares the renegades she is pursuing that they nearly disappear in their shaking boots. As the narrator, speaking for one of the men Calamity is hunting, puts it, Calamity "scorns men too much to let a *lover* speak to her. She is as pure as she is ugly when killin' times comes. She plays a hard game for money and revenge, as all our band have had to learn. I must get out of here."

Equally unbelievable is the appearance of Jesse and Frank James, the notorious train and bank robbers, who show up in the Black Hills. Jesse sees through Calamity's disguise, as she does his. Then they throw in together to bring Deadwood to its knees. The author, Reckless Ralph, evidently thought the James brothers came to the Hills, which they did not, and that they became Calamity's sidekicks, which they were not.

In the final pages, the plot moves to a furious close, futilely attempting to tie up the story's many dangling strands. Jesse and Frank James flee quickly. Calamity finally vanquishes all the rascals she has been pursuing. She also meets her father, who, it turns out, had abandoned his wife Constance (Calamity's mother) because of false rumors. Father and daughter return to Colorado to visit the grave of Constance.

Historian James McLaird is right in suggesting that readers ought not to read this dime novel or other fiction like it as merely distorted history. Instead, they should consider what kind of image of Calamity Jane emerges from these flawed fictions. Exactly. The nonstop action, the plotless adventures, the faulty disguises, the revenge and mysterious motives, the superficially realized Deadwood setting—all these were expected ingredients of dime novels in the late nineteenth century.

But there are a few wrinkles of difference in Calamity's image in the Street and Smith novel. Unlike Wheeler, Reckless Ralph does not build his plot around a romance for

Martha Canary, late 1870s or early 1880s.

A few photographs broke from the usual mold by portraying Martha/Calamity as an energetic young woman of the West rather than a hellion on the loose. This little-known photography reflects a less sensational view of Martha/Calamity. Courtesy Robert G. McCubbin photo collection.

Calamity. There is no Deadwood Dick hero here, and Jesse and Frank are not cast as romantic heroes. Instead, Calamity is a gendered oxymoron, combining feminine qualities of beauty and masculine characteristics of strength, virility, and coercive leadership. The same ambiguity exudes from her character. Despite the gambling and killing, Calamity retains her purity. No sinful stains, "none," a worried vigilante asserts. "She'd kill the man that breathed an insult."

The years between 1875 and 1878, especially, but also into the early 1880s were a tipping point in Calamity Jane's life. In less than a decade, Martha Canary had become Calamity Jane, notorious woman of a frenetic frontier. Calamity's appearances in the widely circulated dime novels dramatically and irreversibly changed her identity. Never again would she be known as the farmer's daughter from Princeton, Missouri. Through the sensational and popular works of fiction and the bits and pieces in historical/biographical writings, she had become, by the early 1880s, a frontier hellcat, a Wild West heroine worthy of mention alongside historical figures like Custer, Billy the Kid, Wyatt Earp, and Belle Starr, as well as imagined characters such as Deadwood Dick, Rattlesnake Ned, and Hurricane Nell. In the next two decades, Calamity was increasingly identified as a lively female protagonist of the "yellowback" novels. These continuing moments of recognition were not always pleasant for her. When journalists or other writers quoted lurid lines about her from dime novels, Calamity usually blew up in anger, labeling the stories and descriptions a pack of lies.

But underneath the layers of sensation was a needy woman who seemed, for some of the time, to find a stable and happy existence. That searching heroine took to the road in the early 1880s.

5

On the Road Again

When Calamity rode out of Deadwood in the early 1880s, her identity as a popular figure of the frontier West was coming into focus. Now in her mid-twenties, she was well traveled in the northern West. Although visiting and staying at many locations in Montana, Utah, Wyoming, and South Dakota, especially at forts or in new mining and railroad towns, Calamity had not found a stable home. She had worked variously as a dishwasher, laundress, dance hall entertainer, and perhaps a prostitute, but few of the jobs lasted more than a few months, some a matter of days. Alcoholism, the absence of a supportive family or spouse, and the lack of education and training were increasingly undermining her life.

But counterbalances existed. Calamity's persistence, her splendid energy, and thirst for adventure offset some of the limitations that threatened to weigh down her life. And new vistas beckoned. As the frenzy of the gold rush in the Black Hills subsided, railroads, farms, and other new towns were springing up to the north. Montana first corralled Calamity.

Even though some patterns still dominated Calamity's life, several changes also defined her life from the early 1880s to the mid-1890s. She experienced motherhood, giving birth to a son and then a daughter. Some of her occupations also transitioned. Thus far a domestic worker, and sometimes involved in male occupations such as driving teams, Calamity now tried to become an entrepreneur, without much success. And during this decade and a half she shifted from being a dance hall woman to participating in Wild West shows. Finally, Calamity spent much of this period, serially, as a companion to two men, William (Billy) Steers and Clinton Burke. She even tested legal matrimony for a brief time.

Calamity's many trips in the 1870s and 1880s and thereafter were not entirely aimless. A discovery-by-travel pattern characterized her ramblings. As transportation networks expanded, Calamity made use of the newly constructed roads and especially freshly laid out railroad lines. In parallel fashion, Calamity visited new mining and farm towns, not so much to settle permanently as to explore them as occupational or temporary residential sites. Most of all, Calamity wanted "to see the elephant," as nineteenth-century Americans phrased it; to visit and experience the new.

In the late 1870s and early 1880s, old patterns first dominated Calamity's journeys. Just as the Deadwood boom began to calm, enthusiastic rumors drew Calamity to new railroad towns sprouting to the north along the new Northern Pacific line in Montana. She enjoyed the company of men, perhaps feeling more comfortable with them than with women who found her appearance and actions questionable, if not repugnant. Also, Calamity's work patterns still brought her to places where incoming men wanted drinking and entertainment outlets. First rambling out from the Black Hills in the late 1870s and early 1880s to other areas in South Dakota and perhaps into Wyoming, Calamity then traipsed on to Montana. That's where most of the new action Calamity was accustomed to seemed to be happening. By 1882, she was in eastern Montana in the expanding town of Miles City.

"To the remote territories of the Far West," one historical account of Montana opines, "the railroads meant everything." Such was the case for many small communities in Montana in the 1870s and 1880s. They hungered and thirsted for a rail line that could become a new transportation and economic lifeline for farmers and ranchers, as well as for miners and mining companies in the western part of the ambitious territory. But the Northern Pacific (NP) was delayed in coming. Stalled first by money problems and the disastrous Panic of 1873, the NP finally recovered financially and entered the eastern section of Montana in 1880, with tracks extended west into the Yellowstone River valley in 1881. In 1882 and 1883 construction crews, simultaneously working on both western and eastern segments of the NP, pushed on rapidly to link up near Gold Creek, Montana, in September 1883.

As the railroad crews moved into an area to survey, prepare roadbeds, and lay rails, new towns rose up along the route to serve the workers, to provide the endless entertainments they coveted, and to furnish needed connections for farmers and ranchers already in the area. Miles City, named after Indian-fighter Gen. Nelson A. Miles, was established in 1877. The rowdy frontier settlement had uncertain beginnings, having been founded by sutlers and other suppliers of whisky evicted from nearby Fort Keough. Railroad crews moved into the area shortly afterwards and added to the new town's social liveliness. When Calamity arrived in the early 1880s, Miles City already was well known regionally as a wide-open, sometimes unruly Wild West hamlet.

"Calamity Jane is in the town," the *Miles City Yellowstone Journal* trumpeted on 4 February 1882. The following June, the same newspaper declared that Calamity was "now living on a ranch near Graveyard Bottom." Located about twenty miles west of Miles City, the area was so named because of its numerous Indian graves. During the summer other newspaper stories revealed that Calamity often visited Miles

City from her Rosebud ranch. One journalist noted that, although she was "as well known on the frontier as any living person," Calamity looked "as if she had seen hard usage of late." In fact, the reporter continued in a negative vein, "she is a freak of nature."

Other Montana newspapers indicated that Calamity was operating a "ranch" west of Miles City or even a tavern in town. Sometimes a "ranch" described a stopping-off place along a trail where men could secure drinks and entertainment. Still other accounts told of Calamity's homesteading with a man named Frank King in the nearby Yellowstone Valley. Then came a little-known story: Calamity had become a mother. In November and December of 1882, newspapers revealed that Calamity had given birth to a "bright boy baby, which she calls 'little Calamity.'" Perhaps King was the father, but that possibility was never confirmed. Unfortunately, the little boy soon died. His presence was never mentioned again until Calamity spoke of him in an interview in the mid-1890s.

While in the Miles City area, Calamity sat before the camera of L. A. Huffman, later a well-known frontier photographer. Although dated as about 1880, the photograph was probably taken in 1882 or 1883 since Calamity had not yet arrived in Miles City by 1880. Calamity posed formally in a dark, stylish dress, trimmed with a frilly collar and cuffs, and also wore a white collar bow and a large hat. Bangs of pin curls were particularly noticeable. Calamity seemed a bit tense and uneasy, staring past the camera. A vibrant young woman in her mid-twenties, she was not unattractive and communicated a much more feminine image here than in the often-reprinted photographs where she was dressed in bulky, masculine buckskins.

True to form, Calamity remained on the move, in and out of Miles City in 1882–83. As the tracklayers from the East made their way westward, so did Calamity. Sometimes

"One and Original 'Calamity Jane.'"

The well-known western photographer L. A. Huffman took this photograph, most likely about 1882, when Calamity arrived in Miles City, Montana. Calamity's image here diverged markedly from the hellcat-in-red-britches representations that appeared in other photographs and dime novels in the 1870s and 1880s. Courtesy L. A. Huffman Collection, Montana Historical Society (MHS 981–573).

she seemed virtually on their heels. Calamity sightings in the Billings and Livingston areas surfaced in fall 1882.

The reports about Calamity in 1882–83 are as jumbled and dramatic as the life of their subject. Indeed, once the reputation of Calamity was established in newspaper stories in 1875–77, in the Deadwood histories and drama in 1877–78, and particularly in the numerous dime novels from 1877 onward, it was difficult not to wild up Calamity. In Miles City she was said to enliven the town during the summer of 1882, then travel nonstop to Billings in September, Livingston in December, near Bozeman in January 1883, close to Missoula in February, and back in Livingston in March. She may even have made a quick trip to Rawlins, Wyoming, early in 1882.

In their rapid-fire stories trying to keep up with the ever-on-the-move Calamity, newspapers played on sensational topics. Calamity had become a mother but lost her baby, she was running a saloon, she and a male companion were arrested for selling alcohol to Indians. Montana journalists appeared to sit on their hands if they could not find a story—or invent a tale—about Calamity to tantalize their readers.

Two other stories, certainly exaggerated and perhaps apocryphal, captivated Calamity followers and would be reprinted dozens of times in the coming decades. The first of the blowzy yarns concerns one Madame Bull Dog in Livingston. Kitty O'Leary, known as Madame Bull Dog, was a former resident of the Black Hills and, arriving about the same time as Calamity, had opened the Bucket of Blood saloon. One source says the huge woman weighed nearly 300 pounds, serving as her own bouncer. Another less weighty and more salacious account claimed that Madame Bull Dog "tipped the scales at 190, stripped. And stripped she was most of the time." She and Calamity quarreled and got into a titanic wrestling match. In one version Calamity won the first clinches, but soon the heavier woman got her down—until Calamity bit her ear. Another account stated that "Madame Bulldog tossed Calamity Jane into the street, as easy as licking three men." Although "Calamity was tougher 'n hell, . . . she wasn't crazy" and threw in the towel.

None of this may have happened. The sources are suspect, secondhand, and mostly distant from Livingston in the early 1880s. But frontier journalists rarely overlooked the possibilities of grabbing readers with another Calamity stretcher, even if the facts did not hold up and imagination replaced eyewitness reports.

The second story, equally dubious, focused on Calamity's doings in Canyon Creek, a location about ten miles to the west of Billings. Some ingredients of the narrative ring true. While in that region, Calamity cooked at a nearby stage station, cut fence posts to sell in Billings, and perhaps delivered firewood. Others living in the same area were reputedly horse thieves. Indeed, the place where Calamity resided in a cabin or dugout and the place where her rustling neighbors lived became known as Horsethief Cache. Charley (Rattlesnake Jake) Owens and Charles Fallon probably stole horses, and later they were gunned down in a shootout in Lewistown.

But Calamity does not appear in stories published about the horse thieves in midsummer 1884. In fact, she probably did not live at Canyon Creek until the early 1890s. Stories that linked the rustlers and Calamity, suggesting that she participated in their thievery, probably owed more to Calamity's living later in the Horsethief Cache and the tendency of writers in the late 1870s and 1880s to link Calamity with those who broke or bruised the law. A thirst for Wild West yarns sometimes led to including Calamity in lively tales that were neither valid nor believable.

Other tidbits about Calamity in the years from 1882 to 1884 were less controversial. Some even provided humorous relief. The *Black Hills Daily Pioneer*, like other Deadwood newspapers, delighted in keeping tabs on Calamity, reporting stories about her whereabouts and doings after she left Dakota Territory. In December 1882, the Deadwood journal published a story from the Miles City newspaper entitled "Calamity Jane's Simplicity." Although well-to-do matrons in the East might pay as much as $250 "for a single pair of stocking supporters," the story revealed, "our Calamity . . . is satisfied with an old pair of her husband's suspenders to hold her four dollar stockings in place." Here was but another example, the *Pioneer* indicated, of Calamity's "simplicity during her long residence in Deadwood." Calamity did not appreciate the story and its references to her attire, so she vented her ire on the Billings editor who had reprinted the piece.

In the fall of 1883, Calamity was involved in another incident that reveals her fun-loving character. Teddy Blue, a man whom Calamity had met in Deadwood and who became a well-known cowboy, ran into her again in a Miles City hotel lobby and talked her into a humorous prank. Teddy's stiff, moralistic, and no-nonsense cattle boss, a Mr. Fuller, needed a comedown, his wranglers believed. So Teddy dared Calamity to jump into Fuller's lap, kiss him effusively, and confess her desires for him. She did just that, among the many kisses asking Fuller, "Why don't you ever come to see me any more, honey? You know I love you." The incident spawned infectious chuckles since Calamity's reputation as a rounder was well known in Miles City. Sputtering and spitting and wiping off his mouth, Fuller "left the hotel and that was the last we saw of him that night."

After the two years Calamity spent sauntering through Montana towns, her career took a new turn in early 1884. As the railroad towns along the Northern Pacific transitioned out of their diapers into youthfulness, Calamity's attentions waned. Then an enticing rumor of a new mining strike in northern Idaho, not too distant from the NP route across the Idaho panhandle, caught and held her attention. Fresh experiences and a new occupation beckoned. Calamity would become an actress for the first time, although she was already a veteran yarn-spinner about her exaggerated past.

Sometime in 1883, probably soon after the NP was completed in September, Calamity ventured even farther west, following the railroad into Spokane, Washington. How long Calamity stayed is not clear, but the *Spokane Press* indicated at her death twenty years later that, though she was far removed from her usual territory, she was participating in her usual activities. She worked as a faro dealer in a saloon while serving up drinks. "'Calamity' quickly became one of the show features of the town, and no stranger ever quit our domains without first visiting her place of business," one early Spokane resident recalled. Another remembered Calamity's dress and actions. "Jane wore a man's suit, her nether garments tucked into the tops of rawhide boots," and "while dealing (cards), her custom was to peacefully chew tobacco and smoke a cigar at the same time." Perhaps a ranch worker caught the essence of the good/bad Calamity when he said of her: "She was a good woman only she drinked."

In 1883–84 a series of mineral strikes in the Coeur d'Alenes of northern Idaho set off a new stampede. As previous rushes had for nearly two generations in the American West, the strike in the Coeur d'Alenes triggered an explosive population movement. One source estimated that two hundred men a day were flooding into such overnight boomtowns as Eagle City and Murraytown (also Murrayville, or Murray) in winter and spring of 1883–84. With men came the thirsts of drink and entertainment. More than forty saloons appeared quickly in the region. The boomtowns and their thirsty populations caught the attention of Calamity Jane, a veteran of saloons and dance halls. Responding to the call, Calamity made two quick trips to northern Idaho in early 1884.

Drawing on her experiences in Deadwood working for Al Swearingen, Calamity recruited female entertainers and brought them with her. J. McDaniels, a theater owner in Eagle City, invited Calamity to bring her "troupe" to the mining camps. Calamity and her girls may have come from Spokane in the west rather than from Montana to the east. The journey to the isolated, cold Coeur d'Alenes was arduous and time-consuming. Leaving the NP at Rathdrum, the female entertainers secured a stagecoach to Kingston and then rode horseback over the Jackass Trail and finally down into Eagle City. A journalist, probably putting words in Calamity's mouth, reported that she said of the difficult journey, "Hell, I could have gone to New York and back in the time it took to maneuver transfer points to get to Jackass Junction, and the agony of the trail was another Hell."

On 22 February 1884, in a thrown-together tented barroom, Calamity starred in what is said to be the "first dance and social event" in Eagle. The big doings featured a four-fiddle orchestra, Calamity's opening monologue of her frontier life, the dancing girls, and then a come-all dance to include the miners—already fueled by the warmth of the hall and their drinking—with the eight women dancers. Calamity was touted as the "star of the evening" in this "motley assemblage of frontier life, rowdy, rough, tough and noisy!" The bouncers were kept busy to break up the fights as night turned into early morning. Then the remarkable affair was over. In leaving, Calamity reportedly told the dwindling crowd, "At least we ain't cooking in the hot boxes of hell. We'll be a-wishing we were when we hit the commodious Jackass Trail. I'll be back when the birds are a-twittering in the spring."

Calamity returned—even earlier than she promised. In March she made a second trip. The *Coeur d'Alene Nugget* reported that Calamity had come back to the Coeur d'Alenes, but evidently not as an invited guest, to lead another social. In fact, the *Belknap* (Montana) *Enterprise* stated that Calamity had "arrived in town . . . penniless, not even able to pay for her lodging." But the next morning she landed a job cooking in a restaurant. "It was a big card for the restaurant," the reporter added, because "many had a desire to see the charming old lady."

A strong rumor in the region, persisting into the twenty-first century, indicates that Calamity had planned an even earlier trip into northern Idaho. But she turned away when she spotted a comely competitor who might steal all the customers. This story centers on a young Irish woman, Molly Burden (later known as Molly b' Dam). Reportedly speaking to Molly on the train on the way toward Eagle City, Calamity concluded that her younger, prettier competitor would sideline her own efforts with the miners. So, Calamity did not then tramp into the Coeur d'Alenes, but waited two or three weeks before coming as a dancer-entertainer. No contemporary evidence substantiates this story, but Molly b' Dam's reputation as a pretty prostitute and nursemaid lives on. Annual activities and sites continue to celebrate her name in the region.

Interestingly, another legendary Old West figure was in Eagle City at the same time as Calamity. At the end of January 1884, Wyatt Earp, his common-law wife Josie, and his brother James Earp arrived in Eagle City. They were there when Calamity arrived a month later. Earp was operating the White Elephant saloon, but Calamity did not host her dance there, and they did not mention one another.

Calamity's two stops in the Coeur d'Alenes lasted but a few days. On 14 March, the *Livingston Daily Enterprise* reported that Calamity, "the most noted woman of the western frontier and the heroine of many a thrilling nickel novel," had been living recently in Livingston but had "pulled up stakes and joined the stampede for the Coeur d'Alenes." A month later, probably attempting to stiff-arm the gold rush drain to Idaho and tout its own site, the same newspaper told readers that Calamity was back in Livingston. She had "successfully escaped various trials and tribulations incident to a trip to the Coeur d'Alenes." She "had enough of the mines and abuses that country in round terms."

But the trip to Eagle City had introduced Calamity to a new possible occupation—public performances as a Wild West woman. A new opportunity for another venue of this type surfaced soon after Calamity returned from the Coeur d'Alenes in spring 1884. Tom Hardwick, a man Calamity had known in Deadwood, offered her a spot with his new group, the Great Rocky Mountain Show.

Although Hardwick's show likely opened in May, Calamity probably joined the troupe in late June or early July. Hardwick was attempting on a smaller scale what Buffalo Bill Cody launched a year earlier in his Wild West show and continued into the twentieth century. A headliner for Hardwick's entourage was John (Liver-Eating) Johnson, who reportedly devoured the livers of Crow Indians he killed because, he was convinced, they had murdered his family. Another featured attraction was Curley, an Indian scout, controversially said to be the only survivor of the Custer debacle eight years earlier at the Little Bighorn. Several Crow Indians, cowboys, and scouts were also part of the traveling troupe. Altogether, the Hardwick show was advertised as "a vivid and thrilling illustration of wild western life." A Montana newspaper revealed in late June that Calamity had left Montana "to join the Liver Eating Johnson troupe." Even though Calamity was never listed as a headline attraction in the Hardwick come-ons, some Montana journalists referred to the show as the "Calamity Jane–Liver Eating John Combination." What specific role Calamity was to perform was never clear, but she was reported on several occasions to be a member of the Great Rocky Mountain Show.

From the beginning, Hardwick was plagued with financial problems. Even though the troupe attracted large audiences and received strongly positive newspaper reviews, rumors of fiscal difficulties surfaced as Calamity was traveling to

Calamity Jane in stylish buckskins.

In Montana, in Idaho and Washington, and certainly in Wyoming in the 1880s, Calamity dressed up in buckskins, probably to participate in parades, shows, and other celebrations. This photo may have been taken in the 1880s in Evanston, Wyoming. Courtesy J. Leonard Jennewein Collection, McGovern Library, Dakota Wesleyan University.

join Hardwick. In early July, after performances in Wisconsin, the money problems deepened. After delays Hardwick's performers left for Chicago in mid-July. Then, the financial roof fell in when Hardwick was unable to pay his troupe members, and some were forced to sell their ponies to pay for return-trip tickets to Montana. On 16 August the *Livingston Daily Enterprise* revealed that the "Calamity Jane-Liver Eating Johnson-Crow Indian-Cowboy combination called Hardwick's show, busted in Chicago." Calamity retreated to Montana, but soon announced she was leaving for Wyoming.

In the Civil War era and in the years immediately following, Americans were newspaper addicts. According to historian James McPherson, Americans had become "the world's preeminent newspaper people, with by far the largest per capita circulation of any country." Or, as the American author Oliver Wendell Homes put it, "We must have something to eat, and the papers to read. . . . Everything else we can do without. . . . Only bread and the newspaper we must have."

This insatiable appetite for newspapers and the local, regional, and global news they carried increasingly influenced the stories about Calamity Jane in the 1880s and 1890s. Needing lively occurrences and anecdotes to feed their hungry readers, publishers and reporters found the nonstop and controversial deeds of Calamity eminently newsworthy. Exaggerated tales of how she bruised and broke social expectations of women in the northern interior West were especially attention-gathering. One was unlikely to hear that she had become a mother or legally married a man in the 1880s, but hundreds of column inches were devoted to her masculine dress, drinking, and errant behavior. The journalists, nearly all men, rarely depicted Calamity as a pioneer woman, or as dressed like one, and desiring family and stability. Rather, the stories emanating out of

Wyoming, Montana, and nearby areas from 1884 to 1894 depicted her as a Wild Woman of the Old West. Once established, this stereotype allowed for little variance in the newspaper stories published in the decade.

After the collapse of the Hardwick show, the initial newspaper accounts placed Calamity in Wyoming. A rumored mini–mining rush took her first to northern Wyoming, but by the end of 1884 she was said to be in the Lander area. Perhaps she visited that area to see her sister, Lena, and her brother, Elijah (Lige). As noted earlier, at age sixteen, Lena had married German immigrant John Borner in 1875, and they had begun a large family. Lena and John had moved to an area just south of Lander, a site that later became known as Borner's Garden. No contemporary account reveals that Calamity came to visit her sister and brother, but family traditions of a much later time, nearly all from the Borner side of the family, indicate that Calamity visited the Lander area in 1884. If not then, a bit later.

But the Borner stories differ markedly in what they said about Calamity. Some of Calamity's Borner nieces or nephews, or their offspring, remember that John Borner detested his sister-in-law and wanted to keep her distant from his family. A religious man who had begun training for the ministry before he left Germany and who knew his Bible, chapter and verse, Borner forbad Calamity from coming to his home. A Borner descendent recalled that when Borner's preschool daughter Hannah began to mimic her aunt's florid profanity, John shut the door on Calamity. She was not welcome.

The sisters may have fallen out too. One Borner family member repeated the story of Lena's upbraiding Calamity for her drinking and carousing, and Calamity's vociferous defense that she had turned to prostitution early on so she could help Lena and Elijah. That often-repeated story is suspect, unfortunately, because it is not based on contemporary evidence but on stories told well after the 1880s.

Only one or two glancing newspaper accounts deal with Calamity in the Lander area in 1884–85, but later stories deal with those years. Some suggest that Calamity and Lena jointly ran a laundry in Lander for a short time, perhaps as early as the 1870s, or even in the 1880s. (If John Borner's clear dislike of Calamity is entirely true, she and Lena probably did not cooperate in a business.) One more sensational rumor has Calamity, well into her cups, running stark naked up Lander's main street, yelling, even howling, calling attention to herself.

Tobe Borner, Calamity's nephew, saw his Aunt Martha in a very positive light. First, he discounted the crazy rumors of her as a Wild Woman of the West, pointing instead to another "dance hall girl" who cavorted in and out of saloons in Wyoming masquerading as Calamity. His aunt drank some, as more than a few frontier women did, but she "was not the gun-toting, hard drinker that she has been pictured." Again, the stand-in Calamity Jane, acting as her double, was behind these distorted myths about his aunt. Tobe was unwilling to accept any of the lurid tales that were appearing in regional newspapers about Calamity.

Tobe's memories more than a half-century later were often off-track, as were the Borner family's stories about Calamity and the Canary family. Calamity's nephew remembered her as entirely kind and helpful, "possessed of some excellent qualities." He added that she had even been present at his birth in 1877, according to his father, John Borner. That story seems unlikely because Calamity was reported dancing and working in Deadwood saloons at the time and because of John Borner's negative reactions toward her.

Whether Calamity spent much time in the Lander area in 1884–85, or even a bit later, is not entirely clear. But a few newspapers placed her there. The *Cheyenne Democratic Leader* of 21 March 1885 noted that Calamity would now "make Lander her permanent place of abode." And eight months later, a stringer for the *Cheyenne Daily Leader* located and interviewed Calamity in Lander.

Before and after these Lander stops, Calamity was sighted throughout the southern half of Wyoming. Her itchy feet and instability had her repeatedly on the road. A Cheyenne newspaper in November 1884 reported that Calamity, having left Buffalo, Wyoming, was now in Fort Washakie "leading a quiet life." One biographer even speculated that Calamity had found another "husband" for a time in that area. From 1885 through 1888, Calamity was irregularly in Rawlins. On other occasions she was spotted in Cheyenne, Laramie, Casper, Rock Springs, and other locations. In none of these places did she stay long, even though she often promised journalists that she planned to settle in one or more of them.

Calamity's own stretchers about her life make it difficult to trace with precision her whereabouts in Wyoming and elsewhere in the years following 1884. In her unreliable autobiography, Calamity claimed that after leaving Montana in 1884, she "went to California," passing through Ogden, Utah, on her way to San Francisco. Next, she abandoned the West Coast for Texas, where in 1885 she married Clinton Burke. She alleged that she bore him a child in 1887 and that they "remained in Texas leading a quiet home life until 1889." Contemporary newspapers in Wyoming and other parts of the northern, interior West, however, told much different, more believable stories.

Rawlins did most to grab Calamity's attentions in the 1880s, with her controversial actions becoming grist for lurid headlines in several Wyoming newspapers. In 1884–85, and perhaps as late as 1888, Calamity was in and out of Rawlins. There, she found temporary work, "married" at least two "husbands," gave birth to a second child, and even got legally married for the only time. These symbols of stability are misleading, however. The years of Rawlins

Calamity Jane in Wyoming in the 1880s.

More often than not, Calamity wore a dress rather than
buckskins. Here she may have been photographed in
Rawlins, Wyoming, where she resided part-time in the mid-
1880s. Courtesy Denver Public Library (F-38793).

were troubled, including several episodes of drunkenness, alienation, and violence.

The central figure in Calamity's tumultuous life in Rawlins was William A. (Bill) Steers, a railroad brakeman whom Calamity probably met about 1885. Born in Iowa in 1865, a younger son in a large family, and perhaps a replacement sibling for an older brother—also William P. Steers—the younger Bill Steers evidently left his family home while a teenager. He probably arrived in Rawlins when he was fifteen and was listed in the census of 1880 as staying in the Smith family boardinghouse with nearly thirty other men. Isolated from his family, a bit adrift, and perhaps adopting some of the unacceptable behavior of his older fellow boarders, Steers soon gained a reputation as an unsavory young man. No one had much good to say about Steers. In 1885, he would have been twenty, nine years younger than Calamity.

Steers and Calamity were first reported as a couple in 1885. Interestingly, in early 1885—indeed, into 1886—Calamity was also identified in Rawlins and other Carbon County documents as Mattie or Nell King. Was this a suggestion that she might have taken on a "husband" named King in the Rawlins or Lander area, or she was still being considered the "wife" of the King in Montana? Rumors circulated up from Meeker, a boomtown south of Rawlins, just over the Colorado border, that Calamity and Steers were in Meeker and that in July 1885 both had been arrested, perhaps for disorderly conduct. A year later Calamity swore out a warrant asking for Steers's arrest, accusing him of hitting her with a butcher knife handle and splitting her lip with a rock. Steers was fined and jailed, but on his release Calamity agreed to go north with him. "They both started out . . . afoot," a Rawlins reporter noted, "Jane carrying the pack. They are a tough pair."

The fights between Calamity and Steers continued into the next year. They were numerous, noisy, and sometimes violent. In September 1886, Calamity and Steers got into another drunken rumble, during which Steers smacked her head with a monkey wrench, opening a bleeding gash. Although Calamity was arrested and taken to Hotel Rankin (the jail), Steers dashed out of town, headed south. A Rawlins journalist described Steers as "one of the most worthless curs unhung." Another story in the same issue of the *Carbon County Journal* revealed that, though "her postoffice name is Mrs. Martha King," Calamity had just returned from Meeker with Steers, "her 'best man' who deserves a hangman's knot." About a week later Steers was apprehended and sentenced to a month in jail. Again, a reporter—perhaps the same journalist—indicted Steers as a "miserable stick" and a person who deserves "a more severe punishment than a month's free board, but the law will not allow it." Reporters who bludgeoned Steers were much kinder to Calamity. She is "not half as bad as the human ghouls that abuse her," one wrote, but is instead a "victim of passion, with generous impulses . . . a poor pilgrim [who] has been made the scape-goat of the outlaw, the assassin, the tin horn, and at last the out cast of man." He added, "Kind Christians, what will you do with her?"

The litany of drunken brawls and jailings continued, and sometimes Calamity seemed in near poverty, but some way or another she got around. In late 1886 she was reported living in a dugout near a creek and adjacent to the roundhouse in Rawlins. But an early morning fire destroyed the slipshod place. The following March, after "an absence of ten or eleven years," Calamity reappeared in Cheyenne in "very dilapidated condition." She was also sighted in Crawford, Nebraska, and, uncertainly, in the Casper area.

The most unusual of her journeys was a trip to the Midwest in early June 1887, if everything Calamity told a Cheyenne reporter was true. She and Steers had traveled to visit his relatives in Wisconsin, and they were now back in Cheyenne where a reporter caught up with her and assembled a revealing story about her past and present. It was the most important interview Calamity gave in the late 1880s.

The reporter framed his interview with his own comments before quoting Calamity extensively. Calling her Mary Jane Steers, he asserted that she was "a genuine character in Western history" and then tipped his interpretive hand: Calamity will "be remembered in the annals of Wyoming long after more useful and better members of society are forgotten." He added that several citizens of the area would recognize her, whom they recollected "as a beautiful and dangerous courtesan, who seemed to take a devilish delight in fascinating her victims and then casting them aside as a child does an old toy." Here was the "wreck of what was one of the most beautiful women in the West."

Then the writer turned to Calamity and quoted her own words. Not surprisingly, Calamity recalled lively incidents in such places as Deadwood and Rawlins—and Bismarck. In the latter Dakota town, she said two men fought a duel over her favors, with one of them being killed. Calamity, scared since he was a town favorite, barely made it south to Deadwood, where she took up men's clothes and then bullwhacking as an occupation. Obviously, Calamity seemed to be pulling the reporter's leg since there is no evidence a man was killed dueling for her, or that she got her start in Deadwood after scurrying for safety out of Bismarck.

The stretchers went on for another paragraph. After being at Deadwood and tiring of life in the Hills, she had moved out to Lander, where, within twenty-four hours, two other men vied for her attentions, with a cowboy killing a storekeeper in the melee.

The reporter, plying Calamity with a variety of questions, asked her about a "history of your life published in an Eastern paper some time since." He wanted to know: "Was it true?" Was the reporter referring to Mrs. William Loring Spencer's novel *Calamity Jane: A Story of the Black Hills* (1887), which had been serialized in the *New York Tribune* before its book publication? The reference is not clear, but Calamity's pointed response is. "I read that. [Was she able to?] No it was a pack of lies. I very seldom talk about myself, but when I do I tell the truth. I can prove every word I've told you by people right in this town." Obviously, Calamity was unable to tell the whole truth and nothing but the truth. Most interesting is what she chose to tell, even when spreading mistruths.

For instance, for the first time Calamity now revealed that she had "married Mr. Steers" some "two years ago" in Rawlins. But news of the marriage had never been announced in the papers and surely would have been, and Calamity had never announced the marriage before June 1887. Now there was a reason. Soon after being interviewed, Calamity, betraying her "overruling passion . . . for strong drink," had gone on a bender and been arrested. But she was released because she was able to present "a physician's certificate that she was in a rather delicate condition." Calamity was pregnant, and, obviously wanting signs of respectability, spoke of a marriage date that had never occurred.

Calamity's earlier biographers and most since often overlook a bundle of incidents that reveal how much Calamity wanted to be like other pioneer women, despite much evidence of how she countered societal expectations. In her several references to "husbands," to being married, and to "living the quiet life," Calamity indicated her desire for respectability. Here, in Cheyenne in June 1887, she provided still another clue of her wish: she did not want her unborn child to be fatherless—or in the word of the day, a bastard.

In her brief autobiography of 1895–96, Calamity tells us that on "October 29th, 1887, I became the mother of a girl baby." The girl was said to be "the very image of its father, at least that is what he said, but who has the temper of its mother." The statement was vintage Calamity: part fact, some fiction. Every indication is that Calamity did indeed give birth to baby daughter Jessie in October 1887. But Calamity tells us the father was Clinton Burk[e], whom she met in Texas and married in August 1885. Evidently, she did not worry about claiming ten years earlier that she had married Bill Steers in 1885, at the very time she indicated she was marrying Burke in Texas. In all likelihood, Steers was the father of Calamity's daughter since he was her more or less steady companion from 1885–86 to 1888. Calamity was again trying to provide signs of stability and respectability in the mid-1890s because she was more recently with Burke and did not want to mention the unruly Steers, who was absent from all of Calamity's statements about her past after 1888.

Wyoming newspapers hinted at why Calamity's relationship with Steers was so troubled and sporadic. One month before the birth of Jessie, the *Sundance Gazette* provided a very negative portrait of her one-time "husband." "Wm. P. Steers is the husband of the famous Calamity," the profile began. Next the reporter quoted a damning Steers letter to a friend in which he wrote that he had "succeeded in 'getting away with the old woman's watch and chain.'" Then the understated conclusion: "The dime novel heroine's husband is a slightly built, sickly looking and unassuming genius, about 25 years old."

Despite all the difficulties with Steers, Calamity ached for social acceptance. Another evidence of that persisting desire came one year later. On 30 May 1888, "Miss Martha Canary" and "Mr. William P. Steers," both of Pocatello, Idaho, appeared before Justice of the Peace A. W. Fisher and were united "together in the bonds of matrimony." As "officiating Magistrate," Fisher had "satisfied [himself] that neither of the parties to such marriage had living at the date thereof any legal husband or wife and that no other impediment existed to hinder the said marriage"—so, he

Calamity Jane marries William P. Steers, 1888.

This marriage certificate is on file in the Bingham County (Idaho) Marriage Record Book A, p. 132. Although William Steers and Calamity are listed as from Pocatello, Idaho, they were not residents of that city.

had performed the ceremony. Calamity and Steers were not, of course, residents of Idaho Territory, but no one seems to have checked on residency requirements before the ceremony.

Calamity now had her husband, but, more importantly, a father for her seven-month-old daughter. Even though, as the *Sundance Gazette* reporter indicated, Calamity and Steers "separate[d] about four times every year, and as often reunite[d]," Calamity had pushed ahead with the marriage. Then Steers disappeared. Had she sent him on his way? No evidence answers the question. We do know, however, that soon after the marriage Steers moved to California, where he resided for almost forty-five years before his death in 1933.

There is a vague hint that Calamity divorced Steers, which may have been true, since his death certificate reveals that Steers married again in California. But there is no official record of a divorce. If Steers was not divorced, of course, he was guilty of bigamy in California.

What happened to Calamity's daughter, Jessie, has remained a long, unsolved mystery for biographers and historians. For nearly a century, Calamity followers argued back and forth about whether she actually had a daughter, and about whether the young girl who was often with Calamity during much of the next decade was her daughter, the child of someone else, or perhaps the daughter of one of her husbands.

Over time, snatches of evidence piled up, and then a breakthrough occurred early in the twentieth-first century connecting the dots of Jessie's rather obscure life. Some of the first evidence came as Calamity traveled to the Black Hills in the mid-1890s. She was accompanied by a young girl about eight or nine she wanted to put in school, perhaps in the Catholic school in Sturgis. When a Deadwood writer visited Calamity's home, the young girl, named Jessie, returned home from school. Even when Calamity went on the road during the 1890s there were stories about Jessie. At Calamity's death in 1903, a story leaked out that she was already a grandmother, meaning that Jessie had become a mother by age fifteen.

Jessie then disappeared. For thirty years she seemed out of sight and then resurfaced in the 1930s through a series of inquiring letters to people and institutions in the northern plains. Calling herself Jessie Elizabeth Oakes Murray, she seemed confused or wary in what she wrote, first explaining that she was Calamity's granddaughter, not her daughter, that her mother was Belle Starr, and that she had a half-brother, Charlie Oakes, from whom she had been separated for many years. As we shall see, these controversial bits of information about Jessie surfaced at nearly the same time that another woman, Jean Hickok McCormick, announced that she was the daughter of Calamity and Wild Bill.

During the first half of the 1880s, Edward Wheeler's Deadwood Dick dime novels continued to appear, sometimes as often as three or four a year, and five in 1881. As the previous chapter revealed, the plots, characterizations, and scenes followed familiar lines in the thirty-three dime novels published in the series. It was the recognizable—not the innovative—style and content that helped the Deadwood Dick series to become as widely known as any dime novels in the 1870s and 1880s.

In the 1880s another book-length work of fiction about Calamity appeared. It was much less influential than Wheeler's Deadwood Dick series in spawning popular myths about Calamity in the 1870s and 1880s, but it did indicate that other well-known authors were writing and publishing about her.

Calamity's image as a woman is colored with variant hues in (Mrs.) William Loring Spencer's novel *Calamity Jane, A Story of the Black Hills* (1887). In some ways she resembles her dime novel sisters, but in this, the only full-length novel on Calamity before the 1930s, she stands out from her dime-novel roles. When she crashes a picnic of well-to-do women, her form of dress, for example, separates her from that of the social belles; she also mocks their pretensions, but they, in turn, think she looks "more Indian than white." She seems something that has come in from the wild to represent an as yet uncivilized West. As one character muses, "She had heard of Calamity Jane whose eccentricities were so numerous and daring, so remarkable, that she was suspected to be in every deviltry from robbing trains to playing faro." Still, some of the women in the novel come to value Calamity's courage and loyalty. And when the leading man denounces Calamity as an unworthy visitor to his home (he has never met her), his stock as a sympathetic character falls quickly and precipitously.

By the end of her novel, Spencer has created a rather complex Calamity. The author achieves this complexity by playing on the gender tensions between Calamity's masculine dress and her feminine movements. That duality reverberates from one especially apt description: Calamity's "pretty foot and ankle" attract attention as she springs "into her saddle." True, some of the snooty ladies treat her as a social skunk, but the empathetic heroine, Meg Stevens, is drawn to Calamity like a loving sister. Spencer's Calamity may injure social codes, laws, and community ties, but she appreciates Meg and other women and exhibits love and concern for several characters. Hating/loving her life, this novelistic Calamity displays more ambiguities and depth than the other women in the novel. In Spencer's work, we see some of the inner life of Calamity, through her own admissions and revelations, as well as from the insights of onlookers, the feminine Meg, and crude miners alike.

There is no evidence Mrs. Spencer ever met Calamity, even though, as the wife of Alabama senator George Spencer, she honeymooned in the Black Hills in 1877. Although Spencer's hackneyed descriptions and shallow characterizations undermine her fiction, she wrote the only full novel about Calamity during her lifetime and provided more than a few glimpses of how a sympathetic author might get at the residual femaleness of Martha Canary even as she disappeared under the deluge of male-dominated depictions, fictional and those said to be factual, that portrayed a Calamity Jane solely as a wild woman of a Wild West.

The years from 1887 to the early 1890s exhibit the periodic instability that often ruled Calamity's life. First, motherhood with the birth of Jessie in 1887, then marriage to Bill Steers and his disappearance in 1888, and in fall 1888 the death of Calamity's sister, Lena, after a farm accident—these events seemed further to unhinge Calamity. Rather than remain in one or two places, as she had for the most part in Lander and Rawlins in the previous four or five years, Calamity was incessantly on the road in the next two or three years. She appeared in Wyoming, but also in Nebraska and Montana. No more than scattered scraps of her life are available in regional newspapers and personal memoirs.

Between 1888 and 1890–91, Calamity stumbled from town to town in western, central, and northern Wyoming. For example, in 1889 alone, she was reported in Lander, Rock Springs and Green River, Cheyenne, the Newcastle area, and Casper by the fall of the year. She may even have ventured down into Nebraska. Contemporary newspaper reports, as well as later reminiscences, furnish scattered details of Calamity's frenetic life. They speak of her invading new towns on railroad spurs, of drinking too much, and of frequently getting involved in altercations and sometimes being sent to jail. In July, she was rumored to be in a bawdy house in Tubb Town, near Newcastle. But one female observer in Tubb Town also watched, fascinated, as Calamity entered a dry goods store, "caressed" a piece of attractive cloth, purchased it, thinking it "so sweet and girlish." Later, early in 1890, Calamity was off to Wendover and then Cheyenne. Before the end of the year, she was in Fort Washakie and then back to northeastern Wyoming.

Perhaps the information missing from accounts of Calamity's incessant travels is as revealing as the published details. For the most part, journalists and memoirists do not speak of Calamity's young daughter Jessie. Where was she staying, at age two or three, especially when Calamity was in her cups? Since Lena was now gone, and since Calamity had no other family in the area, who took care of Jessie? Perhaps the Steers family, some of whom lived in the Lander area, cared for the child. Neither did the reports speak of any jobs that Calamity held during these years, except possible employment at the house of prostitution in Tubb Town. And once Steers disappeared from the scene, Calamity was without a "husband." One might speculate: the relationship with Steers, despite its violent and unsatisfactory nature, at least gave Calamity a semblance of a home. But when Steers disappeared and Calamity was without a male companion, her life seemed to lose all signs of order, even though she had become a mother of a very dependent child. Now in her mid-thirties, Calamity was obviously having difficulty fighting off the hold of alcoholism and finding employment; she was seemingly on the verge of early ruin.

The pillar-to-post jaunts continued in the early 1890s, although facts about Calamity's whereabouts in these years are even more scanty and scattered. Perhaps taking advantage of new railroad lines, Calamity may have roamed through Wyoming and may have visited mining boomtown Creede, Colorado. She was sighted as far east as Omaha, telling a reporter that she was traveling to Iowa to visit relatives. She may have abandoned Lander for good, but later in 1893 was reported in Rawlins and Laramie, in the company of a former "husband," a Mr. King, and had with her a little girl. Gradually she moved north, said to have been driving bull teams in Sheridan and even staying at the Sheridan Inn. One rumor told of her drinking with Buffalo Bill in Sheridan, although sources on Cody do not mention such an incident.

Calamity made her way north through Wyoming and returned to the Billings area, probably in 1893–94. Several reports put her there and comment on her activities. Many years later, Jessie recalled that she and her mother were in Billings by 1893. Others living near Billings remembered that Calamity. A young man living on a ranch near Billings reminisced about Calamity's hauling wood to town to sell as fuel. She also worked cleaning hotel rooms and taverns, as he recalled.

During the year or so Calamity resided in a cabin outside town—and perhaps in town—she participated in one dramatic set of incidents that led to a little-known photograph of her. The Panic of 1893 that disrupted the U.S. economy also engulfed the northern West. The next year, a clutch of angry miners, upset with the tightening economy and lack of jobs, made off with a Northern Pacific train and drove it east to Billings, planning to join Coxey's Army in its famous

Calamity Jane among the railroad men.

In 1894 Calamity was in Billings when a Northern Pacific Railroad strike occurred. She is photographed (fifth from the right) with men called out to protect the train. Courtesy Montana Historical Society, MHS NRR box (strike image).

march on Washington. On the tracks near Billings in spring 1894, Calamity, as the only woman, stood with a dozen or two soldiers and other men and boys, evidently guarding the engine against further takeover by the miners.

Despite this and a few other reported incidents, Calamity's life seemed almost ordered and placid in 1893–94, as compared to the frenetic and nearly aimless wandering of the previous five years. Undoubtedly she hoped to prove some semblance of family and home life for Jessie, who we know was with her in Billings. Perhaps, too, a new male companion furnished additional balance to Calamity's often shaky life.

Sometime in the early 1890s, Calamity met the young Clinton E. Burke, and he became her "husband" for as much as three or four years. In identifying Burke, one has to set aside Calamity's "facts" about him because they are not only wide of the mark; they have led Calamity's biographers to false conclusions for nearly a century. Calamity claimed in her suspect autobiography of 1895–96 that she had met and married Burke in El Paso, Texas, and had a child with him before they returned north. All those assertions were patently false, but one journalist in the 1960s created a six-column story placing her in Texas and portraying her as spending "happy years in El Paso." None of that story is based on substantiated facts.

Clinton E. Burke (1867–1929) was born in Saline County, Missouri, the son of a minister. His father died in 1887, which may have been a reason young Clint (or Charley) headed west. In eastern Montana, Burke met a young man about his own age who had known about Calamity in the Black Hills. Burke told the new acquaintance that he had met Calamity when she was cooking in a logging camp and that "she's my wife." The informant also indicated, "They had a little girl that I assumed was theirs." Calamity and Burke would be together until about 1896, or perhaps a bit later. Burke, like Bill Steers before him and Robert

Clinton E. Burke, one of Calamity Jane's "husbands."

Calamity Jane met Clinton E. Burke, the son of a Missouri minister, probably in the early 1890s. They lived together sporadically for several years. Etulain collection.

Dorsett after him, was considerably younger than Calamity, who turned forty in 1896. When teased about her younger handsome men, Calamity reportedly told on acquaintance, "I never had a fellow with a h—— of a lot of money; I always did pick a good looker."

But it was too much to believe that Calamity could settle down to a stable, rooted life. By summer 1894, she was back in Miles City, where she had moved into a tumble-down shanty behind the Grey Mule saloon. Near her shack was the Hi Astle stable, where she met W. H. (Wirt) New-com, a recently retired trail-herd cowboy. She introduced Wirt to Burke, and they became friends. Unfortunately, Calamity could not avoid trouble and was arrested. She was released on bail so she could earn enough to pay off her fine. Immediately, she invaded Newcom's stable, informing him she had been jailed because she "was a celebrity." Even though she was broke, she importuned Wirt to take her to Deadwood, a distance of more than 175 miles. Unable to leave the stable unattended, Newcom talked a cowboy into taking Calamity to Deadwood. They went by Calamity's cabin, where she rustled up "her war bag and . . . carried out a cheap suit case, and all that was good old Jane's 'forty years' of gatherings." Before she left in the middle of the night with her driver, Calamity told Wirt to inform the sheriff "he ought to be ashamed of himself" the way he had mishandled her in the arrest. Tell the sheriff, she added, that "some day I am coming back here to Miles City and I will whip h—— out of him."

Calamity never made it to Deadwood—not on this trip in summer 1894. Instead, she, Burke, and Jessie ended up near Ekalaka, then known as Pup Town, a small cowtown in southeastern Montana, about twenty-five miles west of the northwest corner of South Dakota. It was to be their home for most of the next year. Burke secured a job as a cowboy on the sprawling William "Cap" Harmon 22 Ranch. The threesome lived in a tent about a half mile from the ranch house, which was located about eight miles east of Ekalaka.

J. R. (Dick) Harmon, son of the ranch owner, vividly recalled Calamity sixty years later. "Jane wore overalls and dressed just like a man. She would often engage in wrestling matches with Jack [Clinton] and she often won the match," Harmon remembered. "She smoked and chewed and was almost as profane as her husband, who swore and cursed in a loud voice at the horses he was plowing with." Calamity also was adept at "borrowing" milk from the cows until Clinton was relieved of that chore. After Calamity and Burke left the ranch, young Harmon, while riding near their tent site, discovered a hole overflowing with chicken heads and feathers, solving the mystery of where so many of the ranch chickens had disappeared.

Ekalaka stories also placed the couple in town for some of their stay. They reportedly lived in Broncho Sam's cabin located at the edge of town. Another source indicated that Calamity had taken care of a sick woman, an act that made her "well liked" in the town.

But Calamity did not cotton to this kind of life. It was too boring, she told residents in Deadwood when she arrived there in early fall 1895. A few scattered sources reveal that Calamity—and probably Burke as well—had tired of the difficult work and low pay of farm and ranch labor. Perhaps Calamity, having seen the possibilities lying before her as a Wild West performer in the Coeur d'Alenes and with Hardwick in the mid-1880s, hungered and thirsted for more excitement and remuneration as a Wild West actress. At any rate, in 1895, before the dissatisfying work in Ekalaka ended, Calamity began to look elsewhere. Months before she returned to Deadwood, she had begun writing (probably Burke wrote the letters), begging for travel expenses to the Black Hills. How the details were worked out is not clear, but on 5 October 1895 the *Black Hills Daily Times* headlined a story "'Calamity Jane!' The Fearless Indian Fighter and Rover of the Western Plains, in Deadwood." The return to the scene of her earliest notoriety would be a high point in the final eight years of Calamity's life. Sadly, more low than high points followed.

6

The Decline of a Life

Calamity's actions in her first weeks back in Deadwood after a sixteen-year absence illustrated her up-and-down journey of recent years. The upbeat initial reactions to her return soon turned downward in her drinking binges and lost opportunities. Then the chance to go on the road with a dime museum show brightened the future, but that too ended in disaster. So did a parallel opportunity in 1901, with a similar downturn. Meanwhile, the splendid energy and vivacity of Calamity's earlier life were slowly but persistently disappearing under a growing load of alcoholism and dissolute living. Calamity's inability to fend off difficulties and to shift for herself was increasingly evident and leading downward in a dark spiral.

In mid-fall 1895, the sunshine of return and pleasant memories shone on Calamity. In a headlined, front-page story on 5 October, the *Black Hills Daily Times* trumpeted: "Calamity Jane's in town"; she had arrived the previous day. A driver at the depot picked up two passengers. One was "a short, heavy set, dark complexioned woman of about 43 years, clad in a plain black dress, and beside her sat a little girl who has seen probably nine summers." When a few old-timers of '76 recognized the woman, a crowd soon gathered, and Calamity, taking a seat in the sheriff's office, quickly granted a *Times* reporter an interview and spoke for nearly an hour to others congregated there.

Calamity told the listeners that she, her husband (Burke, who would come later), and her daughter had been living on a ranch fourteen miles outside Ekalaka. But she "did not like that kind of life" and so had returned to Deadwood. She hoped to find "some respectable employment that . . . [would] afford herself and the little girl a living and give her child the benefit of the schools."

Calamity also offered a few hints about what she was thinking and planning. She disliked "newspaper notoriety" because so many reporters lied about her and reported false stories about Calamity impersonators in the East. Besides, even though she had been told "she could make lots of money by traveling with some good show," she did not "like the idea." Still, the *Times* journalist quoted Calamity as stating "her life has never been written, authentic," so "she thought that she would narrate the numerous incidents . . . to some good writer sometime and have it published." As usual, Calamity was pulling legs and not telling the full truth. She had already made contact with a tour group, but had lost that opportunity by missing an appointment agreed on earlier in the year. In addition, some of what she told the newspaperman in early October made its way into her autobiography, published within the year. Calamity might speak of gainful employment in the Black Hills area and schooling for her daughter, but she was also thinking of going on the road as a Wild West woman.

The most extensive and revealing portrait of Calamity's returning to Deadwood came from the pen of Estelline Bennett thirty years later in her book *Old Deadwood Days* (1928). The daughter of the only federal judge in the Deadwood area, a young woman in her late twenties in the 1890s, and definitely from Deadwood's upper crust, Bennett provided a much more sympathetic picture of Calamity than those found in most Dakota and Montana newspapers in the mid-to-late 1890s. But Bennett agreed with the writer from the *Times* in describing Calamity as "dressed in shabby clothes" and "leading her little seven-year-old girl by the hand." Calamity's dress—a "dark cloth coat . . . never had been good, a cheap little hat, a faded frayed skirt, and arctic overshoes"—particularly grabbed Bennett's attention. Calamity told Bennett she had given away her shoes to a woman whose footwear would not have stood up to a South Dakota winter, leaving her to wear her overshoes.

Even more significant were Bennett's observations— probably arrived at much later—that Calamity represented a Deadwood of the past. A generation had passed since Calamity stormed into the boomtown with Wild Bill in the "Summer of '76." Now Deadwood had evolved into a town no longer entirely driven by extractive mining. But it was the Deadwood of memory to which Calamity was linked. As Bennett noted, "No one like Calamity Jane ever had come into Deadwood Gulch. She not only was typical of old Deadwood. She was old Deadwood." It was exactly these connections to an Old West past that Calamity would capitalize on and take on the road and market in the coming months.

The next day Calamity moved to nearby Lead, with both similar and divergent outcomes. The *Lead Evening Call* reported that after Calamity sauntered into town, "a large crowd soon gathered on the opposite corner of the bank to catch sight of this much noted woman." As had happened in Deadwood, old-timers in Lead welcomed Calamity as a returning celebrity. But the next day, when she made her way back to Lead, she came with "a fair sized jag on board, and this, together with a vile cigar which she smoked, made her look anything but the beautiful woman which novelists and story writers have said so much about." In fact, Calamity was so tipsy, she "had to be assisted into a hack" by an officer, "to whom she used vile language." She was asked to leave town.

After their initial welcome and support of her, some reporters and other observers began to change their minds after Calamity's actions in the coming weeks. Her controversial activities blunted some of the initial open-armed acceptance Black Hills denizens displayed. But she was not without sympathy. Cognizant of her needs and her stated desire to educate her daughter Jessie, some residents of Deadwood sponsored a fundraiser for Calamity at the Green Front, a notorious saloon in the shady parts of Deadwood. A considerable amount was raised. Unfortunately, when the purse was given to Calamity, she quickly set up drinks for some of the sponsors. The purse was rescued but not before a large amount was spent on liquid refreshment.

Not to be outdone by their neighbors, Lead residents announced a "Bloomer Ball" to raise support for Calamity. The masquerade ball was meant "as a benefit for the noted Jane," who was otherwise trying to support herself by selling her photographs on the street corners. The guest of honor at the Lead festivities never arrived. As one reporter put it, the "grand old ruin was in temporary retirement at Hot Springs, so her presence was necessarily dispensed with."

In November and December, Calamity continued to make the rounds in the Hills selling her photographs. Several newspaper accounts roundly criticized her for undisciplined drinking and obscene actions. Calamity defended herself from one especially hostile account of her activities in Hot Springs by saying she had never abused women and that she was not guilty of the uncivilized hijinks of which she was accused.

In late 1895, before Calamity went on the road with a dime museum show, she enrolled Jessie in St. Edwards Academy in Deadwood. When that option failed, Calamity in early 1896 took Jessie to St. Martin's Academy in Sturgis. These schools were generally not a good experience for the girl, even though she gained some education her mother had never obtained. One schoolmate years later recalled that Jessie was teased and harassed, called "Calamity Jane, Calamity Jane." Boys pelted her with rocks and chased her from the school grounds. Those were distraught days for the shy little girl.

In early 1896, journalist M. L. Fox furnished what proved to be one of the most revealing glimpses of Calamity's entire life. Fox caught up with Calamity as she, Clinton Burke, and Jessie were living in Deadwood and preparing to go on the road with the Kohl and Middleton traveling troupe. Fox, who wrote much less positively and sympathetically about Calamity several years later, revealed more in this 1896 interview about the feminine side of Calamity than any other interviewer during her lifetime. No other journalist, male or female, provided as much insight about Calamity's dreams as a pioneer woman. Contemporary newspaper stories about Calamity came from male journalists; Fox was one of the few—or perhaps the only—female writer.

Fox queried Calamity primarily about her roles as frontier woman, as a wife and mother, not about her sensational activities as a Wild West character. Calamity, in turn, revealed much about what she had not accomplished and yet wanted to do to aid her daughter. She also added a few fragments about her Old West activities.

Fox began her written account of the interview by setting the scene, by describing Calamity's appearance and her abode. The journalist also tried to capture Calamity's rural, vernacular speech. When Fox appeared at the door of California Jack's house, where Calamity was staying, she asked for Calamity. "That's me. Walk right in. Rather dirty-lookin' house, but we've been 'bout sick an' let things go." Calamity was also concerned about her appearance: "I ain't combed my head to-day; looks like it, too, I 'spose."

Fox's physical description of Calamity paralleled what the Black Hills reporters had said of her. "She is of medium height, robust, rather inclined to stoutness, and looks to be in the prime of life, but I believe," Fox added, "she is past

153

that, though her hair, which is long, still retains its natural brown color; her eyes are dark gray, and their expressions are many. Her chin is firm and mouth decided."

When Fox asked Calamity about her background, she told the interviewer she was "past forty-three: everybody says I don't look it, but it's 'cause I've lived outdoors so much an' had good health." Actually, Calamity would be forty in 1896, but she would claim 1852 the birth year in her autobiography published about the same time as Fox's story. Calamity filled in a few details that most contemporary biographical accounts omitted. "I was born in Missouri, but my folks moved to Montana when I was quite young. We lived all over the West, an' father and mother died when I was nine year ole." As an orphan, she lived "near a post, an' them soldiers took care of me. I didn't know nothing 'bout women ner how white folks lived; all I knowed was how to rustle grub an' steal rides behind the stage-coaches an' camp with the Injuns." Those who did know the story of Calamity's life could see she was combining actual events with exaggerations, as she would in her autobiography and in her presentations with the traveling troupes.

Fox contrasted Calamity's rough unkempt appearance and rude language with those of her "husband" Clinton Burke and daughter Jessie. "Mr. Burk," Fox wrote, was "a young-looking man, whose white linen and good clothes looked rather out of place in the room, that would have been quite home-like but for its disorder." Calamity told Fox that "I'm honestly married to this man. I had to go to Texas to get him. . . . Nobody'd have me here." She and Burke had tried "to live decent"—on a Montana ranch, in a logging camp, and then with a business in a mining town that went broke and "we lost everything."

But it was in Fox's depiction of Jessie and Calamity's maternal feelings for her that the journalist provided a side of Calamity that no other contemporary account did. As they were chatting, Jessie returned from school. Fox described her as a "neatly-dressed girl," "shy and embarrassed," and "about nine years of age." She "had a bright face, and her manners were very good for one whose opportunities had been so few."

Calamity turned very emotional in describing her feelings for Jessie. "All I ask is to be spared an' have my health so's to give my little girl an education, so when I do go she will have some way to support herself if she don't get married. . . . I don't care what they say 'bout me, but I want my daughter to be honest an' respectable. . . . She's all I've got to live fer; she's my only comfort. I had a little boy but he died." And then Calamity broke down in tears.

Calamity also hinted a bit about her plans for the near future. She was not going to stay in Deadwood; "we're [she and Burke] on our way East." She would leave Jessie in a convent school and would take her chances with "shows an' the like in the East."

But as Fox rose to leave, Calamity took her hand and testified to a larger goal she had. "I'm so glad you come; it seems so good to talk to somebody decent." Then came the testimony: "I've been tough an' lived a bad life, an' like all them that makes mistakes I see it when it's too late. I'd like to be respectable, but nobody'll notice me; they say, 'There's old Calamity Jane,' an' I've got enough woman left 'bout me so that it cuts to hear them say it." Again Calamity broke into tears, and Fox was sure "they were bitter with regret."

In her final paragraph, Fox provided a brief interpretation of her meeting with Calamity. She "wondered how much better anyone else would have done, placed in the same position." Others often told her that when persons were in need, Calamity helped out; she would "do her best to help." Calamity "has a kind heart, or her jolly good-natured manner belies her, and she has done a lot of good in the world." Fox's conclusions were much more positive and empathetic than nearly all the newspaper reports emanating out of the

Black Hills in 1895–96. No one before or afterwards provided such a revealing portrait of Calamity's maternal feelings and her desire to live the "respectable life" of a pioneer woman. Had other writers about Calamity portrayed her in these terms, how different might have been the mythology surrounding her in the more than century that has followed.

Two other happenings illuminate other parts of Calamity's path on the eve of her joining the Kohl and Middleton group. Undoubtedly, these occurrences took place in light of her going on the road as a Wild West woman. Probably the tour directors—and Calamity herself—realized that she needed more than just her self-exaggerated oral stories to "sell" her to interested audiences.

Sometime in late 1895, Calamity had a new photograph taken. This one, taken in the Locke and Peterson Studio in Deadwood, included several poses, some seated, some standing. The best-known of the group portrayed a sturdy, stocky woman, dressed in a long, fringed buckskin coat and pants, a vest, neckerchief, and a slouch hat, staring directly into the camera. These photographs were likely those she sold in the Black Hills and on her tour with the Kohl and Middleton group. A year or two later, a similar group of photographs, taken in Livingston, Montana, also featured some of the same clothes. In each pose Calamity held a rifle. These photographs became the vintage presentation of Calamity as a Wild West woman, ready to market herself as the scout of Crook and companion of Buffalo Bill and Wild Bill. After Calamity's death, the clothes made their way into the collections of artist Frederic Remington and, eventually arrived in the Buffalo Bill Historical Center in Cody, Wyoming, where they presently remain.

Still another occurrence did much more to get Calamity's story out to a larger audience. In the last part of 1895 or early weeks of 1896, again in preparation for her forthcoming tour, she assembled—or more likely had prepared

Calamity Jane on the road.

Shortly before Calamity began her tour with the Kohl and Middleton Dime Museum group she sat for photographer H. R. Locke in Deadwood. She posed in several positions and later sold the photographs during her many travels after 1895–96. Courtesy Montana Historical Society (MHS 941-417).

LIFE AND ADVENTURES

......OF......

Calamity ⊚ Jane.

BY HERSELF.

Calamity Jane's autobiography, *Life and Adventures of Calamity Jane, By Herself.*

In late 1895 or early 1896, Calamity evidently worked with a ghostwriter to craft her brief autobiography of less than ten pages. She offered it for sale in the last years of her life.

for her—a brief autobiography of eight small pages. Since Calamity was illiterate, unable to read or write, she undoubtedly told her story to a writer who put together *Life and Adventures of Calamity Jane, By Herself*. For the remaining seven and half years of her life, as a performer and roaming saleswoman, she peddled her pamphlet and her photos wherever she traveled.

A close look at *Life and Adventures of Calamity Jane* shows it to be largely an unreliable source for Calamity's life, but not entirely worthless, as too many of her critics have asserted. Instead, the pamphlet includes helpful biographical information, alongside the numerous stretchers needing to be dismissed.

Consider the organization and content of the autobiography. The first two pages provide solid evidence of her birth in Missouri, the trip with her parents to Montana, and information on the wandering orphan after the death of her parents. But the stretchers begin on page three when she falsely claims being with General Custer at Fort Russell, Wyoming, in 1870, having accompanied him to the Southwest to fight Indians, and returning to take part in the "Nursey Pursey Indian outbreak in 1872." Calamity was never with Custer, he was not Fort Russell or in the Southwest, and the Nez Perce conflict occurred in 1877. In making all these "windy" claims, the autobiography, as historian James McLaird aptly notes, had "degenerated into frontier fiction."

Other misinformation followed. Although not overplaying her relationship with "Hickock" [*sic*], Calamity claimed, falsely, that she "had grabbed a meat cleaver and made [Hickok's assassin, Jack McCall] throw up his hands." Similarly, she bragged of a nonevent: rescuing a mail stage and taking it on safely to Deadwood after its driver, John Slaughter, had been shot by Indians.

Much of the personal information cannot be trusted either. There is no evidence to substantiate that Calamity traveled to California, the Southwest, and Texas in 1883–89. She met Clinton Burke in the northern West, not in Texas, and Bill Steers, not Burke, is the likely father of Jessie, who was born on 29 October 1887. If the "girl baby" was "the very image of its father," that would have been Steers. If the young daughter had "the temper of its mother," that opinion is not in evidence.

The final section of the autobiography explains Calamity's preparation for going on the road, but fails to mention that she made contacts as early as spring 1895 to try to catch on with another touring troupe. A slightly revised version of *Life and Adventures of Calamity Jane*, published in the next year or two in Livingston, corrected a few mistakes in the initial version and named the author as "Marthy Cannary" rather than Martha. Some copies of the revised version added the name "Dorsett" and "(ca. 1896)" after the "Mrs. M. Burk" of the first version.

The autobiography likely achieved its purpose of selling Calamity as a notorious Old West woman. It clearly and thoroughly touted her as an important scout for Generals Custer and Crook; as the captor of Jack McCall; and as a courageous stagecoach driver and bullwhacker. Most of these assertions can be proved false, or as more puffery than truth. And as a record of Calamity's less sensational doings, the brief story was also unreliable. Even though it made some helpful references to Calamity's whereabouts through the years, those facts were offset by an armload or two of impossible or implausible happenings. Although *Life and Adventures of Calamity Jane* would parallel the line of stretchers Calamity told in her public performances, it did not square with what seem to be more veracious accounts appearing in contemporary newspapers and reminiscences of acquaintances.

After three months back in the Hills, Calamity set off on her tour with Kohl and Middleton. A representative of the traveling museum group had visited Deadwood and invited Calamity to take part in their programs for dime museums.

A Hills newspaper revealed that Calamity would be making her first trip to the East, with an eight-week contract for $50 per week, and appearing in several midwestern and eastern cities. Another account suggested that she would be under a yearlong contract and visit Minneapolis, St. Louis, and other places on her way to the East Coast.

Kohl and Middleton was but one group of dime museums that had fanned across the United States at the end of the nineteenth century. Veteran circus, dime museum, and tour show director George Middleton and one of his partners, C. E. Kohl, had established a string of very successful dime museums in the 1880s and 1890s. Learning much about the business of showcasing "freaks" (often disfigured or physically unique humans and animals) from the original barnstormer P. T. Barnum, Middleton launched, with several partners, dime museums in such cities as Chicago, Milwaukee, Cincinnati, Louisville, St. Paul and Minneapolis, and Cleveland. All save the museum in Cleveland "paid handsomely," as Middleton indicated in his memoirs. The dime museums were, like Barnum's earlier circuses and traveling exhibitions, "places of amusement." Often the museums were divided into two sections, one featuring permanent or semi-permanent exhibits of mummies, petrified artifacts, and weird and fascinating oddities; the other part of the museum was set aside for traveling music programs, dramatic shows, and "curiosities." Calamity obviously fit into in the second category, at least as Kohl and Middleton defined the divisions. On other occasions the noted midget Tom Thumb, Harry Houdini (the contortionist/magician), and "Big Winnie" (a huge woman who had to be transported by railroad car) were "curiosity" headliners. Although Calamity was promised a $50 weekly stipend, "Big Winnie" pulled down $300 a week—and repeatedly filled the amusement sections.

So Calamity was not starring in a show headlining the West but instead one featuring weird and wonderful freaks.

Three years earlier at the Chicago World's Fair or Columbian Exposition, Buffalo Bill Cody's Wild West arena show pulled in hundreds of thousands of spectators through the spring, summer, and fall of 1893. In fact, it's estimated that nearly twenty-five thousand persons flocked daily to the Wild West extravaganza, meaning that about five million people saw the show. Put another way, about one of five visitors to the Chicago World's Fair also experienced the Wild West. Calamity was not with Cody in Chicago, even though several biographers mistakenly place her there in 1893.

Perhaps Calamity's expanding reputation as an Old West star drew on the popularity of Cody's Wild West and other such traveling shows. By the mid-1890s, Buffalo Bill had been on the road for about a dozen years, had traveled his show to Europe, and was said to be the best-known man in the United States—until surpassed by Teddy Roosevelt in 1901. Clearly, Calamity was touted as a remarkable Old West figure, but it was among human and natural world oddities that she traveled in 1896. She was not with Indians or cowboys, riders or raiders, or any other western characters. Instead, Kohl and Middleton took her on the road with snake charmers, "manufactured freaks" (such as tattooed people), or "faked freaks" (those who claimed to be Siamese twins or armless but were not. Such unwestern comrades did not seem to bother Calamity, or least she did not mention them when interviewed along the way.

In mid-January 1896, Calamity hopped on the train for Minneapolis and her first performance for Kohl and Middleton. Clinton Burke was with her, having also been hired to work with the troupe. Jessie, meanwhile, would stay with the Ash family in Sturgis while attending school. As she prepared to leave, Calamity told the *Black Hills Daily Times* she didn't think she would "ever come to Deadwood again to remain any length of time."

Kohl and Middleton lost no time in selling Calamity as a curiosity coming from the Wild West. The poster announc-

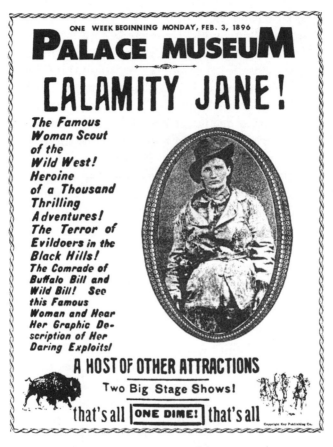

ONE WEEK BEGINNING MONDAY, FEB. 3, 1896

PALACE MUSEUM

CALAMITY JANE!

*The Famous
Woman Scout
of the
Wild West!
Heroine
of a Thousand
Thrilling
Adventures!
The Terror of
Evildoers in the
Black Hills!*
The Comrade of
Buffalo Bill and
Wild Bill! See
this Famous
Woman and Hear
Her Graphic De-
scription of Her
Daring Exploits!

A HOST OF OTHER ATTRACTIONS
Two Big Stage Shows!

that's all | ONE DIME! | that's all

Copyright Kay Publishing Co.

Calamity Jane, the Wildest Woman of the West.

The advertisements for Calamity's presentations with the Kohl and Middleton Dime Museum group were sensational and extravagant. They touted her as the most heroic and daring woman of the Wild West.

ing her performances at the Palace Museum in Minneapolis spewed out pure hype and hyperbole. Viewers were invited to come see "The Famous Woman Scout of the Wild West!"—the "Heroine of a Thousand Thrilling Adventures!"—the "Terror of Evildoers in the Black Hills!"—"The Comrade of Buffalo Bill and Wild Bill!" They must hear and meet this "Famous Woman and Hear Her Graphic Descriptions of Her Daring Exploits!" If the exaggerated billing was not enough, the sensational graphic of her might be. The advertisement announcing Calamity's first show on 20 January pictured her as a buckskin-clad, dangerous woman, with a rifle standing at ready on her right side and a vicious-looking knife clenched in her teeth. None of these words or the artwork was true to reality, of course.

After about a week in Minneapolis, the troupe was off to Chicago, where the sensational publicity continued. The same portrait appeared with Calamity billed as "The Most Famous of All American Women," "Scout, Trapper and Indian Slayer," "The Woman who made Buffalo Bill eat his words," and as having "the bravery of a lion and the tender heart of a woman." Calamity was to appear at the Clark Street Dime Museum with, among others, Ralston, Rattlesnake King; Unzie, the Aboriginal Albino Beauty; and Wm. Lee Roy, Nail King.

How long Calamity was in Chicago is not clear, but she continued for several days to capture dramatic newspaper headlines and stories. The *Chicago Daily Inter-Ocean* interviewed Calamity and shoveled several falsehoods into its story that she had trotted out in her autobiography and that she probably used to spice her daily presentations. Again, the journalistic portraits were of an extraordinary figure from a Wild West. As the *Inter-Ocean* put it on 28 January, "The most interesting woman in Chicago at the present time arrived here Sunday night [26 January] from the West." The story went on to state that Calamity had married a rancher ten years earlier, but that he was now dead. (The macabre reference to Burke suggests he must have left Kohl and Middleton by this time.) Calamity was traveling and performing so she could pay for her daughter's schooling in Deadwood. The advertisement of Calamity's appearances now touted her as a "Terror of Desperadoes, an Unerring Shot, and the Participant in Many Lynching Bees."

The remainder of Calamity's tour is lost to history. Newspaper articles reveal that she was in Chicago as late as 9 February and intending to stay another week, but she disappeared from headlined stories. One later letter from Cincinnati suggests she was there later in February; probably she went on from there to the East to fulfill her contracted appearances through the first of May with Kohl and Middleton. This lack of information led previous biographers, including this writer, to mistakenly assume that alcoholism and Calamity's inability to stay on task led to a premature ending of her tour. But recently uncovered evidence shows that the touring continued for most of four months and suggests that Calamity returned to the Black Hills at the end of May because a letter from Sturgis revealed that Jessie was sick and needed her mother. Such upsetting information was enough for Calamity to terminate her tour.

A pertinent question arises: How well did Calamity do as a presenter with Kohl and Middleton? She was no orator, not a public speaker, and had little experience before groups—except, perhaps, in regaling tipsy audiences over the years in a multitude of western saloons. Limited evidence indicates that she did surprisingly well in her daily talks. A Chicago newspaper reported that her presentations were "proving very popular functions." A surprising number of women had come, suggesting, the reporter added, "that heroine worship is quite as popular a fad as hero worship." Calamity's approach was clear and straightforward: "she tells in her simple manner the stories of her thrilling adventures among the redskins and of her experiences as a government scout." One attendee, who knew Calamity in the West, saw a presentation in Chicago and reported, "She was the same old Calamity and kept her audience entertained all the time by her wit."

One wonders, however, if Calamity might have felt boxed in and censored at times. Since Kohl and Middleton advertised their presentations as family entertainment, such words as "damn" and "hell" and many other swear words that Calamity employed were verboten at her talks. All "blue stuff was banned."

Whatever the challenges and barriers of tour traveling and presenting, Calamity hurdled them at this point. In early June the *Black Hills Daily Times* reported that she had returned from the East, would remain in the Hills for a few months, and then begin again as a touring star the next fall. She had "proved to be a drawing card" and so would appear at Huber's well-known Palace Museum in New York City. She may, indeed, have made another tour to the East in 1896–97, but no one has turned up evidence to confirm or dismiss that possibility.

Once back in the Hills, whether in 1896 or in 1897, Calamity resumed her rambling. For the next three to four years, she traveled through the northern West, especially in Montana. For most of this time, she tried to earn a living selling her photographs and recently published autobiography. These were increasingly difficult times for Calamity, as her energies flagged and her health gradually disintegrated. These times also revealed a truism about Calamity's adult years: when she was under the "rule" of sponsors (such as in 1896 and again in 1901), she did best; when in charge of her own schedule, her life usually went off-track.

The off-track pattern came to the fore once Calamity returned from her work with Kohl and Middleton. Her renewed sauntering commenced. Picking up Jessie in Sturgis, Calamity began traipsing from town to town, first in Wyoming and then in Montana. Once in Montana, she remained there most of the time, until 1901. Trying to eke out a living selling her autobiography for fifteen cents and her photographs for a dime or more, Calamity rarely found other work that lasted more than a few days or weeks.

One of Calamity's first stops was in Newcastle, Wyoming, where, she claimed, she intended to establish a home. But in a few days she was in Sheridan. One of those she visited was dentist Will Frackelton, who had heard of but not met her. (He would meet her again the next year near Yellowstone Park.) The visit in Sheridan with Frackelton resulted from her need for fillings of several cavities.

Frackelton's pen portrait of Calamity discloses her appearance and attitudes as she turned age forty. Before she came to the dentist's office, she had had a run-in with the Sheridan newspaper editor, telling him to keep her name out of his columns, as he had done when she first arrived in town. Her words to the editor, wrote Frackelton, were "very much to the point." She didn't need—or want—"more publicity," as she "warned him profanely."

Frackelton wondered how she would act in his dentist chair. He "braced [himself] for a flood of billingsgate," but it did not come. In fact, Calamity revealed the other side of her "dual personality," by talking "quietly" to him and insisting on paying her bill in silver. One of the dentist's friends, reflecting on her attack on the city's editor and then her quiet demeanor in Frackelton's office, observed: "That's Calamity. When she wants to be a lady, she's as good as any of them. But let her get into a saloon or gambling joint and she'll outswear any man in the place."

The dentist added revealing descriptions of Calamity's appearance and character. Calamity "was fairly good-looking, of average size, with red-hair streaked with gray." Her face was pock-marked and her "keen eye . . . seemed to go right through one." When Calamity returned for a second session in the dentist's chair, she was more relaxed and chattered on. "She was not an educated woman," Frackelton noted, "and profanity was as useful as the other words in her vocabulary. It simply dropped out naturally and never in an effort to seem hardboiled."

Concluding comments added to Frackelton's insightful observations. Residents of Sheridan had a "confused attitude toward" Calamity, he noted, because she was both a hard worker and a ministering angel in camps of the sick and needy but also promiscuous and profane in her behavior. In thinking that romantic writers had not yet spun their nonsense about Calamity, Frackelton obviously did not know about Wheeler's dime novels or the sensational come-ons from Kohl and Middleton.

Soon thereafter, Calamity was off to Montana. During some of her first escapades there, Clinton Burke and Jessie appeared to be with her. The Montana newspapers also spoke revealingly about Calamity's increasing stoutness and evidence of her aging. On a few occasions, too, they took a more illuminating view of Calamity's presence in the northern West. In August 1896, for instance, a writer for the *Anaconda Standard* observed that "Calamity probably has a larger experience and [a] more varied and checkered career on the frontier than any other woman of her class." What the writer meant by "her class" is obscure, but at least he was thinking comparatively.

Unfortunately, such perceptive comments were often buried under an avalanche of journalistic balderdash and mistaken facts. In one story, said to be reprinted from the *Baltimore American* and appearing in newspapers from the east to west coasts, journalists revealed how little they knew about Calamity. And how much more they were willing to rely on Calamity's suspect autobiography than do additional, investigative research themselves. Any story that opened with the assertion that Calamity had "killed more than five score Indians" and "met and conquered a dozen bad men" and had participated "in more deadly rows than falls to the lot of a hundred average men" should have been killed before making it into print. Then followed a story of stretchers linked to Calamity's autobiography, including her rescuing a stagecoach and capturing Jack McCaul (*sic*) and helping to string him up. The story also had Calamity riding with General Custer in a Nez Perce campaign of 1872–73 (a war that occurred in 1877) in which Custer and Calamity Jane took no part. How Montana editors could reprint this error-filled story just twenty years after the events that happened nearby is a mystery. Ironically, too, Calamity could be raucously upset with newspaper stories that presented false facts about her, but in this one she had provided some of the hyperbole in her autobiography.

From August to November of 1896, Calamity—and evidently Burke and Jessie with her—hopscotched through the Montana towns of Livingston, Helena, Anaconda, Deer Lodge, and Castle. These quick, short jaunts illustrated how much the interior West, in such areas as South Dakota, Wyoming, and Montana, had filled in with new spur-line railroads. These new railroads made it possible to travel much more quickly and easily than a generation earlier. Later, when Calamity lacked the financial means to pay for all her tickets, she played games with railroad agents to try to avoid paying fares, or simply begged to ride gratis.

In these brief stopovers, Calamity sometimes spoke of wanting to settle down. She wished to make a permanent home, she said. In Castle, the local newspaper spoke of "Mr. and Mrs. M. Burke" having established a café there, but the shaky venture collapsed after a very brief existence. Although Calamity, usually with Burke, tried to launch a business or operate a boardinghouse or hotel, the establishments usually folded after a few days or weeks. Adding to their inexperience as entrepreneurs, Calamity and Burke also reportedly got into legal battles in Castle for not paying their bills.

Other news stories in spring and early summer 1897 were more on the mark. One reporter, reminding readers that Calamity was one of the first women to invade the Black

Hills and thus an eyewitness of the dramatic events there, nonetheless wondered about the worth of her autobiography. As he put it, some "Black Hillers . . . regarded [it] . . . as a very tame presentation of remarkably stirring facts." A month and half later the Lewistown, Montana, newspaper reported that Calamity had been in that town "for a couple of months" hawking the *Life and Adventures of Calamity Jane.* But, the writer added, she was planning to rejoin the Kohl and Middleton troupe in early August. She would dress in buckskins to "impersonate the female scout" and would receive $100 a month to perform.

Later in the summer, after a brief stop in Livingston, Calamity was back in Billings. Then off to the Yellowstone Park area. By making use of the expanding railroad networks in Montana, she was now exploring the park environs as a new, remunerative sales area for her photographs and autobiography. In fact, she obtained a "Special Permit" on 19 July 1897 to sell her postcards in the park. She also spent time in the Gardiner area just north of Yellowstone. Probably she did not, as one historian has surmised, establish a "joy house" to support her "old-age assistance plan."

Some time in these months, Calamity switched partners. She and Clinton Burke separated, and before long she was rumored to be living with Robert Dorsett. Although Calamity repeatedly claimed to have married Burke in Texas in 1885 (probably to establish paternity of Jessie by Burke rather than the devilish Bill Steers in 1887–88), they most likely did not meet in the northern West until the early 1890s. Burke and Calamity were together, off and on, until about 1896 or 1897, but he does not appear in stories about Calamity after 1897. Burke did reappear in Deadwood, however, shortly after separating from Calamity. Even though details are obscure and sketchy, Burke is reported as driving a hack in Deadwood in the late 1890s. Operating much as a modern taxi driver, he gained a good reputation for taking travelers anywhere in the Hills near

Deadwood. But, over time, financial problems arose. Burke was accused by his manager of pocketing fares—or portions of fares—and not reporting them. Deadwood pioneer John S. McClintock, an eyewitness, succinctly stated: Burke "became an embezzler by appearing to trust his customers and making excuses for not turning in cash receipts, until his collections amounted to one hundred and seventy dollars. With this in his pockets he absconded and was never again heard of by either his family or his employer." Many years after McClintock wrote these words, Burke did turn up—in Texas, where he married and worked as a watchman. He died at age sixty-two of throat cancer in 1939 in Houston.

In early summer 1898, Calamity burst out of isolation. In the previous year, almost nothing about her had appeared in Montana, South Dakota, or Wyoming newspapers. Then in June the *Klondike Nugget* of northwestern Canada surprised Calamity followers by revealing that she was in the Yukon. How she got to this distant area and how long she stayed remain a mystery. The *Nugget*'s stories were filled with a not unexpected mix of revealing facts and misinformation. The first sentence of an early story from the newspaper of 23 June contained a mishmash of helpful and distorted facts. The account opened with Calamity Jane "of Deadwood and Leadville fame, and one of Wells Fargo's trusted detectives, is in Dawson." Despite the reporter's claims, Calamity was not of "Leadville fame," and she had not been a detective with Wells Fargo. The tortured ambiguity continued: Calamity's life had been one of "wild adventures," and "on more than one occasion she ha[d] been forced to take human life in defence [*sic*] of her own." Still, she "is as gentle and refined as any of her eastern sisters," although her "steel-blue eyes . . . , warn the unwary, and a glance at the half-sad face indicates that her life has not been all sunshine." Other accounts reported that she had even performed a bit while in the North Country, at about the same time Jack London was in the Klondike hoarding experiences he would pour out later in his northland novels and short stories. Calamity spent little time in the Yukon, perhaps no more than a few days.

In August she was back in Livingston, peddling her photographs and autobiography and moving on. This time to the east, to Custer and Crow country in southeastern Montana. Even though Calamity had claimed on more than one occasion that she had served with Custer, there is no evidence—only her own boasts—to substantiate the wild claim.

A gathering of fragmentary evidence does substantiate Calamity's whereabouts and activities at the end of the 1890s as she moved into her early forties. Much of 1898 and 1899 she spent in the Billings area, in and out of jobs cleaning houses, fishing, gambling, and taking in washing. Railroad lines expanded into Billings in 1898–99, allowing Calamity to move about even more freely and rapidly. She visited the Yellowstone area again, and while there was photographed by noted travel writer Burton Holmes. The rather attractively attired Calamity is pictured selling her photos or pamphlet autobiography. Holmes describes her as "the original, Simon-pure 'Calamity Jane,' who twenty years ago was famous as a woman-scout, and served our generals faithfully in many of the Indian wars."

Sometime during these months, Calamity gained a new "husband," Robert H. Dorsett. Not much is known about Dorsett, even during the time he was with Calamity. But when Calamity Jane biographer Roberta Beed Sollid traveled through central and eastern Montana in the late 1940s interviewing elderly men who were acquainted with Calamity, several recalled Dorsett, although they were often mixed up on exact dates and names after fifty to sixty years. Two old men in Livingston, for example, recalled Dorsett in that area and nearby but mistakenly placed him there as an adult in the mid-1880s. Dorsett, born in Missouri in 1874, would have been about 14 or 15 in 1888–89, but about 24 or 25 when he and Calamity became a couple. Like Bill Steers and Clinton Burke before him, Dorsett was much younger—nearly twenty years, in fact—than Calamity, who was 42 to 43 in 1898–99.

A handful of references place Dorsett and Calamity together as early as late 1898, but primarily in 1899. The relationship was, by several accounts, short and stormy. In April 1899, for instance, the *Billings Gazette* reported that Calamity strode into Billings from Bridger, where she was then living, to check out a rumor that Dorsett had hived off "with a young and handsomer girl." Dorsett worked at a nearby ranch and also as a laborer hauling water containers to Bridger, just south of Billings. Rancher Philip Korell remembered years later that Dorsett and Calamity had worked on his place near Utica, where they may have remained nearly a year.

As usual, Calamity got mixed into lively incidents that eyewitnesses recalled decades later. Korell, even misdating Calamity and Dorsett's time with him by a decade, remembered that Calamity referred to Dorsett as her husband and endearingly referred to him always as "Robert Dear, providing she was on the Water Wagon." On one occasion she asked Korell for a loan of $2.50 so that she could go to the next dance in town "and smoke up the town for them, just to show them Jane can still handle a 45." He refused, telling her no loan as long as he was Justice of the Peace. At another time in nearby Gilt Edge, Henry Parrent was losing badly in a card game, being done in by a "tin horn gambler . . . taking my money away from me right and left." Then, a booming voice behind him ordered him to "stay right where you are young fellow." Calamity pulled a gun and promised, "I'll see that you get fair play." The gun or his luck—maybe both—changed things, and he "came out

Calamity Jane in Utica, Montana.

In 1897–98, Calamity was in and out of Utica, in central Montana. The horse was evidently borrowed from a cowboy for this street scene in Utica. Courtesy J. Leonard Jennewein Collection, McGovern Library, Dakota Wesleyan University.

a winner by a whole lot." Parrent saw Calamity again in Utica, where she lived in one tent and washed the clothes of freighters and sheep shearers in another.

On still another occasion, the bartender in the Judith Hotel Cafe, where Calamity was working, played a trick on her. He slipped into the room where she was staying, stole some of her underwear, and tacked it up over the bar. Hearing of what had happened, Calamity strode into the bar, packing a gun. After a bit of tense negotiating, the bartender mollified Calamity by providing her free drinks for a week.

The best known of those who saw Calamity during these months was the noted trail-drive cowboy E. C. (Teddy Blue) Abbott. In an often-repeated story, Calamity bumped into Teddy near Miles City after not meeting him for at least fifteen years. When they encountered one another in Gilt

Calamity Jane with Teddy Blue.

Early on, Calamity became acquainted with famed cowboy E. C. (Teddy Blue) Abbott. In this photograph taken in Utica or Gilt Edge, Montana, Calamity and Teddy have exchanged hats and are about to enjoy a reunion drink. Courtesy J. Leonard Jennewein Collection, McGovern Library, Dakota Wesleyan University.

Edge, he recalled the fifty cents he had borrowed earlier and had promised to repay. Now he wanted to do so. She had told him in 1885, "I don't give a damn if you ever pay me." Now, Calamity accepted the repayment—but only if they could drink it up. They did. Blue and Calamity met once more, and he asked her how she was getting along with the do-gooders trying "to get [her] reformed and civilized." In response she teared up and told the cowboy, "Blue, why don't the sons of bitches leave me alone and let me go to hell my own route?"

Calamity's brief relationship with Dorsett may have come to an end because of a heart-wrenching deed in those months—perhaps before the end of 1898, or shortly thereafter. A persistent but unsubstantiated rumor in contemporary newspaper stories and later remembrances claims that Dorsett, concluding that Calamity could never fulfill her maternal responsibilities to Jessie, snatched the girl away and took her to his single mother in Livingston to raise. Many years later in the 1930s, Jessie and Dorsett added other vague information, suggesting that Jessie had indeed left Calamity's side about this time. After separating from Calamity, Dorsett eventually moved to Colorado, where he and Jessie may have reconnected in the 1930s.

The ending of Calamity's relationship with Dorsett leads to a step-aside observation. Dorsett was the last "husband" of her life. Over time, an illuminating pattern in Calamity's life comes into focus. Save for the destructive time when she was with Bill Steers, Calamity's life was more stable and less chaotic when she had an ongoing relationship with one of her male companions. Particularly was this true when she was with Burke. Compare the rambling, disintegrating trajectories of her life *before* her time with Burke and *after* the brief stay with Dorsett when she was in charge of her own life, except for the months with Kohl and Middleton and later with Josephine Brake in 1901. Clearly, in her last decade Calamity seemed unable to eke out a living and live a balanced life without a male partner or leaders she was following. What those "husbands" seemed to offer was more traditional home times, more financial support, and certainly more stability for Jessie. Without the male consorts and group leaders, Calamity seemed to travel endlessly, with no hope of providing stability for her daughter.

Calamity's tracks in 1900 are indistinct and contradictory. One account vaguely places her in the town of Horr, near Yellowstone Park. Bartender Billy Jump, seeing that Calamity was nearly destitute, joined with a half-dozen others to support her through the winter. Jump allowed Calamity to remain in his bar during most of the winter days, spinning improbable but entertaining yarns for his saloon habitués. Another competing account has her in the town of Columbus, where according to that story she spent parts of two winters. Young Jim Annin was afraid of Calamity, "spooked" by the tales he heard about her. In the winter of 1899–1900, she lived in the "pest house," a log hut set aside for those suffering from communicable diseases. Calamity existed on a pittance, buying only absolute necessities from Annin's father at the Columbus Mercantile store and paying cash for her purchases. "We breathed easier when winter broke earlier than usual and she had visited Columbus for the last time," Annin recalled. "A young lady who claimed to be her daughter, came to get her." Toward the end of the year, Calamity may have been in Butte and Helena, including a day or two spent in the Helena jail, where she hallucinated, yelling out in terror that she and her soldier companions were valiantly fighting Indians. Calamity's gradual descent into serious alcoholism was beginning to attack her life more dramatically.

The events of 1901 are clearer and possibly even more action-packed. Indeed, the downs, ups, and downs of Calamity's undulating later life are never more traceable than they were in 1901. Saved from the precipice of disaster by an unexpected offer, Calamity undermined that new, promising future with her own untoward actions, and then descended again to despairing depths.

In early 1901, Calamity's return to Miles City after an absence of nearly five years was covered in regional newspapers. Then, in quick fashion, from 3 January to mid-February, she skipped from Miles City to Billings, White Sulphur Springs, and to Livingston. Warning signs of increasing health difficulties quickly emerged. Calamity took seriously sick and, unable to pay for her care, was placed in the county poorhouse in Bozeman for two or three days in mid-February. Soon bouncing back, she was dismissed and on her way, again selling her photos and autobiography.

Calamity's very brief stay in the poorhouse caught the attention of regional newspapers.

The Rocky Mountain Daily News reported that Calamity had come to "such a poor pass in her old age that she has been compelled to apply for admission to the poor house in Gallatin county." The *Anaconda Standard* added that since Calamity had "no friends [in Bozeman] nor money . . . [she] was sent to the poorhouse." It was the "first time in the eventful career of 'Calamity Jane' that she was obliged to accept aid from the county." And the *Rocky Mountain Herald*, in the most extensive account of the poorhouse stay, predicted that the Old West heroine was likely "to end her melodramatic career in an almshouse." The reporter told readers that Calamity had "outlived a dozen husbands," had "killed as many Injuns as the next man," and "it was doubtful if she ever had a skirt on in her life." But now "poor old Calamity Jane has at last turned her back on all of her old-time glory and gone over the hills to the poorhouse."

The poorhouse stories led to other results. Friends and other acquaintances urged Calamity supporters to raise funds to ensure that she would not be forced again to face the ignominy of the poorhouse. She was back on her feet, but she needed support to keep her off county charity. On the road and after brief stopovers in Red Lodge, Montana, and Cody, Wyoming, Calamity landed in Livingston in late April. There, she met writer Lewis Freeman, and his story, first published in *Sunset Magazine* and later in book form after her death, added much to a portrait of her.

One evening near midnight in Livingston as Freeman was making his way home, a gruff voice called to him out of the darkness. "Short pants . . . oh, Short Pants—can't you tell a lady where she lives?" Freeman edged nearer to the voice, answering, "Show me where the lady is and I'll try." Back came the reply, "She's me, Short Pants—Martha Cannary—Martha Burk, better known as 'Calamity.'" That startling beginning and the events of the next few days, Freeman opined, "ushered in the greatest moment of my life."

Freeman, with a clutch of Calamity saloon buddies, found her hotel. Because Calamity had lost her room key, they boosted her "unprotesting anatomy in through the window by means of a fire-ladder." Checking on Calamity the next morning, Freeman found her smoking a cigar and cooking breakfast, which she shared with him. When he asked her about her past, she, in an almost hypnotic state, repeated her story presented in the dime novels and printed in her autobiography. When he tried to break in with contradictory information from dime novels titled *The Beautiful White Devil of the Yellowstone* or *Jane of the Plain*, she loudly swore and vehemently dismissed those fictions as lies of no historical value.

Freeman's reactions to Calamity's physical presence provide a revealing portrait near the end of her life. She was "about fifty five [aging her by 10 years] . . . and looked it," he began. Her "deeply-lined, scowling, sun-tanned face and the mouth with its missing teeth might have belonged to a hag of seventy." But "the rest of her," including the swing of "her leather-clad legs," "might well have . . . belonged to a thirty-year old cowpuncher just coming into town for his night to howl." And, as did so many others wanting to balance Calamity's darker side, he found her large-hearted,

Calamity Jane in Livingston, 1901.

Writer Lewis Freeman briefly met Calamity in Livingston, Montana, in 1901 and wrote entertainingly about her in *Sunset Magazine* and his book *Down the Yellowstone* (1922). This photograph shows Calamity preparing breakfast with a cigar in her hand. Another in the series portrayed her seated among beer barrels behind a saloon. Courtesy J. Leonard Jennewein Collection, McGovern Library, Dakota Wesleyan University.

willing to help anyone in need. He had heard, falsely, "that her last illness was contracted in nursing some poor sot she found in a gutter."

The next morning Freeman went to see Calamity again, but "dressed in her buckskins," she had ridden off toward Big Timber to the northeast. Calamity hadn't paid her bill, but she would, the hotelkeeper promised. You could count on that.

In the next month of May the out-of-control drinking continued, and Calamity was sick once more. Observers wondered if death weren't eminent. But the Grim Reaper was kept at bay by Calamity's resilience and pluck. She continued as a traveling saleswoman, especially returning to the Yellowstone Park to offer her photos and autobiography to travelers and tourists.

The earlier poorhouse story, however, had fanned across the country and caught the attention of an ambitious eastern woman, Josephine Winifred Brake. The energetic and unusual endeavors of Brake would dramatically change the course of Calamity's life for two months in the summer of 1901. But the failure of Brake's dream, perhaps unrealistic from the beginning, also led to another downward turning point in Calamity's journey. If a trip to Buffalo, New York, in summer 1901 offered possible redemption, the possibility, once lost, never reappeared.

The unusual story of Calamity's journey to the Pan-American Exposition in western New York had remarkable origins. The beginnings were two-pronged, with eastern and western births. Josephine Brake's exact motivations never became clear, but the poorhouse story evidently convinced her that she should go west, find Calamity, and talk her into coming east, where her financial future would be secure. Was Brake also planning to use the notorious Calamity to further her own career? More than bits of evidence suggest she was. Or did Brake sincerely want to help Calamity, motivated by more than selfish material drives? Some of Brake's subsequent actions indicate she honestly wished to aid the increasingly troubled Calamity.

Whatever her motives, Brake arrived in Butte in early July 1901, moving on to Livingston when she heard Calamity was now there. Her search for Calamity led her to the "hut of a negress at Horr, near Livingston." Brake promised Calamity she would take care of her if the western heroine would come east. The exact terms of the offer were not spelled out, but two ingredients seemed clear: Calamity would have to go to New York, and Brake would look after her. Critics of Brake—especially the most cynical of the commentators—accused her of ulterior motives, of planning to use Calamity and her Wild West reputation to reap some unnamed reward for Brake. When Calamity accused Brake of taking advantage of her and the honeymoon ended in late August, naysayers quickly puffed their journalistic cheeks with evident satisfaction.

Information about Calamity's trip to and her appearances at the Pan-American Exposition in July and August is surprisingly limited and varied. Nearly all the information comes from contemporary newspapers in Montana and New York. Brake and her friends never wrote or spoke about the intriguing fiasco.

As part of the bargain, Calamity apparently promised to behave herself, not to drink, for example, unless or until she had Brake's permission to do so. Probably, Brake was not entirely aware of the large challenge of keeping a lid and leash on Calamity. Even though a report circulated that "dissipation" rendered Calamity "faded" and "worn and weary, twisted and bent, on the rapid decline," she was an extraordinary assignment for Brake on the way east. A mid-trip report from St. Paul on 19 July revealed that Calamity was "no stranger to corn juice and about four times a day," but she was letting Brake know about the imbibing. She was also smoking big black cigars. Newspapers were likewise taken with the story that Calamity showed she was a neophyte in facial care. She "sprinkled that [face powder] around in a promiscuous fashion on her bright blue shirtwaist, black skirt, face and hair. She was a sight to behold when Mrs. Brake opened the door and surveyed her." And when Brake registered at a St. Paul hotel, an observer thought "her hand writing . . . [showed] plainly that she was more or less agitated and nervous."

Toward the end of July, the pair arrived in Buffalo. On 30 July, Calamity participated in a much-enjoyed trip to Niagara Falls in the company of Brake, Col. Fred Cummins, and a trolley-load of other visitors. Following the trip, Calamity was feted at a reception in her honor. The *Buffalo Enquirer* reported that at the social gathering Calamity seemed "rather out of atmosphere." She "wore her battlefield attire . . . the buckskin trousers and beaded blouse of chamois . . . capped by a sombrero." Another Buffalo newspaper observed that the speeches about Calamity at the reception indicated that "her word is as good as her bond and she was loved and respected by everybody in the West." Perhaps the actions of Colonel Cummins were a bit more tinged with financial concerns: told of Calamity's traveling east to the Buffalo Exposition, he "hastened to secure her for his concession [the Indian Congress] and succeeded in closing a contract."

On the last day of July, "Elks' Day," Calamity made her Pan-American debut. She was placed near the back end of a huge, long parade driving a team of 100 mules. With help from others, Calamity "managed the reins of the team nearest the wagon as if she was an old-time Western coach driver." Indian groups seven hundred strong, Winona the Sioux girl, and hundreds of others were to march in the extravaganza. Next, Calamity took part in "Midway Day," when perhaps as many as one hundred thousand spectators watched the grand parade. She appeared sandwiched among the Indian Congress Band, Geronimo and a group of Apache warriors, and as many as five hundred other Indians.

How Calamity exactly fulfilled her obligations to Mrs. Brake and also to Frederic Cummins as part of the Indian Congress is not entirely clear. A western friend watching Calamity perform in Buffalo spoke of her audience appeal—"she stole the show"—when she galloped dramatically into the ring. Most of the other initial reports were similarly positive.

Calamity Jane at the Pan-American Exposition.

In summer 1901, Calamity traveled with Josephine
Brake to participate in the Pan-American Exposition in
Buffalo, New York. Discontented with that assignment,
Calamity joined the Fred Cummins Indian Congress at
the Exposition. She is pictured here in the Cummins
area of the Exposition. Courtesy Library of Congress
(LC-USZ 62-47390).

But the sunshine of acceptance and adulation of Calamity
soon disappeared under the clouds of discontent. Calamity, thinking that Brake was manipulating her, gradually
separated herself from her eastern benefactor and moved
into Cummins's camp. Calamity complained to her visiting western friend that she had difficulty following Brake's
attempted proscriptions against her drinking. She also concluded that Brake and others were keeping her rightful wages
(the amount of the wages was never revealed) from her, giving her only pennies to spend. Perhaps, with good reason,
they wanted to keep dollars out of her hands that she would
likely spend on alcohol and the enticements of the midway.
A little-known but revealing account suggests that Brake
was serving as a publicity agent from the Pan-American

Exposition and had worked with that organization to lure Calamity east as a sensational Old West attraction, much as the Apache leader Geronimo was. Calamity concluded that Brake cared little for her, except as a crowd pleaser. But Brake's subsequent actions suggest that she did sincerely care for Calamity and her troubled future.

Increasingly, Calamity became part of the Cummins Indian Congress. Modeled somewhat on Buffalo Bill's famed Wild West arena show, Cummins's troupe was also more ethnographic in its emphases. The Indian Congress featured multiple Indian groups, in all kinds of dress and presentation. But the stress was on Indian life and cultures rather than dramatic competitions. Calamity would provide an additional more dramatic component, as a sensational westerner. Cummins's program of 1901 never listed Calamity as a participant, probably because she came onboard too late to be showcased in his publicity. But, when a later program did include Calamity, the information therein suggested how little Cummins and his publicists knew about her. The later account opened by telling readers that Calamity "was known for her daring courage, as a spy, during the Civil War, wearing men's garments." (Calamity was nine years old in 1865!) The writer also wrongly asserted that Calamity "was never connected with any other public exhibition." This assertion was also well wide of the mark.

Not surprisingly, in a few days Calamity's actions were off-center. The *Buffalo Evening News* carried a story on 9 August that "Mrs. Mattie Dorsett, the original 'Calamity Jane' of Wild West fame and who has been with the Indian Congress during the last month, spent last night behind prison bars." Found reeling in drunkenness by a patrolman, Calamity was detained one night before being "released on suspended sentence." Calamity told officers that "it was the first time she had been arrested." In the next few days, Calamity was drinking again and involved in other altercations, including disruptions in the Indian Congress. Needing a break from her mounting upset at the Pan-American celebration, Calamity made a quick four-day trip south to Pennsylvania to visit Byron Hinckley, whom she had met at the exposition.

Calamity then determined to flee the East; the West was not such a confining, dull place after all. She belonged back in Montana, South Dakota, and Wyoming. But she had no money. So, needing funds, Calamity sought out Buffalo Bill Cody, whose Wild West show arrived in Buffalo on 26 August. A newspaper carried an account stating that Calamity had told Cody, "They've got me Buffaloed, and I wanter go back. . . . Stake me a railroad ticket and the price of meals, an' send me home." Buffalo Bill did just that, and Calamity was soon on her way west.

The return home did not go smoothly. Two major hiccups delayed Calamity and got her off track. Although Buffalo Bill's ticket for her was probably through to Montana, Calamity may have cashed in part of it to satisfy her thirst for liquid refreshment along the way. At any rate, a Billings newspaper reported in late September that Calamity was stranded in Chicago and had agreed to perform a few days at a dime museum to pay for the remainder of her trip west. Nearly three weeks later, a similar story emerged from Minneapolis, where Calamity, again lacking funds to return, was working at the Palace Museum, where she had starred back in 1896.

Finally, Calamity arrived home in November—not in Montana as expected, but stopping off in Pierre, South Dakota. Even before Calamity returned to South Dakota and Montana, westerners were buying into her contention that easterners had "flim flamed" her, using her "for exhibition purposes." "Calamity may not be possessed of all the feminine graces," one reporter admitted, but "she is a better citizen than Emma Goldman any day in the week." The vague reference pointed to Goldman's reputed influence on the assassin of President William McKinley, whose deadly deed occurred in September 1901 in Buffalo at the exposition.

Another informant, in an undoubtedly embellished recall, was more humorous. When Calamity got off the train later in Billings and stood on the platform, he reported that, "she kicked off those high-heeled shoes about twenty feet in the air. 'God damn 'em,' she hollered, 'I could not live with 'em any longer.'"

Calamity remained in Pierre through the winter of 1901–1902, but generated surprisingly little coverage in the local newspapers. One young schoolgirl, remembering back thirty years later, recalled that Calamity holed up in a run-down shack near the river, "where the poorer people lived." She did not dress in her western buckskins but "in an old pink gown." Calamity quickly established herself as a skilled and helpful midwife, and sometimes aided needy families—with mixed results. On one occasion she agreed to help a sick mother with her flu-ridden children. When the offspring acted up, Calamity yelled at them, "Damn you . . . you little devils, now you stay there." And there were the other usual activities—hanging out in saloons, drinking and gambling.

During Calamity's stay in Pierre, photographer R. H. Kelly captured an unusual image of her. Dressed stylishly—perhaps in some of the attire she obtained for receptions the previous summer in Buffalo—Calamity presented an attractive presence. Wearing a high-necked blouse or sweater, a well-tailored coat, and a huge, flowery hat, Calamity appeared slim, healthy, and not prematurely aged. Kelly's photograph proved that Calamity was not yet in precipitous decline.

But the semblance of stability that reigned in Pierre fell apart when Calamity returned to her incessant rambling. By March 1902 she had taken to the road. Wandering first to eastern South Dakota and then north to Montana, Calamity left a few traces of her perambulations. In March and

Calamity Jane returns west.

In fall of 1901, Calamity, disgusted with her experiences in Buffalo, New York, returned west to South Dakota. Photographer R. L. Kelley took her picture in Pierre, with Calamity dressed in the stylish clothes she probably obtained in the East. Courtesy, Montana Historical Society, MHS Jack Ellis Haynes Collection, Box 14.

April she tracked through Huron and Aberdeen and then doubled back for return visits. One eyewitness remembered that Calamity lived in a boxcar in Huron, staying with a family sick with the flu. When Calamity was in Aberdeen, she castigated Josephine Brake, her erstwhile eastern sponsor, as having misused her, cheating her. Navigating her way toward Livingston, Montana, and following indirect railroad connections, Calamity stopped off in Oakes, North Dakota. While in Oakes, Calamity reportedly "shot up" a saloon while getting revenge on a remuda of cowboys "josh[ing] the old lady." Pulling out two guns, she made the ridiculing cowboys dance to her tune. "You have had your fun," she yelled at them, "and now it's mine." In addition, she denigrated their manhood, telling onlookers that the dancers "don't know as much as the calves on my Montana ranch." Perhaps the rumor that Calamity had spent $30 on liquid refreshments that day in Huron partially explains her actions. Whatever the full truth of the incident, it gained numerous column inches in newspapers across the country.

The next day Calamity arrived in Jamestown, North Dakota, not feeling well. But she was soon back on the trail, with brief, unplanned stops in Mandan and Dickinson, and in Billings after staying away for nine months. During her days in Billings and the months immediately following, Calamity's decline came quickly, like an out-of-control stagecoach careening down a steep incline. Her affinity for the bottle had fully captured her. She seemed to give up.

Other shadowy consequences followed Calamity's increasing alcoholism. In early June, suffering from a lingering illness while staying in Gardiner in a shack, she was taken to Livingston to be committed to the county poorhouse, where she could be treated. Understandably, given her lifetime of individualism, she refused to go. She "objected vigorously" despite the promise that the institution would give her "medical assistance" and "take care of her." Local officials in Livingston urged her to "move on," which she did after borrowing money for drinks and a ticket out of town. At about this time, a wretch "rolled" Calamity, stealing her watch. But he got off free when she failed to show up to testify against him.

Hearing of Calamity's dire circumstances, some of her friends and acquaintances mounted a drive to gain a government-funded pension for her. Spearheading some of these efforts was Josephine Brake, after she heard of Calamity's destitution. Brake and others based their case on Calamity's having served as "a scout and Indian fighter." Now that she was "no longer able, physically, to take care of herself," advocates for a pension were calling on the government and "old soldiers and their friends" to support the pension effort. But one Montana editor, speaking for many others, dissented. The push for the pension, he pointed out, was "not being received with hilarious approval by the public at large. . . . It is an open question," the journalist added, "whether or not this frolicsome lady is deserving of the consideration which some now propose to bestow on her." Eventually, the humanitarian move to support Calamity foundered, probably because no one could prove she served as an official government scout.

Calamity's drink-fueled wandering continued into the fall. In November in Billings, after taking on a huge liquored jag, Calamity was arrested on a "charge of disturbance." A reporter stated that, after "drinking freely for the past two months" Calamity had turned violent. She had entered a store, become fascinated with a scalp she wanted to have, and threatened a young female clerk with a hatchet. Arrested, Calamity was sentenced to sixty days in jail, but released when a doctor diagnosed her with severe rheumatism. A short hospital stay and then renewed drinking brought an end to her stopover in Billings. Declaring Billings "a tenderfoot town" because of its recent treatment of her, Calamity headed off to the Black Hills.

After a few days stay visiting and partying with acquaintances in Deadwood, Calamity went north just a few miles, to the town of Belle Fourche. Once there, she seemed serious about reforming and about supporting Jessie, who accompanied her. (If the later rumor was correct that Calamity became a new grandmother just before she died the following August, Jessie might have been expecting a child. Was the discovery of Jessie's pregnancy the reason for their later alienation? No one has yet to turn up information to prove that Jessie was actually a new mother at age fifteen.) Whatever the situation with Jessie, in mid-January the *Belle Fourche Bee* reported that Calamity had arrived the previous week, looking for work to support herself and her daughter. Calamity told the *Bee* reporter that she had "tired of travelling" and wanted to find a place where she could "earn her living in a honorable manner" and "spend the balance of her days in peace and quiet."

A few days later, Calamity secured a job cooking and doing the laundry for sex workers at Dora Du Fran's "house of joy." In her very brief account of Calamity written three decades later in the early 1930s, Dora, who became a famous madam, reported that she and Calamity had first met in 1886. In one succinct sentence she depicted Calamity as a very complex person. "This ignorant, uneducated, untamed, unmoral, iron-hearted woman, who had been thrown among unfit associates from babyhood, played the part of a ministering angel in the life of the frontier." But Du Fran did not tell the truth about her own establishment, stating instead that Calamity "went [to work] in a dance hall and boarding house" rather than in a house of prostitution.

Calamity worked assiduously at Du Fran's place for about four to six weeks in January and February 1903. Then, she fell off the wagon. Taking her wages, she went on another disastrous spree. "For five days she whooped it up," Du Fran wrote, "then came back asking for her job back. As she was a wonderful cook she got it and was back on the job the next day." But the resolve disappeared like snow before a warm chinook wind, with Calamity soon embarking on another series of diurnal wanderings.

Du Fran's abbreviated account provides a revealing snapshot of Calamity's situation at the beginning of the last year of her life. She was extremely poor, the madam said, carrying all her goods—the buckskins she wore, two or three calico dresses, underwear, a few other items—in a small, battered suitcase. "Her whole fortune lay in her strong arms and her desire to work," Du Fran asserted.

Critics needed to be more understanding, madam Dora argued, seeing how Calamity's tragic and unfortunate beginnings shaped her later life. Good women "brought up with every protection from the evils of the world and with good associations" were likely to replicate their upbringings as adults. But Calamity had no such protective origins; she grew up the "product of the wild and woolly West. She was not immoral; but unmoral. . . . With her upbringing, how could she be anything but unmoral."

The empathetic Dora had to admit, however, that Calamity's behavior sometimes went beyond the acceptable. She drank excessively and tried to take on too much. And then there was her howling, which often broke out at night when coyotes sounded their own barbaric yawp across the Black Hills. Their howls stirred her up, setting her off to join in with them. And, Du Fran concluded, "Believe it or not, Calamity had any coyote, or band of coyotes, beaten to a frazzle for sustained howling."

Like Fox's notable interview with Calamity in Deadwood in 1895–96, Du Fran's account provided another feminine perspective on Calamity. It too exuded feelings of sisterhood and empathy missing from so many of the masculine-driven accounts of Calamity.

In the next few weeks, Calamity made brief stops in several locations. In March she was said to be cooking at a ranch near Belle Fourche and then traveling to Hot Springs, hoping perhaps to soak away some of her persisting rheumatic sufferings. Then Calamity headed back to Rapid City—but never arrived.

Instead, she turned up, unexpectedly, for the first time in Sundance, in northeastern Wyoming. She was not in good condition. As one account put it, "all traces of her former vitality and aggressiveness were gone. She was but fifty-two years old [actually, forty-seven], but looked to be eighty. Dressed in a dark-colored garment of poor material; her stringy gray hair twisted into a careless knot at the nap of her neck; her skin wrinkled and sallow, she was indeed an object of pity."

Calamity may have remained in Sundance for several weeks. Moving into an old, vacant hotel, she lived off the townspeople. An older man whom she had known in Deadwood helped Calamity with money, and another resident provided furnishings for her room. She wandered into the seven saloons in town and also frequented a furniture store just to chat. Calamity claimed she had come to Sundance to find her husband, indicating that a sick man named Chrissy was that man. She nursed him through his final days in Sundance.

On one occasion, a group of younger women of the town paid a social visit. When the conversation turned personal, however, Calamity "became decidedly indignant," and the visitors "left in a hurry." Without any means of support, Calamity mooched off others for everything. As one observer remembered, she "had no scruples about asking for anything she wanted." Since Calamity had "given freely in her day, [she] rather expected the same treatment from others." Then, as so often happened, Calamity was suddenly gone.

One train conductor remembered Calamity on her way back to Deadwood, or on another ride about this time. Calamity was seated in the men's smoker section, not in good condition. "She was poorly dressed," he recalled, "dirty, unkempt, not alert and she seemed down in the dumps." Calamity told the trainman she was going to Deadwood to die. When he requested her ticket, she showed him her baggage claim. He left on his rounds, promising he would return for the ticket. When he came back, she was near tears, confessing she had lost her ticket. Hearing of Calamity's dilemma, other passengers took up a collection, paying for her ticket and providing for food.

By July, Calamity was back in the Black Hills. After quick, brief visits to several towns, she returned to Deadwood. She wandered in and out of town during July, meeting friends and making new acquaintances. One journalist, understating the facts, found Calamity "not as robust nor as picturesque as she was ten or fifteen years ago." Still, Calamity liked having her picture taken, as photographers in Deadwood and nearby Whitewood discovered. The two photographs in these two communities taken just a few days before her death reveal her as an ailing, rather emaciated, prematurely aged woman. But she continued to drink, often appearing groggy to most observers.

On 24 July, Calamity boarded an ore train for the mining town of Terry, a few miles out of Deadwood. There seemed no reason for the trip. Soon after her arrival in Terry, an incapacitating illness overtook her. An acquaintance, H. A. Scheffer, took her to his hotel and called in a doctor. But the medic indicated he could do virtually nothing for Calamity; she was too far along on her downward path. She also refused to take the medicine he prescribed for her. During her last days, Calamity told her visiting acquaintances that she was dying and accepted that fact. She may also have told them that she was now a grandmother but alienated from Jessie; she would not give information about the where-

Calamity Jane near death.

John B. Mayo photographed Calamity in front of Wild Bill Hickok's grave in the Mount Moriah Cemetery in Deadwood. The picture was taken in July 1903, the month before her death. Courtesy J. Leonard Jennewein Collection, McGovern Library, Dakota Wesleyan University.

abouts of her daughter, rumored to be in North Dakota or Montana. Calamity may also have told some of these listeners that she wanted to be buried next to Wild Bill Hickok in Deadwood.

The end came on the afternoon of 1 August. The official diagnosis was death from "inflammation of the bowels." Probably the main cause of Calamity's demise at age forty-seven was from chronic alcoholism. Calamity refused to take care of herself. Even as her health declined and her finances were nearly nonexistent, she seemed determined to live on straight whiskey and other strong drinks. Her addiction to John Barleycorn most assuredly led to her premature death.

The details of the days immediately following Calamity's death remain murky. Some think Calamity's funeral and burial followed Calamity's wishes, expressed to acquaintances in her last hours in Terry. In their account, she asked that Black Hills pioneers take care of the details and bury her next to Wild Bill. A competing, less certain story indicates that a group of drinking cronies, including some pioneers of the area, gathered in a saloon, and after a few drinks and hearing of Calamity's death, decided "it would be good joke on Wild Bill if she [Calamity] would be buried alongside him in the Mount Moriah Cemetery." Wild Bill would be mighty upset "if he knew he would lay up with Jane for all eternity."

Even more macabre were tales leading from Terry back to Deadwood and to the funeral service. One young observer later recalled seeing Calamity's corpse prominently displayed in a wagon on the way back to Deadwood. Her body was seated—and tied—to an upright chair, and when the wagon jolted ahead, her "head nodded gently up and down as if to bow to friends who had come to the street for a last farewell." Another strain of this gruesome story had the driver stopping several times en route for liquid refreshment while Calamity's remains remained in plain sight in the wagon.

The Robinson Funeral Home in Deadwood took charge of preparing Calamity's body for burial. Two little-known photographs were taken of Calamity as she lay in her casket. But the mortuary family had to guard the body from curiosity-seekers who wanted to take a clip of her hair. Some did before a protective wire was devised to protect her head.

The funeral service, said to be the largest to date in Deadwood, took place in the town's Methodist Church. The church was packed with an overflow crowd of friends and acquaintances of Calamity; others merely wanted to participate in a memorable event. (It was rumored that many of the "saloon crowd" who attended the service gathered in

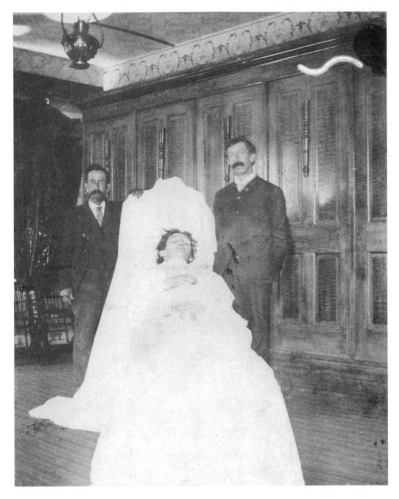

Calamity Jane in repose.

Calamity lies in her casket on 4 August 1903, three days after her death in Terry, South Dakota. Standing beside her casket are Henry and Charles H. Robinson, undertakers. Courtesy Western History Collection, Denver Public Library (F-23387).

taverns afterwards to celebrate.) Declaring that every person deserved a good Christian service and burial, Charles B. Clark, the father of the future well-known writer Badger Clark, officiated at the service. Dr. Clark chose to emphasize Calamity's humanitarian actions. Drawing from Psalm 90, Clark, stressing the uncertainties of life, praised Calamity's "deeds of kindness and charity . . . [she was a] heroine." Like other Deadwood pioneers, she had helped to establish what residents a quarter of century later now knew and counted on. Calamity should be remembered, Pastor Clark

Calamity Jane in the Mount Moriah Cemetery.

Calamity was buried in the Deadwood cemetery next to the grave of Wild Bill Hickok. Her burial spot, adjacent to his, became a favorite tourist site after her death. More recently, Calamity's grave site, much transformed, is largely overshadowed by an imposing sculpture on Hickok's grave. Courtesy J. Leonard Jennewein Collection, McGovern Library, Dakota Wesleyan University.

concluded, as one who helped the needy, nursed the sick, and stayed with the depressed and lonely.

After the service, a hearse took Calamity's remains to the Mount Moriah Cemetery. There, she was buried near Wild Bill's grave. The close companionship Calamity may have wished for in life seemed possible only in death. Madam Dora Du Fran, having promised to take care of Calamity's grave, paid for a sculpture to be placed on the grave.

Calamity's gravestone read:

Mrs. M. E. Burke
CALAMITY JANE
Died
Aug. 1, 1903
Aged
53 YRS.

Ironically, in the town best known for Calamity's in-and-out presence, her tombstone misspelled her name and gave a wrong birth date and age. This combination of facts and erroneous information had marked her life and legends while she was yet alive; now it went on. The marriage of truth, distortion, and myth, as we shall see, has continued to define Calamity Jane in the more than a century since her death.

7

Imagining Calamity

Launching a Legendary Heroine, 1903–1930

Even before Martha Canary celebrated her twenty-first birthday, she had been transformed into the Wild West heroine Calamity Jane. Once the dramatic heroine came on stage, the orphan farmer's daughter from Missouri largely disappeared from the scene. Calamity Jane she had become before she rode into booming Deadwood with Wild Bill Hickok in midsummer of 1876. Already commented on as an independent-minded, free-spirited female who dressed, rode, and drove teams like a man, and maybe served informally as an army scout, Calamity soon emerged as a notorious figure, a rousing drinker, and perhaps a part-time prostitute.

These sources of information did much to shape images of Calamity as a frenetic frontier woman in the 1870s and beyond. Most important in the creating and broadcasting of the rambunctious, eccentric Calamity were local and regional journalists of the northern interior West. Knowing they had to turn new residents into subscribers and realizing that sensationalism and controversy appealed to readers (as they always have), newspapermen rarely overlooked opportunities to bring startling people or events onto their pages. As one historian of frontier journalism has put it, newspaper publishers and editors "knew that sensationalism sold newspapers." Nor, the same scholar writes, were they above "the practice of embellishing articles to enhance otherwise dull reading." The new, unknown Calamity, with her unorthodox behavior and controversial actions, was exactly the grist needed for these journalistic mills. Wherever Calamity went from the mid-1870s onward, she became a subject for writers and readers hungering and thirsting for lively copy.

The second force in shaping Calamity's burgeoning reputation was eastern writers, or at least writers outside the area of her usual perambulations. Journalists from Minnesota and Chicago, for example, provided some of the first dramatic stories about Calamity in the 1875–78 period for readers in those areas and even for the much larger national readership. Most important of all in turning Calamity into a continentally known figure were the dime novels of E. L. Wheeler in the Deadwood Dick series. True, as biographer James D. McLaird perceptively notes, little of the Calamity Jane of the dime novels surfaced in later biographies, novels, or films about her. But Wheeler made her a well-known name in the late 1870s and early 1880s. No one acquainted with the heroes and heroines of American popular fiction, particularly those focused on the American West, would have been unaware of Calamity Jane by the mid-1880s.

Third, Calamity herself had a large hand in molding her popular image during her lifetime. She did it by eliding much of her pedestrian and depressing beginnings and replacing nondescript events with sensational happenings. Although Martha was about eight years old when the Canary family left Missouri to take its arduous, dangerous trip west to frontier Montana and about eleven when she became an orphan, her earliest statements avoided the truth of what her father and mother had become. If the scattered segments of what others gathered first from Martha and later from Calamity are true (as well as the stories her younger sister, Lena, told her children), Calamity sometimes replaced Robert and Charlotte Canary with her birth and orphanhood in a soldiering family in the northern Rockies. And, as the years passed, she spoke often of her rollicking—and largely imagined—roles as a scout and soldier for Generals Crook and Custer, her heroic work as a veteran bullwhacker, and superb rider.

As noted in the previous chapter, Calamity's pamphlet autobiography *Life and Adventures of Calamity Jane, By Herself* (1895–96) provides the best example of her reshaping of her own life. Although speaking truthfully, for the most part, about her birth in Princeton, Missouri, years in Montana, and the loss of her parents early on, Calamity loads up her account with misinformation. She speaks much of scouting and soldiering that never occurred, a legal marriage to Clinton Burke that never took place, and of nonexistent travels and homes. Moreover, she erases her only legal marriage (to Bill Steers), omits her saloon dancing and gambling, and understandably makes no mention of drinking and possible prostitution. Calamity sold herself as an authentic Old West heroine for much the same reasons frontier journalists capitalized on her: stories of an unusual, dramatic frontier woman drew attention and corralled readers and show attendees. Calamity needed people to come to her presentations as a dime novel performer and to buy her autobiography and photos. As noted, Calamity herself played a central role in shaping the Calamity Jane legends that have paraded before the American public in the past 110 years and more.

In the years after Calamity's death, as in the twenty-five years or so before it, images of her have been neither monolithic nor static. During her lifetime, journalists often tried to balance the less palatable facets of her controversial character—the cross-dressing, drinking, and promiscuity—with counterbalancing images of an Angel of Mercy. Even before her Deadwood days, there were accounts of Calamity speaking approvingly of her willingness to nurse the sick and help the needy, unhappy, and destitute. These early and much later positive treatments included her care for smallpox victims, her aid to the poor, her attentions to mothers

Calamity Jane as Pioneer Woman.

Rarely before, or immediately after, her death in 1903 was Calamity pictured as a well-dressed pioneer woman. Some stories associated with photographs like this one touted her as a nurse and helper for the sick and indigent. Etulain collection.

and children, and her bailing out the penniless. Few pre-1903 accounts omitted these positive aspects of Calamity's life, even while castigating her as an increasingly destitute, drunken, wretched wreck of a woman.

Missing in nearly all accounts of Calamity during her lifetime, however, was her desire to be a rather traditional pioneer woman, with a family. Only a handful or two hints survive to reveal this desire. Calamity wanted to be married, to be with a "husband," to be near children. In 1895–96 she told a female interviewer that her daughter, Jessie, was her reason for living, that she wanted to make sure Jessie got the education she had missed. Calamity visited and perhaps worked with sister Lena until her untamed actions built a barrier between her and the Borner family in Wyoming. Calamity also had warm feelings for her "little brother" Elijah, or Lige, and wept openly when she heard of his difficult life in western Wyoming.

Calamity mentioned family and parenthood much less frequently than she paraded her Wild West activities. Increasingly, the emphases on Calamity as a Wild West woman, by others and by herself, meant that few interpreters ever depicted Calamity as a wannabe traditional pioneer woman. Yet most of the two-dozen photographs of Calamity portray her in women's clothing of the late nineteenth century, and many of the private reminiscences recall Calamity dressing and acting like a wife and mother. Those domestic images of Calamity were sidelined during her days in Deadwood and never reappeared with any consistency before her death. Calamity Jane had become identified with a romantic Old West and never broke free from its constrictions.

Still, these close and tight links between Calamity Jane and the Wild West, although clear and large at the end of her life, did not continue unchanged in the passing decades. As we shall see, the legends surrounding her have undergone considerable transformation in the more than a century since her death. Indeed, these changes, particularly in regard to her reputed relationship with Wild Bill Hickok and the possibility of her bearing his child, repeatedly redirected—and often distorted—the images of her in numerous biographies, novels, and films, among other venues.

The obituaries of Calamity, and the first retrospective stories about her in August 1903 and in the months and years soon thereafter, revealed a good deal about legends surrounding her in the immediate coming decades. These first post-grave musings also disclosed how little writers knew factually about Calamity and how willing they were to shovel out misinformation about her.

The obituary in the *New York Times*, viewed by many as the country's leading newspaper, clearly displayed both the Wild West imagery surrounding Calamity as well as the false facts peddled as truth. Obviously, the *Times* writer was whistling in the dark, as far afield in his details as he was distant from the deceased person he was profiling.

The obituary in the *Times* appeared on 2 August, one day after Calamity's death in faraway Terry, South Dakota. Unfortunately, the writer, perhaps devoid of other information, relied heavily on Calamity's unreliable autobiography and thus repeated much of the misinformation contained in that brief source. The subheads of the obit introduced the multiple errors that followed. Calamity is declared to have been a "Woman Who Became Famous as an Indian Fighter" and who had "Served with Gens. Custer and Miles." The writer adds that Calamity became "the most eccentric and picturesque woman in the Old West," and "thousands of tourists went miles out of their way to see her." After these breathless beginnings, the obit writer largely follows Calamity's account in her stretcher-riven autobiography.

The *Times* story does include bits of authentic biography. It correctly cites her birthplace as Princeton, Missouri, rightly mentions the trip overland to Montana (but gets the date wrong), the death of parents, and her first years "in the rough camps of the plainsmen in Montana [Wyoming]." Then off to the races with Calamity's falsehoods about scouting, serving with Custer, carrying the mail on dangerous routes in the Black Hills and points west, and capturing Jack McCall (Wild Bill's assassin) with a threatening cleaver. The post-1878 years are crammed into half a paragraph, and when her husband Clinton Burke died in 1895 (!), it is attested she "returned to her Montana ranch." The final sentence reads: "In her dotage speculators fenced in her home and charged an admission fee to tourists."

The *Times* obituary runs aground on two shoals. First, the excessive number of factual errors as already noted. Second, the extraordinary omissions. Nothing is said about Calamity as a public performer, especially the well-publicized months with the touring Kohl and Middleton dime museum group in 1896 and the weeks in Buffalo at the Pan-American Exposition in 1901. Also, one learns very little about Calamity's life in Montana, Wyoming, and South Dakota, even though all are mentioned. Nor does the writer allude to Calamity's sensational depictions as a dime novel heroine.

If the *Times* obituary is a harbinger of things to come, Calamity will be seen almost entirely as a romantic, adventuresome woman who served in the army and fought Indians. The Deadwood years and the last two decades of Calamity's life will be sidelines, and almost nothing will be said about her as a pioneer woman. And her challenges concerning alcoholism, prostitution, and increasing poverty will get little attention—if any at all. Another obituary, published the next day in the *New York Sun*, was but a condensed version of that in the *Times*. It too spoke of an assertive woman who fought Indians with Generals Custer and Miles. Personal details in the *Sun* account were as scarce as correct information.

At the other end of the continent, the *Portland Oregonian*, the leading newspaper of the Pacific Northwest, carried two retrospective stories about Calamity rather than a traditional obituary. (The lack of solid details about Calamity probably led many newspapers to print such stories rather than fact-laden obituaries.) One *Oregonian* story, reprinted from a Salt Lake City newspaper, was about Calamity's shootout with her last husband, "Squint" Squires. In the near-deadly competition, Calamity shot off Squint's arm, and his bullet tore away her ear lobe. The shootout story, as well as the other exaggerated yarns Squint peddled, had no basis in fact; but the Salt Lake City and Portland newspapers printed them as veracious gospel. The second piece in the *Oregonian*, by Amy Maguire, views Calamity from her own perspective as a child who had seen her in the Black Hills and Rapid City. The author depicts a Calamity whom children feared despite her attempts to draw them to her. Her wild riding astride a galloping horse, firing her two guns, and vociferous yelling (shrieking) scared children. But Calamity also "looked harmless" when walking Rapid City streets dressed in a "plaid dress that combined the colors of green and red timi." There, she helped a burdened mother and her child. If true, these remembrances confirm many other accounts saluting Calamity's interest in and aid for the needy and depressed. Although the child Amy "repelled" Calamity's overtures to her out of fear, she "liked her secretly because she seemed so strong and free and good-natured." Unfortunately, Maguire's account is undermined by her acceptance of Calamity's untruthful assertion that she captured Jack McCall after he killed Wild Bill. Nor should Maguire have gone farther with the already well-traveled myth that "Calamity was the original of Bret Harte's Cherokee Sal" in his notable short story "The Luck of Roaring Camp." That incorrect conclusion surfaced as early as 1878 (Calamity was only twelve years of age when Harte's story was published in 1868), and continued strong until the time of her death.

The obituaries and retrospective stories published in the upper interior West where Calamity spent most of her life both replicated and disagreed with the content of those published outside that home region. Several of the regional stories virtually reprinted what the Deadwood (2 August) and Lead (3 August) newspapers printed as obituaries or commentaries. Not surprisingly, the Black Hills newspapers were closer to the truth about Calamity's life in that area and often far from the facts—or even totally fictitious—in dealing with 'events outside Dakota. Headlines in Deadwood and Lead newspapers touted Calamity as a "Famous Border Character" whose mother had been a washerwoman in Montana. Once Charlotte died and the family disintegrated, Calamity became a "rover." She had a "rough exterior but was possessed of a kindly heart and a generous disposition" and often displayed her "woman ministrations" in acts of kindness. The mistaken statements in the two periodicals were especially surprising. Among other errors were stories that Calamity's real name was Mary E. Canary and that in 1895 she had brought a fourteen-year-old daughter with her to Deadwood.

Most of the same information appeared in the *Belle Fourche Bee* (6 August). That writer also added that Calamity had been married several times and that Wild Bill Hickok was "one of her old consorts." The most revealing comment in this brief story was the writer's apt conclusion: Now that Calamity had been buried next to Wild Bill, Deadwood would "have a double attraction to exhibit to visitors from the east."

The journalists in the Hills wrote selectively about Calamity's career. None of them spoke of her work as a saloon dancer and gambler, her drunkenness, or her selling sex. A later Lead obituary suggested what had been undisclosed thus far. In describing Calamity's funeral service and the upbeat sermon of the Reverend Dr. Clark, the *Lead Daily Call* (7 August) reported that the good pastor spoke "feelingly of the good . . . [Calamity] had done, leaving that part of her life which appeared the darkest to be judged by Him who has alone the right to do so."

Newspapers around the northern Rockies sounded similar, ambivalent notes. The *Rawlins Republican* reported that Calamity, whose real name was Jane Burke and who was "nearly 73 years of age" at death, was "familiarly known" in Rawlins. She had been a "member of the Montana vigilantes" and was an "intimate acquaintance" of Buffalo Bill Cody," serving as a scout with him. In addition to these comments wide of the mark, there were also negative statements. Calamity, the writer noted, sat "around on Front Street 'dead drunk' and spent many a night in the Rawlins city jail." She had married William Steers, a one-time resident of Rawlins, but that union had not worked out. Later, Calamity came back to town "with a little girl she had stolen" and claimed a Mr. King as a husband. Because of her disruptive actions, she had been ordered to "move on." The Rawlins account concludes with the mistaken information that Calamity's last marriage was to Squint Squires (5 August). The story in the northeastern Wyoming *Sundance Crook County Monitor* was brief and blunt. The reporter noted Calamity had recently been in town. But, he quickly added, she had become a "habitual drunkard of recent years and her death is said to have been the result of a protracted spree" (7 August).

One the most extensive retrospective accounts following Calamity's death appeared in the *Bozeman Avant Courier* (7 August). After declaring that Calamity was "the most remarkable woman the frontier had developed," the Bozeman writer provided little information about Calamity's actions in Montana but instead launched a series of embellished statements. Calamity had helped lynch Jack McCaul [*sic*] and had "followed the mining booms from Mexico to British Columbia." She had also "scouted and prospected in every state in the west," and a "passion for free, untrammeled existence possessed her." An extensive remembrance of

Wild Woman of the Old West, Calamity Jane.

Many obituaries and early stories about Calamity depicted her as
a nontraditional, masculine, often-wild woman. These accounts
stressed her alcoholism, possible prostitution, and challenges to social
mores. Courtesy James McLaird, from W. G. Patterson, "Calamity
Jane," *Wild World Magazine*, August 1903.

Calamity by Buffalo Bill concluded the story in the *Avant Courier*. As we shall see, that piece by Cody and another by him traveled widely in the American West.

Newspapers in Calamity's hometown of Princeton, Missouri, also carried stories about Calamity's death and career. They too exhibited more truth than fiction in close-at-hand happenings but an alarming tendency to accept stretchers from afar. The *Princeton Telegram* (12 August) briefly mentioned Calamity's origins as Martha Canary and then her immigration "with her parents to Nevada in 1863." She had been "left alone" in Virginia City and fell in "with an unworthy woman of the town." Later, she served with Buffalo Bill, "her life-long friend," before ranching in Missouri and fighting Indians in Kansas. Then came two sensational claims: Calamity "had twelve husbands, only one of which died a peaceful death." The first of the husbands she had "killed with her own hands."

On the same day, the *Princeton Post* (12 August), in a front-page story, provided local comments. News stories about Calamity coming in from elsewhere were of special interest to Mercer County residents, the writer began. Many in the area "remembered her father and mother and a number of whom remembered the woman herself when she was a girl here." Her real name was Jane Canary, and she resided in the Princeton area until going north with her family to Appanoose County, Iowa, and then, age thirteen, on to Montana. Once the writer took Martha/Calamity west, he fell back on Calamity's exaggerated reports in her undependable autobiography. In 1878, the story continued, Calamity "bought a ranch and retired." She had married three times. Pondering the meaning of Calamity's life, the reporter concluded "now, that . . . [Calamity] is dead the curtain of mystery will probably never be lifted from certain chapters of her checkered life."

The *Princeton Post* account appended the same Buffalo Bill story that had appeared in the *Bozeman Avant Courier*. The Buffalo Bill stories that follow were considered important sources of information about Calamity at the time. Recall that in 1903 William F. Cody, internationally known as Buffalo Bill, was the country's best-known purveyor of the romantic history of the Old West. For nearly two decades he had traveled the United States (mostly in the East but some in the West) and western Europe with his immensely popular arena show, the Wild West. It drew thousands—sometimes tens of thousands—to its spectacular performances. That meant Buffalo Bill had immense credibility as a spokesman on the Old West. When Buffalo Bill spoke about or performed in the Wild West show, everyone listened or watched. So it was that Cody's two stories about Calamity drew a good deal of attention, being reprinted widely in newspapers trying to capture Calamity Jane in print.

The first of the stories, written in 1902 but published in 1903, provided a partially positive portrait of Calamity. Much about her appealed to the famous western showman. Cody pointed particularly to her "man's will and man's nerve," electric energy, and courage. "A more daring and eccentric woman, I have never known," Cody added. Unfortunately, he also had to admit that where Calamity had "nearly all the rough virtues of the old West," she also had "many of the vices." "Her weatherbeaten face . . . show[ed] signs of dissipation" when he saw her in Buffalo in summer 1901. It was true, too, that she had been arrested frequently, and it was "quite a matter of course with her now." Once Cody moved past these generalizations and a few facts about Calamity's life, he got lost in several unsubstantiated stories and, perhaps, outright fabrications. Several came in one sentence: "She has shot scores of Indians, assisted in the lynching of many a desperado, saved numerous lives"—all of which were untrue.

Another later story from Buffalo Bill came from London, where a reporter caught up with him while barnstorming with the Wild West show. Much of this interview repeated what Cody had said the previous year: he knew Calamity as a scout, and the last time they met was in Buffalo at the Pan-American Exposition, when he had paid her way back to the West. Then, exaggerations came to the fore once again. When Calamity joined Cody's scouts in 1874 in their "three or four skirmishes with the Indians," she was "always up on the firing line." He also reported that Calamity had been in the Black Hills in 1873, "hanging round to gambling saloons" [*sic*], even though none had yet been established there.

It would be a mistake, however, to place major emphasis on nit-picking, fact-checking in dealing with Buffalo Bill's two stories about Calamity. Readers and journalists of the time seemed less interested in the details than in Cody's opinions about Calamity Jane. After all, many thought of him as America's best-known man and certainly *the* authority on the American West. Since readers and listeners wanted, most of all, to learn what Buffalo Bill thought about that enigmatic woman Calamity Jane, they paid close attention to what he said.

And he was not shy about stating his overall opinions about Calamity. She was, he began, "the most remarkable woman the frontier has developed." He had never met any other woman quite like her. True, she sometimes stepped over the lines of acceptable action and often bruised notions of what a woman ought to do and be, but he quickly moved beyond those points to praising her. She was kind, generous, a "big-hearted woman . . . daring as the most recklessly brave man that ever lived, and a prince of good fellows." Eccentric, willing to paint "the town red," and sometimes a bit inclined to join in violent activities—yes, all of these. But these tendencies were more than matched by her fearlessness, willingness to aid anyone in need, and quickness to join in protecting families. Through these actions—and

213

more—"everyone knew and liked her." They "dubbed her 'mascot' and were generally glad to have her along with the company." Although admitting some of Calamity's shadowy sides, Buffalo Bill liked her, as he made very clear in his two stories.

Others at the time of Calamity's death and shortly thereafter wanted to counter these positive characterizations of Calamity, to show that she was by no means a frontier heroine or ministering angel. Several newspaper editors took the lead in criticizing the "myths" already beginning to cluster around Calamity early in the twentieth century.

More than a few journalists seemed driven to turn out highly critical—even vitriolic—counternarratives of Calamity. They wanted to make sure that the romantic stories being spread about her, which they considered misleading nonsense, were shoved off the scene and replaced with more realistic—in their view more truthful—depictions. Two Montana newspapers sledgehammered Calamity. The *White Sulphur Springs Meagher Republican* declared that Calamity was never a scout, that she lived on a steady diet of whiskey, and that she was a resident of "red light or bad land districts." Her associates were most often "roughs, rogues, rounders, robbers and highwaymen." And lest readers miss the point of her real, negative character, the reporter was even more explicit: "If the press of the state cannot find a more respectable person to eulogize through its columns for the delictation [*sic*] of its respectable readers, better that it . . . throw its presses in the dump pile and embark in the cultivation of rattlesnakes" (14 August). The *Gardiner Wonderland* was more succinct—and savage. Its headlined story of Calamity's death read "Calamity Jane Finally Does the Proper Thing" (6 August).

Even though some newspapermen in the Black Hills and others who had known Calamity there were reluctant to target her downsides, others leveled their critical guns at her. A writer for the *Black Hills Union* in Rapid City underscored Calamity's "wanton waywardness and debauchery." More surprising was the harsh account of M. L. Fox, who had written the memorable story of Calamity as a warm-hearted mother and aspiring pioneer woman in the mid-1890s. Now Fox wanted to discount the romantic silliness about Calamity as a scout or killer. Rather, she was a saloon and dance hall habitué. Indeed, Calamity was "an ignorant woman of most unwomanly habits," unworthy of any more "notoriety."

Other writers who had known Calamity firsthand also wanted to set the record straight, correcting false information and promoting what they considered a more realistic view of her. A widely cited example of these "correctors" was Captain Jack Crawford. A few months after Calamity's death, Crawford penned an essay entitled "The Truth about Calamity Jane." Crawford's piece attracted attention because many readers thought Captain Jack knew whereof he spoke in giving personal information about Calamity. He first met Calamity in 1876 in Custer City, where, serving as a law officer, he had arrested her "for intoxication and disorderly conduct." Crawford scouted for the U.S. government in the Black Hills and later became chief of scouts in the pursuit of Sitting Bull. He claimed to be "well acquainted with every scout employed by the government" and thus thought he could assert, from firsthand experience, that Calamity was never hired as a scout, did not carry U.S. mail, or drive a stage. He likewise dismissed as nonsense the claim that Calamity had been involved in the lynching of Jack McCall because that event never occurred. In addition, he discredited Calamity's story that Captain Egan had given her the sobriquet of "Calamity Jane" during a battle in which the captain was wounded. Again, Crawford pointed out, neither took place.

Captain Jack could be guilty of mistakes, too. He wrongly stated that Calamity had never seen Buffalo Bill. Simply wrongheaded was his assertion that "Wild Bill's name should in no way be associated with Calamity Jane's" because Hickok "did not even know" Calamity. Nor would everyone then or later agree with him that Hickok "was the soul of honor" and in all ways "a good man and law abiding citizen." Some of Crawford's details about Calamity's personal life were shaky too, including his statement that her father was "a dissipated soldier."

Of more interest are Captain Jack's conclusions about Calamity's character. She was, he noted, "a good-hearted woman and under different environments would have made a good wife and mother." But, raised in rough mining camps, "with not a hand raised to protect her, until too late," she grew up in a "wild, unnatural manner." Despite these shaky beginnings and later dissolute actions, however, Calamity retained "a kind or generous heart."

Crawford blamed "yellow journalism" for distorting the truth about Calamity. Journalists were, he thought, too willing to retail rumors and create imagined happenings to sell stories. Newspapers often lionized Wild West heroes as Indian killers, even though some "never did one-tenth that is credited to them."

Readers were also partly at fault. Captain Jack wondered if readers did not want to be humbugged, as showman P. T. Barnum had claimed. Crawford suggested that distortions about Calamity's life and supposed good deeds lived on because Americans wanted to believe them. If so, she would march on triumphantly—but falsely—as an Indian killer, a participant in lynch mobs, and a "pard" of Wild Bill.

Obituaries and retrospective stories flooded out at the time of Calamity's death and shortly thereafter, but the flood soon dwindled to a mere trickle. Indeed, in the quarter century from the end of Calamity's life until 1930, newspaper stories and other small gleanings about her nearly disappeared from the scene, with books almost nonexistent.

The paucity of publications about Calamity is all the more noteworthy because during these years fictional and filmic versions of the frontier West exploded in popularity. Owen Wister's classic, emulative novel *The Virginian* appeared in 1902, and the dozens—almost hundreds—of popular Westerns by Zane Grey and Max Brand became and remained best sellers. Film Westerns also galloped on the scene. Beginning with *The Great Train Robbery* in 1903 and stretching through the Hollywood silent Westerns of Broncho Billy Anderson, William S. Hart, Tom Mix, and dozens of other sixgun and sagebrush heroes of the teens and twenties, the Western became the most popular cinematic genre in the United States by time the first talkies appeared, just before the Depression fell like a huge, wet blanket in 1929.

The first three decades of the twentieth century also witnessed the birth of the American West as an academic historical field. The frontier writings of Frederick Jackson Turner and Frederic Logan Paxson, the Borderlands essays and books of Herbert Eugene Bolton, and the establishment of the Mississippi Valley Historical Association were clear testaments of the rising popularity of the pre-1900 American West among historians. Other writers, usually journalists or lay historians, turned to the heroes of the Wild West as subjects for their new books. The first biographies of such Old West worthies as Wild Bill Hickok, Billy the Kid, Wyatt Earp, and General George Custer appeared before 1930.

Thus, the lack of publications about Calamity in roughly the 1905 to 1930 period is all the more revealing, considering the otherwise burgeoning public interest in the pioneer West. Several large barriers faced those who wanted to write substantively about Calamity. Information about her remained nearly nonexistent, with most of the reliable facts buried in newspapers not of easy access to researchers.

In addition, some of the stories about Calamity, including her own, were unreliable, often more fanciful and downright false than truthful. Third, myths about Calamity were already hardening into assertions: (1) that she had served as a scout, (2) that she was an Indian killer, and that (3) she had been romantically attached to Wild Bill Hickok. Biographers who wished to construct veracious and soundly researched accounts of Calamity had to find their way through or around these barriers that seemed almost impassable or insurmountable.

The first two films featuring cinematic Calamitys illustrated how much myths about her had already solidified in the teens and early twenties. Interestingly, the silent film *In the Days of '75 and '76* (1915) issued not from Hollywood but from the outback of northwestern Nebraska. This early amateurish—even primitive—film uses many stereotypes associated with Calamity while avoiding others. Like later films such as *The Plainsman* (1936) and *Calamity Jane* (1953), this movie is the romance story of Calamity and Wild Bill. Calamity, played by Freeda Hartzell Romine, the daughter of the police chief of Chadron, Nebraska, is a perky, pretty tomboy, who learns to shoot and ride well and carries a sidegun along with her rifle. Known locally for her "sharpshooting and equestrian skills," Hartzell Romine personifies a young, vivacious woman who functions competently in a man's world of riding, scouting, and mining. In many scenes of soldiering and mining, she is the only woman on stage.

In other ways, this film's Calamity differs markedly from earlier stereotypes. The movie opens in Calamity's cabin in Butte, where she lives with her mother (perhaps a widow) and a brattish little brother. Now in her early twenties, this vivacious Calamity wears braids, wards off leering louts like Jack McCall (the villain of the film), and dresses attractively in buckskin-like attire. Calamity is portrayed in a domestic and very positive light, before she marries Wild Bill half-

First Calamity Jane film.

In 1915, a small film company in Chadron, Nebraska produced *In the Days of '75 and '76*. The movie began the long, incorrect tradition of depicting Calamity and Wild Bill Hickok as man and wife, or at least lovers. Freeda Hartzell Romine starred as Calamity Jane, A. L. Johnson as Wild Bill. Courtesy Paul Andrew Hutton.

way through the film and later helps him with scouting and mining. The story carries through Wild Bill's violent death and Calamity's quest for justice against his killer, McCall. At times Calamity seems like one of the guys, but not the slightest bit of immorality or alcoholism is hinted at here. No drinking for her, in fact little or no drinking occurs in the saloon scenes.

The plot of the seven-reel, hour-long *In the Days of '75 and '76* foreshadowed the storylines of Calamity films through the 1950s. She is romantically involved with Wild Bill, and as an attractive, adventuresome young woman accomplishes much in a masculine Wild West. As in most of the early Calamity movies, the gray side of her character—the possible prostitution, aberrant behavior, and alcoholism—is entirely elided. The rambunctious young woman who rides, shoots, and acts outside the bounds of the sociocultural expectations of her sex and who falls in love with an entirely respectable Wild Bill—these were the standard ingredients in the early Calamity films.

There is no evidence that the locally popular film of 1915 had a national impact, but its plot surely suggested what might be the filmic pattern from then on. Obviously, history would take a back seat to popular myths and societal wants. Early movies demanded romance stories and valiant heroes and heroines vanquishing heavies. That's what happened in 1915 in the first Calamity movie. As to historical accuracy, perhaps film historian Kevin Brownlow had it right when he asserted, "No one goes to a Western for a history lesson, so to charge most westerns with inaccuracy is pointless. 'Make it vivid,' said Jack London. 'Truth doesn't matter so much, so long as it lives.'" Clearly, audiences for these early Calamity films seemed more interested in a good story than in historical accuracy; such has been the case for nearly a century of moviegoers.

The second silent film with a role for Calamity, William S. Hart's *Wild Bill Hickok* (1923), is somewhat shrouded in mystery because all copies of the movie have disappeared. Additionally, because of Hart's notoriety as a leading star of Westerners, and his ego-need to be at the dominating center of all his movies, neither he nor Paramount could allow Calamity's character, played by Ethel Grey Terry, to steal the limelight. Nonetheless, Calamity is in action for several scenes: first, as a gambler and "lookout" for Wild Bill as a gambler and law officer in Dodge City; and then later, by chance, they are together in the Black Hills. Calamity longs for Wild Bill, but his eyes are fixed on another woman, Kathleen O'Connor. When Hickok finds out Kathleen is married, he renounces his position and lams out for Deadwood. Meanwhile, Calamity, spurning the attentions of Jack McCall, turns to smoking, drinking, and masculine dress when Hickok abandons Dodge—and leaves her. When they are in the Black Halls, Wild Bill suggests that he and Calamity might forge a life together, but before that can happen, McCall again dashes on camera and guns down Wild Bill. In the final scene Calamity is present at McCall's hanging, staring at him; McCall gnashes his teeth at her just before he's strung up.

Hart flatly declared *Wild Bill Hickok* was historically accurate. In fact, Hart himself had written the screenplay. He claimed to know a great deal about Old West characters

Wild Bill Hickok (Paramount), 1923.

Another film treating Wild Bill and Calamity Jane as a romantic twosome, this movie starred the notable actor William S. Hart as Hickok and Ethel Grey Terry as Calamity Jane. In spite of Hart's claim, the film was wide of the known facts about Wild Bill and Calamity. Courtesy Paul Andrew Hutton.

such as Wild Bill and Calamity. His father had told him about Wild Bill. And when a Nebraska historian wrote to him about Calamity, he found her comments intriguing and wanted "to prospect over that country." Referring to Calamity and Wild Bill, he told the Nebraska writer, "I have studied those characters so much that I almost feel as tho I know them."

Obviously, in the eyes of most moviegoers the historical accuracy of the film, although not insignificant, was of less import than how writers and filmmakers were portraying Calamity early in the twentieth century. The plots of these early movies foreshadow the storylines of many films and writings about Calamity Jane in the coming decades. Just as their graves were next to one another in the Deadwood cemetery, Wild Bill and Calamity would be together in subsequent films and novels. The romantic yarns about Wild Bill and Calamity, while not substantiated in subsequent history and biography (a fact not yet clear in the 1920s), were needed to bring together *the* story of an Old West hero and heroine. With but a few exceptions, it would be several years before Calamity could stand as the center pivot, by herself, in novels and cinematic works.

In the generation and more between Calamity's death and 1930, several writers dealt with her in their reminiscences or in retrospective essays. Most of these treatments of Calamity were rather glancing. Most often, authors were discussing her as part of a larger subject, in a brief profile, or calling readers to consider a new avenue of understanding about her. These fragments added to the mosaic-like view of Calamity coming into focus in the teens and twenties.

A few of the writers dealt with Calamity's tumultuous times in Deadwood, but not all came to the same conclusions. In his memoir *Hard Knocks* (1915), bartender Harry (Sam) Young provided an abbreviated sketch of Calamity as a hanger-on during the Jenney Expedition but offered more extensive comments on her roles in Deadwood. Remembering back thirty years after the events, Young says Calamity did "white slave" work for "Al Swarringer" [Swearingen], was "thoroughly masculine" in her behavior, and "her love of whiskey equaled that of any hard drinker." But, obviously, she had declined badly when she later returned to Deadwood. (Young sometimes erred badly in trying to recall facts. He says, for example, that Calamity died on 2 August 1906, missing the day and the year.) Still, Young has warm feelings for Calamity and Wild Bill, whom Calamity "greatly admired." He closes his section on Calamity, now lying in death's repose next to Wild Bill, with an accepting coda: "May the Supreme Ruler of the Universe forgive their faults, for they had many virtues."

Judge W. L. Kuykendall is much less sympathetic in his account, *Frontier Days* (1917). Kuykendall, the judge at Jack McCall's trial in Deadwood, dismissed as bullshooting nonsense the yarns of Calamity's hobnobbing with men on both sides of the law. To the judge, these stretchers had two purposes, neither of which was admirable: either to magnify Calamity's actions well beyond accuracy or to pull the legs of outsider greenhorns willing to buy these exaggerations.

The most widely cited and perhaps most influential of memoirs about Calamity's time in Deadwood is Estelline Bennett's *Old Deadwood Days* (1928). Published more than thirty years after Bennett's observation of Calamity's return to Deadwood in 1895, the reminiscence furnishes an entirely sympathetic account of Calamity. In a full chapter entitled "When Calamity Jane Came Home," Bennett, the daughter and niece of very prominent Deadwood citizens, catches the significance of Calamity's symbolism twenty years after her heyday in the Black Hills gulches: "no one like Calamity Jane ever had come into Deadwood Gulch. She not only was typical of old Deadwood. She was old Deadwood."

Bennett was not the first to see that the West, and the Black Hills specifically, had moved beyond Calamity in the generation she had been roaming throughout the northern West. Others had come to a similar conclusion as they watched residents of Deadwood view and react to Calamity when she returned to the Hills in the mid-1890s. This idea—a closed frontier bypassing an Old West Calamity—persisted in the years to come. It continued throughout the twentieth century.

Another ingredient enlarged the view that time had roared around Calamity. Deadwood promoters, some of whom were labeled the "stagecoach aristocracy," embraced progress, uplift, and development, none of which they thought Calamity represented. She could drink and roar in the saloons with that sottish crowd and be cheered in Old Deadwood celebrations, but she must not be celebrated as representing what they wanted Deadwood to be now and in the future.

To her credit, Bennett hurdles the class barriers of her mother and other snobbish Deadwood churchwomen and stands instead in the footprints of her tolerant father and uncle. Yes, Calamity bruised several of the Ten Commandments, and she had problems with alcohol and carry-through. But she also loved her daughter, wanted her to get a good education, was willing to give away her shoes to a needy woman, and more than once nursed sick men. Revealingly, three women at much the same time—Bennett in her observations in the mid-1890s, Mrs. William Spencer in her novel *Calamity Jane* (1887), and M. L. Fox in her essay "Calamity Jane" (1896)—gave profoundly sympathetic views of Calamity. Bennett summed up her observations by writing, "Whatever there was of evil in Calamity's life has been long since forgotten. It is not living as anyone's sorrow." One can construct a "full category of her vices," Bennett notes, but then adds, "I never heard anything about them from the people who had known her. Old Black Hillers seemed never to remember her faults. Certainly they attached no importance to them." And neither would Bennett.

A handful of essays in national newspapers and magazines in the 1920s revealed what some Americans were remembering about Calamity Jane. The perspectives were very mixed. In October 1921, Josiah M. Ward wrote a very general story for the *New York Tribune* that claimed "most people" thought of Calamity "as a fictional character." But in his second paragraph the author swung toward an opposite view: Calamity was "the boldest, fiercest, tenderest, most unconventional and best known figure in the old West." That statement came close to capturing the ambivalent, complex popular figure emerging in American popular culture by the 1920s.

Sadly, Ward knows only enough about Calamity to fall into error and to deliver a distorted frontier heroine. Although he follows veracious material about her origins, her life at the Gallaghers in Miner's Delight (misplaced in South Dakota), and concludes she "was the victim of her times and surroundings," his mistakes overshadow the few truisms. She was not, except for Wild Bill, the best shot in the West, did not participate in several outlaw gangs and more than a few lynchings, was not a scout for Miles and Custer, and no one who knew her personally described her as tall, pretty, and very feminine. Ward also questionably makes Wild Bill Calamity's "beau ideal," and then, after declaring Deadwood "the wickedest and wildest place on the earth," telescopes the last twenty-five years of Calamity's life into four paragraphs and places her death in Butte, Montana. A reader without any—or with very limited—knowledge of Calamity would have been led far astray by Ward's essay.

Four years later on 18 October 1925, the *New York Times Magazine* published a similar essay by Seymour G. Pond. A litany of Wild West characteristics dominates Pond's portrait of Calamity: the piece travels her as a sharpshooter, Indian fighter (bearing the "scars of a dozen bullets from Indians and highwaymen"), savior of stagecoaches, and generally "rough and tough." But Calamity's tender and kind side is trotted out too. She nursed the sick, disallowed mal-treatment of wagon-pulling bulls, and stood by soldiers in need. Pond thinks Calamity was married several times and "some children were sent to an orphanage." The author adds a false serendipity by reporting that Calamity died on 2 August 1903, "twenty-seven years to the day after 'Wild Bill Hickok.'" The next month the *Literary Digest* published a condensation of Pond's article titled "Calamity Jane as a Lady Robin Hood." This abbreviated story repeated the central focus of Pond's tough/kind interpretation.

The initial nonfiction book about Calamity, Duncan Aikman's *Calamity Jane and the Lady Wildcats* (1927), reinforced the romantic Old West image already introduced, which would dominate representations of Calamity from the 1920s through the Doris Day movie *Calamity Jane* in 1953. A journalist inflicted with the sardonic wit of his friend the cultural critic H. L. Mencken, Aikman devoted a bit more than a third of his 350-page book to Calamity, along with provocative sections on Cattle Kate Watson, Belle Starr, Lola Montez, Pearl Hart, Madame Moustache, and other Wild West women. Supposedly a work of nonfiction, most of its pages about Calamity reeked of imagined scenes and what-ifs—even though Aikman interviewed a few persons who knew Calamity, read dozens of newspapers clippings, and perused other published information about her. His book overflows with sensational details, contrived characterizations, and invented dialogue. Guessing at happenings, as well as at the reasons for these occurrences, Aikman fills in large sections of his biography with speculations, manufactured events, and supposed contacts. If the author had used only the hard facts of his research—and avoided the artistic verbiage—his account of Calamity could have been condensed into a twenty-five-page essay.

Still, researching more widely than most early writers, Aikman included new information in his book. But the manner in which he gathered and used the sources on Calamity's life led to a decidedly mixed product. His account remained the most widely circulated biographical source on Calamity for more than two decades, with subsequent biographers capitalizing on his disclosures but also victimized by his slanted evidence, misstatements, and blatant fabrications.

Aikman did uncover important documents about Martha Canary's first years. He was the first writer to turn up proof of the land purchases and sales of the Canary family in Mercer County, Missouri. Also, his interviews with two aged citizens—remembering back sixty to sixty five years—gathered important information for understanding Martha's preteen years. His were the first references to the *Montana Post* story that placed the Canary family in Virginia City, Montana, in December 1864. Although Aikman did not uncover the inheritance problems and resulting legal squabbles that did most to drive Martha's parents, Robert and Charlotte, out of Princeton, or the marriage and census records that pinpointed Martha's parents' marriage, her birth, and those of her siblings, he did discover more than any previous researcher.

Regrettably, Aikman misuses some of this path-breaking information. He relies too heavily, for instance, on the long-ago and shaky memories of one or two interviewees. Much of what he says about Charlotte Canary, for example, seems to have come from "Mrs. Elizabeth Collins" (Collings), who recalled Martha's mother almost entirely as a vixen. Fixing on those views—and perhaps on other similar reminiscences—Aikman manufactures a memorable but off-center description of Charlotte: Mercer County residents "could not understand a beautiful, coarse woman who smoked, drank, cursed and publicly flirted, yet refused to be caught in *flagrante delicto*." Nor does the author make clear on what evidence he bases his rather full characterizations of Robert and Charlotte. This repeated pattern—conflating a few facts into several pages of imagined commentary—undermines the value of the volume.

By focusing almost entirely on the gambling, prostitution, and other scorned habits of Calamity and the "Lady Wildcats," Aikman distorts their lives. This tendency becomes clear in his correspondence with the leading historian of Wyoming in the 1920s, Grace Raymond Hebard, a longtime professor at the University of Wyoming. Hurrying to complete his manuscript in the summer and early fall of 1927, Aikman wrote a series of letters to Hebard asking her to turn up more information on Calamity and two or three of the other female vixens he was treating. But he wanted stories about their gambling and shooting; never does he ask about them as wives, sisters, daughters, or mothers. So, when Aikman wrote about Calamity, he was not much interested in her role as a pioneer woman but almost entirely in her actions as a frontier hellcat. He spilled no ink about her giving birth to two children or about the lives of her children and debunks almost entirely her rumored actions as an angel of mercy. Notably, he scorns the possibility of anything between Calamity and Wild Bill Hickok (whose name he consistently misspells). On one occasion Aikman says of his efforts to piece together Calamity's story, "It is all guesswork." The trouble is Aikman guesses too often on too little evidence and seems unwilling to ask other questions that should have been raised. Given his intentions, Aikman found what he wanted: Martha Canary, the wild "lynx's kitten" who becomes a wild woman of the West.

The Calamity Jane who emerges from Aikman's book fits well with the lively Old West heroes and heroines of the interwar period. His Calamity is a worthy companion for the heroes in Walter Noble Burns's *Saga of Billy the Kid* (1926) and newspaperman Stuart Lake's *Wyatt Earp: Frontier Marshall* (1931). These romantic, overly dramatized protagonists had also been made larger than life and inducted into the pantheon of frontier demigods.

No one had written a full-length biography of Calamity by the early 1930s, but historians had been at work on

The first nonfiction account of Calamity Jane.

In 1927, journalist Duncan Aikman published a sensational account of Calamity and other so-called wildcats. Even though Aikman imagined dozens of unreliable scenes and conversations for Calamity in *Calamity Jane and the Lady Wildcats*, he also dredged up manuscript records and reminiscences important to later biographers and historians. Courtesy J. Leonard Jennewein Collection, McGovern Library, Dakota Wesleyan University.

Wild Bill Hickok. Most of their writings on the western sharpshooter also dealt with Calamity and certainly shaped the reading public's opinions about her, particularly in light of the absence of any life stories of Calamity herself. In the early 1880s, St. Louis journalist J. W. Buel wove together a new fabric of fantastic yarns to lionize Wild Bill as the West's leading lawman and nature's nobleman. In his hyped and error-filled version of Wild Bill's life, Buel obviously imagined more than a handful of his many stories about Hickok, but contemporary dime novelists and also novelist-and-historian Emerson Hough repeated the same fabricated stories in his widely popular *The Story of the Outlaw* (1907). The developing and crystallizing story of Wild Bill Hickok as a frontier demigod did not allow much leeway for Calamity Jane to play anything but a very minor role. As the leading authority on Hickok puts it, "The hero-worshiping fraternity [touting Hickok] have steadfastly maintained that Wild Bill would have died rather than share a bed with Calamity." Even though those cheerleading for Wild Bill might admit his dalliance with the Cyprian sisters of frontier demimondes, they stoutly denied any possibility that he would have been attracted to a sluttish Calamity.

By the 1920s and early 1930s, historians were producing biographies of Hickok said to be based on solid, factual research, ones that moved well beyond the first sensationalist and dime novel–driven tomes. Even though these biographers seemed less willing to front for all the extravagant tales being marketed about Wild Bill, they nonetheless quoted a good deal from Buel, without stating reservations about his questionable stories. Nor did they change any previous stances on Calamity Jane.

The most important of the Hickok biographies in the 1920s was *Wild Bill Hickok: The Prince of Pistoleers* (1926) by Frank J. Wilstach. Toward the end of his biography, after a chapter on Wild Bill's attraction to and then marriage to widow Agnes Lake, Wilstach treats the Hickok-Calamity rumors in a full chapter, "The Calamity Jane–Wild Bill Myth." He labels the stories that attempted to link the two Old West worthies as "gossip" or "mere moonshine." Wilstach "investigated carefully" the contention of Deadwood pioneer J. S. McClintock that Calamity was Wild Bill's "consort" and was "unable to find the least justification for it." He then cites a 1925 letter from Ellis T. ("Doc") Peirce, longtime Deadwood resident who knew Wild Bill and Calamity, to conclude that Wild Bill did not associate with "lewd women" (meaning Calamity!) and that Calamity "never made any talk . . . about Bill, or even mentioned his name," at least not in Peirce's presence. In the final pages of the chapter, Wilstach quotes Doane Robinson, the blunt, outspoken secretary of the Department of History of the state of South Dakota. In Robinson's eyes, Calamity was "large and thick . . . chewed tobacco, . . . [and] was among the lowest harlots without trace of refinement." Romantic popularizers, Robinson continued, "magnified" her "good qualities," and "her worst [qualities were] never disclosed." But Wilstach could be less harsh in his portrait of Calamity. He advances a compromise interpretation that gradually gained the support of other Hickok followers. After dismissing the idea of Calamity as Wild Bill's "sweetheart," Wilstach quickly adds that "among the celebrities of that time period [the second half of the nineteenth century] Calamity Jane ranks as an astounding figure." Even though stories of her birthplace and life often collided in controversy, one must conclude Calamity "lived a hard and vicious life, yet she had a most kind and generous heart. She might have "no more use for skirts than an owl has for the Book of Common Prayer," but one need not—and should not—cut her off at her boot-tops.

Here was a middle-of-the-road position for biographers and historians. Wild Bill and Calamity were not romantically entangled. "Those who knew," Wilstach notes, "both Wild Bill and this unfortunate woman have been reluctant to admit that he could have had any interest in her outside a casual acquaintanceship." But having eschewed this nonsense did not mean one should forget Calamity Jane. She was a major, unforgettable character of the Old West, just not Wild Bill's "consort" or "sweetheart." If this mediating, give-and-take, approach satisfied the so-called truth-tellers, historians, and biographers, it was less satisfactory to the myth-makers, the movie directors and novelists, as we shall soon see.

By the end of the 1920s, about a quarter century after Calamity Jane's death, images of her were beginning to congeal but not yet into a coherent single image. Biographers and historians spoke of her as one of the residents in the pantheon of Old West heroes and heroines. They detailed her rowdy and antisocial behavior, sometimes mentioning her prostitution and drunkenness, but balancing that with conclusions about her nursing and kindheartedness. Movie-makers, less inclined to stick to contested facts about her life, imagined stories that had little basis in fact. They also were bent in finding ways to show her as a romantic interest of Wild Bill Hickok.

Surprisingly, newspaper writers, supposedly among the truth-telling tribe, were often willing to spin yarns wide of accepted facts. Perhaps they were relying too much on their archives, their journalistic morgues, rather than on investigating new lines of information. Meanwhile, advocates of Wild Bill Hickok were agreed that Calamity, though she was an acquaintance in Deadwood, was in no way a romantic interest of the famous pistoleer. In the next three decades, novelists, filmmakers, and biographers traveled these paths of interpretation even while they found and followed still other avenues of explanation.

8

The Search for a Coherent Calamity, 1930–1960

In early 1936, when famed movie director Cecil B. DeMille announced his plans for a film on Wild Bill Hickok, with a major role for Calamity Jane, he set tongues to wagging. What would he do with those Old West demigods? Would he place an emotional romance at the center of the film, how would he treat the darker side of Calamity, and would he remain true to history and end the film tragically?

Generally, DeMille's *The Plainsman* (1936) fit comfortably with a growing interest in the Old West that spiraled upward in the 1920s and hit a high peak in the 1930s. The new talkie Western films, starring new leading men such as Gary Cooper and John Wayne, captured large audiences even at the nadir of the Depression. At the same time, Zane Grey, Max Brand, Ernest Haycox, and Luke Short were churning out dozens of popular Western novels. The western frontier was also attracting many academic historians. After a bit of a lull in things western during World War II and immediately thereafter, Western films and fiction climbed to new heights of popularity in the 1950s. Interest in Calamity Jane, especially in films and less so in biography and fiction, remained high during the three decades from 1930 to 1960.

But a counterapproach to the American West provided a challenge to popular treatments of the Old West.

Beginning in the 1920s and sweeping over the country in the 1930s, a tide of regionalism encouraged thinkers to approach the West from an opposite tack. Rather than pursue the West through the dramatic lives of frontier heroes and heroines like Custer, Billy the Kid, Wyatt Earp, Wild Bill Hickok, Calamity Jane, and several Indian chiefs, regionalists wanted novelists, historians, artists, and moviemakers to stress places—regions and subregions— and show how those powerful places shaped the lives of people who inhabited them. If frontier or Old West stories stressed larger-than-life men and women who came *to* a new area and launched into character-exhibiting conflicts with Indians or other opponents, regionalists wanted to tell stories of persons already *in* the West whose lives and characters were being reshaped in situ by their physical and cultural environments.

Stories about Calamity Jane moved through the ebb and flow of these competing approaches to the western past. For the most part, the Old West interpreters won out with general audiences, meaning that stories about Calamity as a Wild West woman would dominate up to 1960. For one thing, strange stories coming from daughter Jessie revealed much about the complexity of Calamity's family life. Of special importance in shaping images of Calamity as a Wild West figure from World War II onward was the sensational announcement by Jean Hickok McCormick in 1941 that she was the daughter of Calamity and Wild Bill. In addition, the essays of Clarence Paine and the brief biographies of Calamity by Nolie Mumey (1950) and Glenn Clairmonte (1959), as well the more critical biographies of J. Leonard Jennewein (1963) and Roberta Sollid (1958), illustrated the fascination with Calamity as an Old West woman. Movies such as *The Plainsman* and *Calamity Jane* (1953) and a novel like Ethel Hueston's *Calamity Jane of Deadwood Gulch* (1937) provided cinematic and fictional depictions of Calamity in a similar vein. But most of the debunking or "gray" treatments of Calamity would not appear until after 1960.

Two women whose stories would markedly challenge existing images of Calamity Jane appeared suddenly on the scene in the 1930s and 1940s. The first was Jessie Elizabeth (Oakes) Murray, who in the late 1920s but especially in the early 1930s, came forward to claim she was Calamity's granddaughter. The best evidence—not gathered until much later—indicated instead that she was Calamity's daughter. The other woman, Jean Hickok McCormick, announced dramatically in 1941 that she was the daughter of Calamity and Wild Bill Hickok. McCormick's story, buttressed by what she asserted were her mother's diary and letters, eventually proved fraudulent, but not before it roiled accounts of Calamity for three or four decades. The reports of these two women, particularly McCormick's, clearly impacted images of Calamity because so little was known of her private life, and Calamity raconteurs were too ready to gather and accept any new yarns that surfaced.

Not much is known about Calamity's daughter, Jessie. For nearly a decade after her birth on 28 October 1887, Jessie tagged along, off and on, with her mother. Several newspaper stories place her with Calamity, particularly in 1895–96 when Calamity returned to Deadwood and just before she went on her dime museum tour. Jessie claimed much later that Calamity's last husband, who was probably Robert Dorsett, stole her away from Calamity. (Jessie all the while was claiming Calamity as her grandmother.) And, newspaper accounts just before and at the time of Calamity's death reported that she had a married daughter in North Dakota, who had made her a grandmother. But Calamity ruefully added that she and her daughter were estranged, refusing to give out further information on her.

Jessie seemed to disappear from all sources for more than three decades. But recently William R. Whiteside, a diligent, energetic researcher, has turned up records of two of Jessie's marriages in 1904 and 1908, both in Montana. After a large gap in evidence, the next information came in the early 1930s when a flurry of stories in Calamity Country newspapers reported that Jessie, claiming to be Calamity's granddaughter, was looking for information about her grandmother, mother, father, and half-brother. Writing to the Adams Memorial Hall in Deadwood and the Colorado Historical Society, among other places, Jessie stated that Calamity, her grandmother, "reared me to the age of ten years old [when] her last husband took me away from her." Jessie was also trying to find out if her real name was "Jessie Oakes or Jessie Hickok," because the married name of Jessie's mother, Calamity's daughter Belle, was Oakes or Hickok. In still another letter, Jessie told an educator that her mother, Belle, was "married three times," and Jessie remembered as a three-year-old playing with her half-brother, Charley or Jack Oakes. Jessie was convinced that there was "not a historian living who really knows the absolute facts of (Calamity Janes) life and her connections." But she wanted it to be known she was "very proud to have been a Grand-daughter of (Calamity Jane)."

In another letter four years later, Jessie, now signing her letters Jessie Elizabeth Oakes Murray, was also looking for her father. He was, she told one correspondent, a "U. S. Marshal for South Dakota in the 80s." He may have died about 1900, and Jessie wanted to find out if he left an estate. Were there any records of what he left? To substantiate her claims, Jessie enclosed an affidavit from Robert H. Dorsett, dated 23 June 1934, declaring Jessie the granddaughter of Calamity, who reared Jessie "as her own daughter." Dorsett claimed to have known Jessie since she was seven, and he wrote as "a confidential friend of Calamity Jane's." Dorsett, the last "husband" Calamity claimed, and the person who probably took Jessie away from Calamity and placed her with his mother in Livingston, must have known that his affidavit supported false information. But he spoke in support of Jessie's claims.

When Jean Hickok McCormick burst on the scene in 1941 to claim she was the daughter of Calamity and Wild Bill, Jessie felt pressure to change her story. Now, Calamity became her aunt, not her grandmother. Based on Calamity's "confession," which McCormick said Calamity left behind at her death, Jessie also had to revise her statements about her claimed mother: she was not the famous Belle Starr, the outlaw. Instead, Jessie's mother, another Belle Starr, "never was in history so you can tell this to the world." And now, to clarify further, as a daughter of William Hickok, she was a second cousin to Wild Bill.

In addition to these confused and often-changed stories about her heritage, Jessie revealed several idiosyncratic characteristics about herself. She was, she told an editor, a "born American molded from American *Soil*, and proud of it! Never have been out of my country, never had any desire to go out of it . . . This USA is *my country*. I say what I like and please! when I say I am of the soil. . . ." Then she revealed something about her mother/grandmother that no one else has stated. "Did I write and tell you," she added in speaking to the newsman, that Calamity "was an Indian! Yes, sir, A real Indian[;] so was my mother, Bell [*sic*] Star. I am more than proud of my Indian blood." Intrigued by what Jessie said about her heritage, the journalist asked for a full report on her background. Jessie never sent the requested information.

From the mid-1940s onward, Jessie was increasingly off-scene. As Jean Hickok McCormick gained the headlines with her claim as Calamity and Wild Bill's daughter, Jessie backed away from the barrage of letters and messages she had issued during most of the previous decade. One suspects that Jessie knew so few facts about her parental heritage that

Calamity Jane's daughter, Jessie Oakes
Murray (1887–1980).

Jessie, probably the biological daughter of
Bill Steers and Calamity, undoubtedly led
a troubled life, with an alcoholic mother
and without a stable home and resident
father. She may have already been a mother
when Calamity died in 1903, was married
several times, and was obviously confused
about whether Calamity was her mother,
grandmother, or aunt. Photograph from an
unidentified newspaper clipping.

she was afraid to disagree with Hickok McCormick's very unusual claim. But even Jessie's less frequent letters had similar requests. Did record keepers have any information on James Butler Hickok, her father who was not Wild Bill? Before being appointed a peace officer, he had served as a security guard on bullion-hauling stages from the Homestake Mine in Lead to Nebraska. Other familiar facts were restated—but in different terms, giving them transformed meanings. "I was raised by an aunt of mine, from a baby up to ten years old, then I ran away from her." This letter never mentioned that the aunt was Calamity Jane; it asked only for information on her father. She wanted to know the date of his death and "who was at his bed side" when he died.

During the next decade Jessie remained quiet, evidently, as before, moving often from home to home. Then, in the mid-1950s another of her letters came to the clerk of Deadwood. It was a petulant—even angry—missive. She had presumably asked Marie Lawler for information on her father William Hickok, not Wild Bill, but Lawler had mixed up the two in her reply. (Both letters are evidently missing.) Jessie fired back to the clerk: "What is the matter can you read? I asked about James Butler Hickok or Bill Hickok not (Wild Bill)." Were the Deadwood people trying to "use my letter, to show something on the [Hollywood] screen"? Then Jessie angrily and erratically added, "Why dont get some thing to get the scum off of your brain Wild Bill). Ha! Ha! [*sic*]."

Meanwhile, Jessie had used some of this information to gain support. In 1939, then living in San Diego, she filled out an application for Social Security benefits, stating she was born 28 October 1887 in Denver, Colorado, the daughter of William Hickok and Belle Jane Somors. She also listed her maiden name as Jessie Oakes, her last name taken from her adoptive stepfather. Jessie lived a long life, dying at age ninety-three in Whittier, California. She may have been institutionalized in her last years. There is no evidence she pursued further her confused identity as Calamity's daughter, granddaughter, or niece after her fiery letter to the Deadwood official in 1957.

The other woman who claimed to be Calamity's daughter, Jean Hickok McCormick, erupted on scene in 1941. Her story astounded listeners and readers. On Mother's Day, 6 May 1941, she appeared on the national CBS radio program *We the People*, hosted by Gabriel Heatter, to declare that she was the genuine daughter of Calamity Jane and Wild Bill Hickok. That dramatic announcement, in written form, soon made its way into many newspapers. "Billings Woman Announces That She Is Daughter of Famed Calamity Jane," the *Billings Gazette* declared in a lengthy feature story on 14 June 1941. A few weeks later, on 12 September, a headline in the *Rapid City Journal* read: "Woman Who Believes She Is Daughter of Calamity Jane and Wild Bill Is Visitor in Rapid City."

The details, although nearly incredible, were rather simple and straightforward. The story of Jean McCormick, briefly summarized, was this. In Kansas, Calamity and Wild Bill first met in 1870 when she had warned Bill about cutthroat killers awaiting him; she nursed him through the injuries resulting from attacks on him. They soon married, and a child Jane (or Janey; and later Jean, her adopted name) was born on 25 September 1873 at Benson's Landing near present-day Livingston, Montana. When Calamity gave birth to Jean, Bill was gone, and she was alone in faraway Montana. Bill relocated Calamity and Jean, helped briefly with their care, and then left again. Saddened by Bill's lessening interest, Calamity offered him a divorce when they reunited later in Deadwood, so he could marry Agnes Lake. Unable to properly care for and support Jean, Calamity gave her up to James O'Neil, a ship captain then traveling in the West. O'Neil and his wife raised Jean; she never learned, growing up, that Calamity was her mother. When Calamity died, a diary she had kept sporadically and a few unsent letters she had written were bequeathed to O'Neil. He, in turn, gave the diary and letters to Jean just before his death in 1912. Learning for the first time her ties to Calamity and Wild Bill, Jean decided to keep her heritage a secret

Jean Hickok McCormick (1873[?]–1951), self-proclaimed daughter of Calamity Jane and Wild Bill Hickok.

In 1941 on national radio, Hickok McCormick sensationally announced she was the offspring of Calamity and Wild Bill. More than a few writers and moviemakers accepted her fraudulent claims. Not until the 1990s was her declaration proven entirely false. Courtesy The Center for Western Studies, Augustana College.

from the public until friends urged her to disclose the full truth.

Jean's story captivated many readers hungry to know more about Calamity and others wanting, one way or another, to unite Calamity and Wild Bill in their romanticized versions of Old West history. In the summer of 1941, the diminutive (about 5' 4", 100 pounds) Jean began appearing as a buckskin-clad rider in rodeos and parades. In the fall at La Crosse, Wisconsin, she attended a Hickok family reunion, having her picture taken with two Hickok cousins. The reporter for the *La Crosse Tribune* (15 September 1941) was so taken with Jean that he declared "the story of her life would make an author of westerns look at his fiction with disgust."

The documents that Jean provided were even more impressive than her presence in substantiating her unusual story. But the content of the diary and the number of letters changed over time, providing a slippery, ever-winding trail to follow. At the beginning, those who made contact with Jean and spoke of her purported Calamity documents referred to an album diary of about fifteen entries, twelve additional entries on separate sheets of paper, a few letters exchanged with Captain O'Neil, a marriage license for Calamity and Wild Bill written on a page torn from a bible, a poem, a last will and testament, and, most curious of all, a so-called confession of Calamity's at the end of her diary. Copies of these documents, or at least selections of them, widely circulated in the last decade of Jean's life, 1941–51. Some writers had access to them, some were deposited for a time in a museum in Fort Collins, Colorado, and sections of others were printed in several newspapers. Most important, Don and Stella Foote, museum owners in Billings, purchased the documents and printed two or three nearly complete versions of the diary and letters. It is rumored that as many as 100,000 copies of the small booklets were printed and sold. If true, that means the publication sold by far more widely than any other publication about Calamity

Jane. The Footes helped Jean through her difficult last days. Death came on 21 February 1951.

Jean Hickok McCormick's portrait of Calamity differed dramatically from what had been said about her previous to 1941. No other journalist, acquaintance, or biographer advanced several of the points McCormick made about her purported mother on the eve of World War II. It was if a new edifice had been built, transforming the horizon.

The most explosive of Jean's revelations was the marriage of Calamity and Hickok and the birth of their child. Previously, there were contested rumors about the relationship. As we have seen, most pooh-poohed the idea that anything besides a brief acquaintance had occurred in Deadwood in 1876, fewer tried to sketch in a previous contact, and still others thought Calamity and Hickok were a bit more than casual acquaintances. But no one had made anything like the case Jean promoted in the so-called Calamity diary. In the 1940s and 1950s, more than a few commentators expressed their doubts about the authenticity of the marital and parental claims, but they lacked concrete information to overthrow the claims.

Others wondered about the personality of Calamity that emerged from the diary and loose-leaf sheets. These sources portrayed Calamity as interested in being a wife, as a warm mother, as much more domestic than the rough, uncouth figure described in so many nineteenth-century sources. McCormick's Calamity suggests little of the drunkenness, possible prostitution, and extreme wildness of other portraits.

The diary also added experiences not in other sources. Calamity says here that she was with Buffalo Bill's Wild West show, that she traveled in England, and that she had spent considerable time in Kansas before coming to the Black Hills. The Calamity diary speaks, too, of her being in Richmond with Cody, her loneliness, and her approaching blindness in her latter days.

Even more noteworthy are happenings the diary omits that were front and center in other sources, including some in Calamity's autobiography published in 1895–96. No mention is made of Calamity's trips to the Coeur d'Alenes, her participation in the Hardwick and Kohl and Middleton touring groups, or her connections with Josephine Brake and her trip to Buffalo to take part in the Pan-American Exposition. We hear little or nothing, too, about her Missouri beginnings, her siblings Lena and Elijah (save a backhanded swipe at Tobe Borner in one of the added pages), or other "husbands" George Cosgrove, William Steers, or Robert Dorsett. And why no references to "the little Calamity" son born in Montana, and especially to the daughter, Jessie Elizabeth, referred to in her interview with M. L. Fox in 1896, her autobiography, and in several newspapers?

One of the other large reservations about the diary was that no one had seen, to date, any writing from Calamity. If she was illiterate, as was rumored, how could she have authored the diary, with its direct, readable style and more-than-adequate vocabulary? Like so many other aspects of the documents that McCormick was touting, the diary seemed the product of someone else besides the Calamity of history and memory.

A reflective aside is in order, which should help illuminate the difficulties of constructing a coherent image of Calamity Jane in the years from 1930 to 1960. Think of the family histories that Calamity, her siblings, and offspring provided for their contemporaries, misshaping the truth and hamstringing those attempting to piece together factual stories of their lives. Neither Calamity, her sister, Lena, nor their younger brother, Elijah (Lige), gave full, dependable accounts of their parents or of themselves. If the 1860 census is correct, Calamity was about ten or eleven years of age and Lena about seven or eight when their parents died. (Lige's birth date is not confirmed, but likely sometime between 1860 and 1866.) The two sisters were old enough to know the true story of their parents, their declines and deaths. As noted earlier, Calamity in her autobiography provided the briefest of details about her family, gave the wrong date of her birth, and misled everyone on many events of her life. Lena manufactured a wholly false origins story to tell her children, a narrative passed on to her grandchildren, and on to the present. Through the years Lena's children and grandchildren stood by her false family history. Lige, when asked about his birth for two different prison records, said he was born in Montana in 1868, two years after Charlotte's death. Jessie concocted a wild account of her origins, and changed those details at least two times after Jean Hickok McCormick came on scene to claim Calamity as her mother.

Why should these fabricated family histories have endured and traveled so widely? One answer, more than several others, deserves major consideration. These smoothed-over stories removed the shame of truthful but negative accounts, replacing them with new, more positive histories. Rather than depict Robert as a gambler and Charlotte as a woman "of the worse kind," they were depicted as ambitious and courageous settlers, victims of marauding Indians. Or, rather than Jessie becoming the rumored offspring of Calamity and a violent and vicious Bill Steers, she was the granddaughter of a caring Calamity Jane, who helped raise her and whom she remembered with warmth. The retold stories provided family histories more acceptable to children and grandchildren; they were substituted for disastrous ones about a disintegrating Robert and Charlotte and Calamity as a drunken prostitute.

One needs to ask, too, why Jean Hickok McCormick promoted a story of her descent from Calamity and Wild Bill. That account contained little proof and was eventually proven fraudulent, so why was McCormick willing to take such a great risk to her credibility and reputation? What needs were being met in peddling a heritage not hers?

The moving story that Jean Hickok McCormick peddled about her reputed mother and father captured many audiences from the early 1940s onward. A number of scholars, biographers, and filmmakers were enamored with the story and centered their works around it. The McCormick followers came on scene in the 1940s and 1950s, but they continued through the next decades and even into the twenty-first century.

Librarian and Calamity biographer Clarence C. Paine was one of those who, at first, believed the McCormick version of Calamity's story. Immediately after Jean Hickok McCormick appeared on the *We the People* radio program to identify her parents, Paine, then a librarian at Beloit College, met with her in Chicago, and they made a verbal agreement. She would provide the Calamity documents, which he would copy and edit for publication. Or, perhaps, he would use the documents in his preparation of a full-scale biography of Calamity. For more than a decade Paine worked on the project, gathering a superb collection of materials, now on deposit at the Center for Western Studies at Augustana College, Sioux Falls, South Dakota.

Paine proved to be a better gatherer than finisher. He seemed so taken with proving the authenticity or falsity of the McCormick documents that he could not move much beyond that demanding task. But he did complete three strong essays important for assessing the status of Calamity studies at midcentury. Two of the essays appeared in the "Brand Books" of Westerners groups, the other in a collection about the Black Hills.

"She Laid Her Pistol Down; or, The Last Will and Testament of Calamity Jane" (1944, 1946) and "Calamity Jane: Man? Woman? or Both?" (1945–46, 1947) illustrate

Paine's approaches to his subjects as well as the difficulties he had in moving to conclusions about Calamity. In the first brief piece, Paine provides a critical reading of the McCormick documents, but hesitates to move to definite judgments. He is convinced that there is "no evidence to justify the belief that she [Calamity] was illiterate," so he entertains the idea that some of the McCormick documents might have been written by Calamity, although he thinks the so-called marriage record of Calamity "can be shown to be a forgery." After looking carefully at the diary, and dismissing the section on Calamity's having served in Buffalo Bill's Wild West as "pure fancy," he concludes, "If the diary is a forgery, it is either the cleverest or the most bungled attempt of which I know."

The second essay replicates Paine's anecdotal approach, a less satisfactory organization than a chronological one for most readers. As he had in the first essay, Paine embraces the findings of one entry in the 1860 census for Missouri and declares that Calamity was most likely M. J. Conarray, a sixteen-year old young woman born in Illinois and an immigrant to Mercer County and Princeton. He dismisses the census listing of Robert and Charlotte that Aikman (whom he criticizes without naming him) followed, but the dismissal is cavalier, without any supporting reasons. Then, in the closing pages Paine introduces the possibility that Calamity might have been a victim of "Hermaphroditism," helping to explain her masculine-like actions and dress. No other scholar before or since has traveled that trail in studying Calamity, although novelist Larry McMurtry also advanced it in his novel *Buffalo Girls* (1990). It was also at the center of the movie by the same name in 1995. This strange, bold interpretation is startling, given Paine's reluctance to provide several other less sensational conclusions.

Paine's third and final essay, "Wild Bill and Calamity Jane" (1952), demonstrates how much revealing information he had gathered about Calamity but also his stubborn holding on to views that subsequent research have proven far wide of the mark. After providing a brief biography of Wild Bill, Paine does the same for Calamity, this time adopting a fuller, more attractive chronological approach. He also digs deeper into newspaper sources. Yet he remains convinced that in the 1860 census Abigail Conorray is the mother of sixteen-year-old M. J., whom he believes to be Martha Jane Canary, the real Calamity. Even though he rightly speculates that James Thornton Canary is her uncle, he cannot accept Robert and Charlotte as her parents. Obviously, after more than a decade of research, Paine had not looked carefully at the Canary family records in censuses from 1820 onward and had left unexamined the documents in the Mercer County Courthouse that revealed the full family of Martha; he seems not to have moved much beyond sources in Montana, Wyoming, and South Dakota. Paine is still pushing his hermaphroditic interpretation, helping him to explain Calamity's man/woman confusion. He mentions but one man, Clinton Burke, as a possible "husband" and dismisses anything serious between Calamity and Wild Bill and does not cite William Steers or Robert Dorsett, who were mentioned more than a few times in newspapers. Revealingly, Paine was now moving beyond all the Jean McCormick contentions save for the alleged marriage license of Wild Bill and Calamity, which he declared a forgery. Paine's closing lines summarize what he might have said in a full-length biography:

> Whatever may have been the eccentricities or sins of Martha Jane Canary, the deeds of Calamity Jane will live forever in the history and folklore of the frontier. Her beginnings were humble, to say the least, and her end miserable. Yet there was a richness and freedom in her life that many never attain, and because of it the heritage of the Hills is greater and more colorful.

By 1952, Clarence Paine had taken a new position with Oklahoma City Libraries and was buried under adminis-

trative duties. But in July he wrote to J. Leonard Jennewein, a journalist, and faculty member at Dakota Wesleyan,
and another Calamity researcher. Paine and Jennewein
exchanged several letters and Calamity documents, and the
librarian disclosed he had just hauled his Calamity research
out of storage and renewed his work on a Calamity biography. "After searches extending literally over many years,"
Paine told Jennewein, "I actually began to write about a
year ago urged on by a New York publisher." But Paine
published nothing more, and before Jennewein could issue
his brief but very good pamphlet in 1953, another Calamity
biographer had published a book.

Noley Mumey was a medical doctor and a diligent
researcher of local western history. In 1950 he published
his curious volume, *Calamity Jane 1852–1903: A History of
Her Life and Adventures in the West* in a privately printed,
two-hundred-copy edition. It quickly went out of print, has
never been reprinted, and thus had little impact on shifting
interpretations of Calamity. But the volume reprinted dozens of key newspaper stories about Calamity, thus providing
a very useful compendium of information no other author
had furnished to that date.

Mumey's volume also included a nearly complete copy
of the McCormick documents. He handled these writings
much as he did the newspaper and memoir quotations—
with little or no comment. But the content of Mumey's
chapters and a few footnotes to the diary make clear that he
is not following the McCormick/Calamity story in his own
narrative.

Mumey was decidedly positive toward Calamity. He
thought far too many writers had been excessively critical
of her. "I fain would cast any smirch upon her character
or degrade her in any way," he wrote in his introduction;
"her drinking and carousing in the saloons of these times
are not of much consequence." His "literary secretary"
Norma Flynn Mumey, who later became his wife, recalled

on one occasion that Mumey refused to speak to a woman researcher from New York who wished to interview him, but he rejected her offer of an interview *after* he became convinced that she had already concluded that Calamity was a negative character. He told her that he had nothing to tell her because she had too quickly decided what she thought about Calamity.

Generally, Mumey was more annalist than analyst. But his views were clear on Calamity. "It is unjust and cruel to harshly judge . . . [Calamity] by our present-day standards . . . for she lived in the true atmosphere of the West, even to the last years of her existence. Calamity Jane could not fit into the new scheme of things when the free life of the trapper, the trader, and the miner were gone." Although he was vague about his volume's purpose, Mumey stated on the final page of text that he had attempted "to check all available sources and to present them to the reader so that he may form his own opinion." Nolie Mumey would never be numbered among the harsh critics of Calamity Jane.

A decade later another biography of Calamity appeared, this one illustrating the staying power of Jessie Hickok McCormick's story and how far a writer was willing to go in adhering to that story line. Glenn Clairmonte's *Calamity Was the Name for Jane* (1959) was touted as "The Only Complete Life of Calamity Jane," with the author promising that "all the material in this story is authentic, and most of it has never been assembled before." But these assertions, and the publisher's labeling it a "distinguished biography," were all wide of their marks.

Soon after Clairmonte's book appeared, J. Leonard Jennewein, the journalist and college professor, unleashed his big guns on the volume. He told a friend in a private letter that the Clairmonte book "should win the prize for the worst biography ever written!" Going on the offense, Jennewein wrote to Clairmonte's publisher, Alan Swallow, asking if "someone pull[ed] a six-gun and force[d] you to publish that Calamity Jane book?" He asserted that Clairmonte had added much to the questions—"the chaff"—surrounding Calamity and then, in three single-spaced pages, listed the egregious errors. Three months later Jennewein's thirteen-page letter to Clairmonte herself was enough to make an author close up shop. His page-by-page comments attacked Clairmonte's research, her points of view, her conclusions, her misuses of sources—in short virtually everything about the ostensible biography. Jennewein would not have won an award for tact, which he more than once admitted, but most of his major criticisms were dead center.

In her decision to tell a sympathetic life story, Jennewein noted, Clairmonte omitted too many damning facts and overemphasized Calamity's admirable actions. One would not know from Clairmonte's account that Calamity had several "husbands" and seemed not too self-conscious about moving from one to another. Calamity's profanity and early drinking are muted. Nor does Clairmonte take up Calamity's possible prostitution, except to deny that it ever happened. In the same way, particularly in the early chapters, Clairmonte shapes Charlotte Canary into an idealized wife and mother.

Obviously, Clairmonte, caught among conflicting sources and possible motivations, could not sort them out. She tried, and failed, to knit together smoothly her two major sources: the McCormick/Calamity documents and Calamity's suspect autobiography. Many valid newspaper sources are also tossed into the narrative, adding bits of authenticity, but they are frequently misquoted and out of chronological order.

The author's possible motivations may have been the major reasons she so often misuses—frequently page after page—her sources. Clairmonte, totally taken in by Jean Hickok McCormick's sources, wants to dramatize Calamity's warmheartedness toward her putative daughter Jean; in doing so, she creates sources and conversations, whole cloth, that can be proven to be nonexistent or for which there is no substantiating proof. Nearly everything Clairmonte says about the Wild Bill–Calamity relationship is imagined, sometimes even more far-fetched than the McCormick story. She has Calamity sharing Bill's bed in Kansas, marrying him and wearing his ring from 1870 to 1873 and beyond, giving birth to his child in 1873, and bundling with him again in Deadwood—after he has married the widow Agnes Lake Thatcher. No other previous biographer had detailed this imagined torrid romance at such length.

Unfortunately, Clairmonte's book, more fiction than fact, was the most extensive "biography" published until several decades later. It was also the farthest from the truth, creating new conversations and scenes based on premises no previous or more recent biographer had touched on. Happily for truth seekers, Clairmonte's book was not widely circulated by its small western publisher, never enjoyed much attention from reviewers, and made little impact on shifting interpretations of Calamity Jane.

Two other biographers in the 1950s, also drawn to the enigmatic Calamity and perhaps encouraged by the upsurge of interest in things western in the decade, produced valuable studies of Calamity. Neither followed the wrongheaded story of McCormick; both helped move some biographers away from that story, which had dominated so much writing about Calamity since 1941. Instead, J. Leonard Jennewein and Roberta Beed Sollid published the most significant and reliable biographical accounts of Calamity appearing before 1960. They remain very useful for understanding Calamity Jane and her shifting images in the twentieth century.

For several years, Jennewein researched Calamity's story, gathering abundant information on her. To collect his facts, he wrote numerous letters, especially to elderly men, who knew Calamity well or were at least acquainted with her. He was also a pioneer in recording oral interviews with his sources. By the early 1950s he had drafted a manuscript of roughly fifty thousand words (150–200 pages), but had severely cut the manuscript to article length because he "felt it was so weak in a few respects," and he was "unable to dig into the blank spots." He put the challenges succinctly in his pamphlet-length book. Early on, he had thought of doing a large-scale biography of Calamity, but then, speaking in first-person plural, "it was slowly forced upon us that we had neither the time, money, nor talent to complete a full-length work on Calamity. The first two deficiencies might have been overcome; the third is definitely restrictive."

But word for word, Jennewein's abbreviated work *Calamity Jane of the Westward Trails* (1953) remains eminently valuable. He briefly addresses the controversial topics in Calamity's life, including her birthplace, death and funeral, her drinking and prostitution, scouting, her physical appearance, and the McCormick stories about her. Consider, for example, his one-line summary about Calamity's drinking: "Alcohol pushed and pulled and pounded on Calamity Jane." Or the baneful problems of sources and previous writers: "Writers have accepted the word of previous authors without checking original sources." But Jennewein had checked the sources. And on the McCormick story, he states: "We buy no stock in the Calamity Jane–Wild Bill corporation." He dismisses the McCormick/Calamity story as a "hoax," but does accept some accounts of Calamity as an angel of mercy. Jennewein's annotated bibliography of about seventy items, stretching to nearly eight pages, and his valuable photos retain their importance after more than half a century.

Still, one wonders about some of Jennewein's emphases and how they shaped subsequent images of Calamity. Because he did not move much beyond South Dakota in his examination of sources, he did not look at the census records in Missouri and Wyoming, and he did not turn up the important *Montana Post* of December 1864, revealing that the Canary family was living near the boomtown of Virginia City. Nor did he know about Calamity's marriage to William Steers in 1888 and his probable fathering of Calamity's daughter, Jessie, in 1887. He missed, too, Calamity's role with the Hardwick and Kohl and Middleton touring groups and, strangely, overemphasized her dress in buckskins and spoke not at all about her being attired more often in dresses. Yet it was not these oversights but the breadth of Jennewein's coverage in his extended article that caught the attention of evaluative readers of Calamity's story. Repeatedly, they urged other historians and biographers to pay close attention to the information Jennewein had uncovered and used.

Roberta Beed Sollid, in many ways, traveled up several of Jennewein's paths, enlarging and paving them over with new research and incisive conclusions. Sollid hardly seemed a candidate for an author of a new biography of Calamity Jane. A midwesterner who gained a bachelor's degree in psychology from Stanford University and who had served in the navy in World War II, Sollid moved with her family to Montana. Smitten by a growing interest in regional history, she enrolled in a master's program at the University of Montana, Missoula, under the tutelage of historian Paul C. Phillips. After being told that Calamity Jane was an actual personage who lived some of her life in Montana (Sollid's mother had laughingly called her "Calamity Jane" when she became too rambunctious as a girl), Sollid decided to do her master's thesis on Calamity. At first she feared there was insufficient material for anything but an essay. She then made a decision that would lift her book well beyond anything else written about Calamity. In the summer of 1949, Sollid decided she would travel to all the sites where more information might be available on Calamity. Via Greyhound buses, she visited places where Calamity had lived in Montana, South Dakota, and Wyoming, and even on to Colorado, Minnesota, and Chicago. (Of note, she did not get to Missouri to examine the Princeton or Mercer County

Roberta Beed Sollid, *Calamity Jane: A Study in Historical Criticism*, 1958.

Sollid's valuable book was the first well-researched, analytical study of Calamity Jane. It remains a useful volume in this new version (1995) with an added introduction by James D. McLaird and an afterword by Richard W. Etulain. Courtesy Montana Historical Society Press.

records.) At these sites, she thoroughly examined newspaper clippings files, local histories, and regional memoirs. She also interviewed more than a dozen elderly informants in the late 1940s who had known Calamity personally.

In writing about Calamity, Sollid was no romantic sycophant. In fact, she may even have disliked the woman. In the first paragraph of her valuable book, Sollid made bluntly clear her anti-romantic intentions. "No career is so elusive to the historian as that of a loose woman," Sollid began. "Calamity Jane was that sort of woman. . . . Like most prostitutes and drunkards she left little behind in the way of tangible evidence which could be used by historians to reconstruct the story of her checkered career."

Sollid did remarkably well, however, in uncovering such information. She devoted sections of her probing study to Calamity's birth, appearance, nickname, husbands, and to her nursing, bullwhacking, performing, jailings, gun handling, and death. It was not a biography that Sollid aimed for but a critical study of the stories told about Calamity and the validity of those narratives. It was not so much a thesis-driven book as one debunking, clearing away misconceptions, lies, and folklore. Sollid would clear up the mistakes; others, building on her clarifications, would have to tell a more full-bodied story of this exotic character.

Sollid achieved much of what she essayed. Basing her account primarily on many newspaper clippings, she was able to pinpoint Calamity's whereabouts more fully than any previous writer. Her careful examination of other sources allowed Sollid to provide the fullest information to date on Calamity's "husbands," particularly William Steers, Clinton Burke, and Robert Dorsett. She also critically examined Calamity's suspect autobiography and pointedly noted where that account was far from the truth. Nor did Sollid encourage readers to pay much attention to Jean Hickok McCormick's materials since "her stories are so out of line with other known facts that they can be dismissed."

But Sollid was not able to deliver a completely dependable study. She badly bungled Calamity's birth and first years by depending too much on Paine's mistaken information and dismissing some correct facts that Aikman turned up in Princeton. Sollid overlooked the Missouri (1860) and Wyoming (1869) census reports, failed to turn up the Calamity-Steers marriage certificate, and skipped over information dealing with Calamity's performances for Hardwick, Kohl and Middleton, and Pan-American venues.

These were minor lacunae compared to the achievements. As well-known western historian Robert Riegel pointed out in his review of Sollid's book, romanticists could be unhappy with Sollid because she not only torpedoed numerous misleading tales, she provided a valuable analytical discussion of a notable Wild West character seldom subjected to such exacting scrutiny. Those who "desire to know the truth about Calamity Jane," Riegel added, would find her book "fascinating." Although Sollid obviously had not set out to pummel previous writers as irresponsible sensationalists, her matter-of-fact treatment of Calamity provided a painstakingly researched story that had eluded earlier writers.

In the decades from 1930 to 1960, novelists exhibited more reluctance than historians, biographers, and moviemakers in focusing on Calamity in their productions. Before 1960, in fact, only two full-length novels (leaving aside the much briefer dime novels) on Calamity had appeared: Mrs. William Loring Spencer's *Calamity Jane: A Story of the Black Hills* (1887) and Ethel Hueston's *Calamity Jane of Deadwood Gulch* (1937). This dearth of novels about Calamity is all the more revealing because American literature was awash in popular fiction about the Old West in these years.

The reasons for the paucity of memorable fiction about Calamity Jane are clear. By the mid-twentieth century, popular stories about the West had solidified—if not calcified—into a recognizable formula. In their hundreds of Westerns, the name given the genre by 1930, such writers as Owen Wister, Zane Grey, Ernest Haycox, and Luke Short had blended the formulaic ingredients: a heroic protagonist; his love interest, the romantic heroine; his competitor, the villainous opponent; and a demanding, almost preternatural, environment. No man deserved heroic status and the hand of the virtuous heroine if he did not dispatch villains and win a taxing contest with a rugged setting.

Calamity Jane, at least what was known historically about her, remained outside the parameters of this popular formula. She could not serve as the deserving mate of the leading man. As an alcoholic and possible prostitute, she fit none of the niches expected of an attractive, feminine woman. On occasion, Ernest Haycox and Luke Short included flirtatious and frisky females in their Westerns, but not those who took up residence in saloons or houses of joy. Any writer who wished to place Calamity at the center of a western novel had to tell a different kind of story and to find a nontraditional place for her in that variant story.

Ethel Hueston attempted to do just that in her historical novel published in 1937. By the late 1930s, Hueston was a veteran writer, the author of dozens of historical, domestic, and religious novels. Her historical fiction, such as *Star of the West: The Romance of the Lewis and Clark Expedition* (1935) and several other novels, smoothly blended historical figures with created characters. That was her approach in *Calamity Jane of Deadwood Gulch*. Hueston drew on published historical sources dealing with Calamity's life, repeating dozens of stories biographers had used. Her novel also featured historic photographs of Calamity, the Black Hills area, and stagecoaches and other well-known scenes, all providing an aura of history.

Hueston's Calamity embodies several of the widespread popular images of her that had emerged by the 1930s. She is a profane, drunken, amoral woman who is also caring and often tenderhearted. Calamity hates Indians ("savages"), dancehall entertainers ("damn chippies"), and moralists (preachers and schoolteachers). Yet she also tends to the smallpox-afflicted, penniless, and lonesome prospectors. Hueston's treatments of Calamity are realistic and, for the most part, persuasive.

Some of Hueston's most appealing verbal touches vividly describe Calamity. A talented wordsmith, the author speaks of Calamity as all accelerator, no brakes. Another woman observes, "If she's on the warpath, Crazy Horse is a Christian dude alongside Calamity Jane." Calamity's actions were often feverish but usually short-lived. The author says of her: "Jane in love was virtually—though not quite virtuously—a monogamist. She loved with passionate singleness of purpose, if not for eternity, at least for a time." Calamity deeply admired Wild Bill, maybe loved him, but moved on after his shocking murder. Calamity's actions often displayed her "untrammeled indecency." She was also a busybody, who "loved news like a magpie." Loving boomtowns and overnight new settlements, Jane always relished a new run; "a stampede was Jane's idea of a paradise on earth."

On the other hand, Hueston's Calamity wanted to help. "If there was anything in the world that gave Jane more genuine, savage joy than a rough and tumble melee at a congenial bar, it was running a pest house." She often and movingly spoke her feelings about aiding the needy. She declares on one occasion, "There ain't nothin' above love. . . . Nothin'." A woman friend, in summing up Calamity's character, may be speaking for the author: "She was always—pretty bad. . . . Always pretty bad—and usually pretty good along with it."

Regrettably, when adopting writerly techniques so popular among historical novelists, Hueston often goes awry. To fulfill the romantic requirements of her novel and to provide alternative viewpoints, Hueston creates several imagined characters. The imaginary heroine is Phoebe Ann Norcutt, a puritanical princess of New England. Daughter

259

of a missionary to Indians, Phoebe sees life through biblical and moralistic images distinctly out of place in the worlds Calamity Jane inhabits. Hueston's forced friendship between Phoebe Ann and Calamity and Phoebe's romance with Len Wade seem improbable, if not entirely impossible. Phoebe's innocence, unyielding religiosity, and her pro-Indian sympathies are huge barriers to a warm sisterhood with a devil-may-care, rough, and Indian-hating Calamity. Similarly, Phoebe's outspoken predisposition and intransigence seem too strong to attract a realistic, tough-minded man like Wade into a romance. Even more unbelievable, the author is guilty of the worst kind of authorial manipulation when she has Wade, among all the thousands of men on the wide plains, become the killer of Phil Red Hawk, Phoebe's lifetime Indian protector.

The obvious strengths and concomitant large limitations of Hueston's novel illustrate the difficulties of writing popular fiction about Calamity Jane. Even though the descriptions of Calamity's character here ring true, as a rough, unfeminine woman she cannot serve as the heroine of a romance story. When Hueston attempts to graft a love story onto a realistic portrait of Calamity, the effort fails badly. What Hueston aimed for and fell short of remained an elusive goal for novelists. Moviemakers, however, sidestepped the problem by creating improbable but heartwarming Calamity–Wild Bill romances.

Filmmakers in the years between 1930 and 1960 discovered that a cinematic Calamity attracted large audiences, particularly if they could romantically link her with Wild Bill Hickok, Sam Bass, or another Wild West hero. Not all of the Calamity films rigidly followed this trend, however.

Of the nearly ten Calamity Jane films made in these decades, two deserve brief mention, two others extensive comment. Jane Russell played Calamity in *The Paleface* (1948). Remembered for her erotic and much-commented-on role in the Howard Hughes–directed *The Outlaw* (1943), Russell took a much different role in *The Paleface*. Playing opposite Bob Hope (Peter "Painless" Potter) in a western comedy, Russell's Calamity gets lost in the hokey plot focused on Hope. The cowardly, humorous, and appealing Hope/Potter steals the scenes from Russell. Part of his appeal comes through in his song "Buttons and Bows," which won an Academy Award for best song. The vivaciousness and sexuality of Russell in *The Outlaw* disappears, for the most part, in *The Paleface*.

Another attractive woman, Yvonne De Carlo, playing Calamity in *Calamity Jane and Sam Bass* (1949), is pushed to the cinematic sidelines by a horse. Known for her glamor and velvety appearance, De Carlo had to play a supporting role to her four-footed competitors. Once the Denton Mare gallops on scene in preparation for a huge horse race—and other later races—De Carlo's Calamity Jane is relegated to backstage, suggesting, one film critic noted, that a man's best friend must be a horse, not a shapely, attractive woman. The holdups, shootouts, and horses, while including De Carlo/Calamity, do not allow much space to develop her character. She remains rather flat, without much attraction or spice.

But two other films, one released in the 1930s and the other in the 1950s, probably did most to shape the dominant romantic image of Calamity from 1930 to 1960. Both movies proved how popular were the stories that romantically linked Calamity and Wild Bill.

The dramatic, sensationalist fingerprints of director Cecil B. DeMille indelibly mark the shape and content of his panoramic *The Plainsman* (1936). Already a veteran moviemaker and later known for his biblical epics and societal spectacles, DeMille also directed Westerns, including *The Squaw Man* (1914, 1918) and *Union Pacific* (1939). DeMille loved circuslike, wide-angle moving pictures. *The Plainsman* depicts the history of the American West as extravaganza. The film opens with President Abraham Lincoln's command that the frontier must be cleared of obstacles, mainly Native Americans, to northern men and their families who needed land at the end of the Civil War. The movie parades Calamity Jane, Wild Bill Hickok, General George Custer, and Buffalo Bill Cody as western giants smoothing the way for incoming settlers.

The DeMille papers on file at the Brigham Young University Library disclose much about the director's preparation for and intentions in *The Plainsman*. A researcher for the director gathered abundant information on Hickok and Cody, but little on Calamity, even though DeMille had selected her to be the female lead. When a rumor leaked out that the film might include a Wild Bill–Calamity romance, fans of Wild Bill and members of the Hickok family sent off fiery letters to the director denouncing the romance story as embodying a falsehood—and, even worse, a slanderous lie. Harold L. Hickok, Wild Bill's nephew, threatened DeMille, telling the director he would pursue him in court if he linked Wild Bill and Calamity in his forthcoming film. "I will not have the name of so brave and great a man coupled with that of a degraded old —— that my uncle never knew and I have proven that fact." William S. Hart had "damaged [Wild Bill's character] and you are preparing to do so once more" by tying "his name with the worst woman in his generation." Similar letters came from the granddaughter of Agnes Lake Thatcher Hickok, informing DeMille that any movie plot that associated Wild Bill with "that notorious woman, Calamity Jane" was "not right." "Wild Bill was not that character of a man, he was not interested in women." DeMille wrote to critics—and to several others—trying to defend his approach to Wild Bill and Calamity. "The story of the picture," he told them, "does not depict any relationship between Calamity Jane and Wild Bill Hickok other than a romantic acquaintance. There is no suggestion of any culmination of this affection, and I am certain that she will in no way minimize the greatness of Hickok's character."

The DeMille papers exhibited more uncertainty about how to depict Calamity than Wild Bill. Would her sexual experiences be made explicit? Was she a whore? Several manuscript notes indicate that DeMille and his cinematic lieutenants wrestled with what other words besides "whore" could be used, and what legal difficulties they might encounter by being so explicit. Unused versions of the script reveal that, early on, the director planned to be unambiguous about Calamity as a sexual being. In these scrapped notes, Hickok is portrayed as jealous of Calamity, angry about her being with other men. Wild Bill says of Calamity "I lost interest in her—she's not good. I loved her but she's a whore." Then a list of possible, less censorable synonyms for "whore" follows.

Part of the uncertainly about Calamity's role in the film led to several discussions about who would play her. Early on, sexpot Mae West and famed fan dancer Sally Rand were suggested as possibilities. Clearly, DeMille planned a film about what he considered the great men of the Old West— Hickok, Custer, and Buffalo Bill. But, wanting a romantic plot at the center of the movie, he thought Calamity would fit that role since she was the best-known woman of the Old West. What kind of Calamity Jane he could depict was less certain—until he selected Jean Arthur to play Calamity.

Jean Arthur was not yet well known by the mid-1930s. Most of her roles in the silents of the 1920s were not particularly memorable. Given DeMille's heroic and romantic predilections, his Calamity (Arthur) must serve as the love interest of Gary Cooper's Wild Bill. She must also act out the feminine/masculine ambiguity that audiences were coming to expect of her character. If Buffalo Bill and his new wife, Louisa, symbolized a coming civilized West—marriage, pregnancy, acquisition of property, and settling down—Wild Bill and Calamity represented a frontier inimical to civilizing.

The Plainsman, 1936.

Cecil B. DeMille's blockbuster film, starring Gary Cooper as
Wild Bill Hickok and Jean Arthur as Calamity Jane, gained
wide attention and strong reviews. DeMille's Calamity is a rambunctious frontier woman who wants to marry. Courtesy Paul
Andrew Hutton.

Frequently, Louisa Cody and Calamity are contrasted as a western lady against a frontier woman not yet a lady. Throughout the film, Calamity/Arthur plays a hybrid character. Early on, she uses impolite words and descriptions—swearing without swearing. She also drives a stagecoach in a wild, masculine manner and swings a long bullwhip like no other pioneer woman. And she is too forward with Bill, pushing at him, touching and kissing him. Yet her form-fitting buckskins are clean and not unattractive, her hair nicely arranged and never much out of place despite the nonstop action. Perhaps she acts like a man in her bull-whacking and whipping, but she also wants to be a woman, wife, and mother.

One memorable scene in *The Plainsman* reverberates with symbolic meaning and encapsulates DeMille's interpretation of Calamity. Preparing to secure help for soldiers pinned down by Indians, Calamity steps out of her nearly ruined stylish skirt, donned earlier in hopes of proving her femininity, and rides for reinforcements in her buckskin undergarment. Moving back and forth from dress to leather pants, Jean Arthur's Calamity personifies the oxymoronic legend of Calamity that had come on scene by the 1930s. Spunky, perky, and pretty but also assertive and courageous (but not boozy or loose), Calamity plays a romantic, vernacular woman of the frontier who wishes to marry.

It was the second film, the musical *Calamity Jane* (1953) starring Doris Day, that featured a romantic Calamity in full flower. Hoping to capitalize on Metro Goldwyn Mayer's very successful musical *Annie Get Your Gun* (1950) with Betty Hutton, Warner Brothers decided to produce one starring their own prize property Doris Day. Western hills— as well as the plains and mountains—were to be alive with music. Most musicals were glitz, uplift, and nonstop action. History fell by the wayside in the dash to entertainment; the past was distorted, denatured, or left blank. The content of *Calamity Jane* embodied these popular aims, deemphasizing a factual Calamity Jane. The movie also proved to be by far the most popular treatment of Calamity before 1960.

Although some critics thought Jean Arthur (remembered primarily for her role as the wife and mother in the block-buster Western *Shane*) was miscast as the heroine in *The Plainsman*, most thought Doris Day ideally suited for the lead in *Calamity Jane*. Already a popular ballad singer with a national reputation, Day was also well on her way to what proved to be a very successful career as a Hollywood actress. *Calamity Jane*, a delightful if innocent musical, showcases Day's singing talents—and her physical attractiveness. Agile and overflowing with vivaciousness, Day represents the romantic, less gritty Wild West Calamity. There will be no alcohol for her, only "sasparillah"; and her swearing is limited to no worse than her denunciation of recalcitrant miners as a "mangy pack of dirt-scratching beetles" or "slab-sided coyotes." Most of all, the movie appealingly blends romance, adventure, frenetic action, and folksy music.

The plotline of *Calamity Jane* follows the heroine's transition from a careless and seemingly carefree tomboy to a woman aching for a man's love and marriage. When Katie, a maid masquerading as headlined singer, comes from Chicago to Deadwood and attracts the attentions of a military man, Calamity's hackles of jealousy are aroused, and she begins to compete with Katie for the soldier's attentions. Calamity rediscovers her femininity, but is disappointed when Katie wins the competition. Only then does Calamity pay more attention to another man, Wild Bill. Gradually, she becomes more womanly, donning dresses and advancing her attractions. The transformation works, and after a marriage ceremony, Calamity and Wild Bill ride out of the Hills atop a stagecoach headed for their honeymoon.

Revealingly, the film invokes familiar themes about Calamity even as it avoids others and dodges history. In the opening scenes, Doris Day's Calamity exhibits masculine dress, speech, and actions, but it is a feminine role that she

Calamity Jane, 1953.

This romantic musical starring Doris Day as Calamity probably remains the most widely known movie about her. Romance, humor, and music push aside historical accuracy. Courtesy Paul Andrew Hutton.

really wants—and obtains—before the movie ends. (In this regard, the plot of *Calamity Jane* follows the story line of *The Plainsman*, released seventeen years earlier.) The transition to love and possible marriage comes front and center in Sammy Fain's Oscar-winning "Secret Love," whose lyrics reveal that Calamity's "heart is now an open door" and "her love is secret no more"; in those lines, Day declares her love for Wild Bill. The musical omits, however, Calamity's alcoholism and sexual explicitness and makes little use of historical facts, including that Wild Bill died in Deadwood a bit less than a month after he arrived in midsummer 1876.

Overall, Doris Day plays a Calamity with a warm "female" heart, bursting with sentiment, love, and, if necessary, jealousy. Day's Calamity is a lively frontier woman who fits smoothly into the then-familiar musical tradition established in the very appealing role of Annie Oakley in *Annie Get Your Gun*. In its excessively romantic depiction of Calamity, however, her role sacrificed nearly all historical veracity on the altar of cinematic popularity.

Biographers, a novelist, and filmmakers added the most commented-on portraits of Calamity in the 1930 to 1960 period, but other pamphlets and parts of books, as well as still other briefer essays, added small segments to the composite Calamity. A handful or more of these briefer sources merits comment.

One of the most intriguing was the pamphlet *Low Down on Calamity Jane* (1932). Said to be written by D. Dee, the pseudonym of brothel madam Dora Du Fran, this abbreviated account included firsthand tidbits from a woman who first met Calamity in 1886 and knew her through early 1903. Whether Calamity "probably . . . worked on occasion as a prostitute for Madam Du Fran in Deadwood in 1886 . . . [and] also in subsequent years," as editor Helen Rezatto asserts in her introduction to a reprint of the booklet in 1981, cannot be proven. But Du Fran knew Calamity personally, and Calamity clearly served as a cook in one of Dora's brothels in Belle Fourche in early 1903. The author speaks of Calamity's excessive drinking and her howling but also her willingness to give her last coin to someone hungry or sick. Du Fran's brief piece is one of the few accounts by a woman well acquainted with Calamity. Du Fran emphasized the positive more than the negative Calamity, but other writers were more inclined to debunk stories about Calamity's helpful activities. Among the debunkers was historian Harold E. Briggs, whose book *Frontiers of the Northwest* (1940) includes a chapter section entitled "The Calamity Jane Myth." Briggs knows his Calamity sources, pinpoints the stretchers in Calamity's autobiography and other smiling writers, and comes to a concise conclusion. Her personal account was "thoroughly imbued with the frontier characteristic of exaggeration," Briggs writes, and "many of the stories [written about Calamity] are pure fabrications and have little or no historical basis." He discounts Calamity as an angel of mercy. He also argues that Calamity greatly enlarged the significance of her youthful misadventures, when, Briggs claims, "her only claim to fame was her absolute lack of respectability."

As substantiation for his ridicule of Calamity, Briggs cites the work of Doane Robinson, longtime administrator at the South Dakota Historical Society. Robinson and his son, Will G. Robinson, also on the staff of the historical society, pummeled Calamity in their writings throughout the first half of the twentieth century. Doane Robinson encapsulated his negative opinions in two especially harsh sentences: "She was a woman low down even in her own class. . . . She was a prostitute of the commonest variety, so vulgar and coarse that she was rarely welcome even in the dives around Deadwood." Will G. followed his father's acerbic condemnations of Calamity. "She was a notorious liar as are all prostitutes and told at least a dozen different stories of her origins." He also touted the Wyoming/Jane Dalton beginnings of

Calamity, asserting repeatedly that if Dr. Valentine McGilly-cuddy backed the Dalton story, it was gospel. Not until Will G.'s letters to the Department of Army record holdings in Washington proved the inaccuracy of the Jane Dalton report did he in the least back away from his harsh asser-tions about Calamity.

John (Jack) Hunton was of the same negative opinion. Hunton, who operated a road ranch on the stagecoach route from Cheyenne to Deadwood and frequently saw Calamity on that route or nearby, decried romantic or admi-rable images of her. She was a prostitute and "among the commonest of her class," Hunton told a journalist many years later. "Her achievements have been greatly magnified by every writer I have read," Hunton continued. He dis-counted all stories of her having served as a scout as bosh, and he also thought, wrongly, that Wild Bill did not know Calamity, had never seen her.

Others moved beyond the debunkers to uncover new information about Calamity. Surprisingly, one of these was a journalist in Calamity's hometown of Princeton, Missouri. During the half century following Calamity's death, resi-dents of Mercer County seemed uninterested in Calamity, perhaps embarrassed by the notorious reputation of Prince-ton's best-known former resident. But in the mid-1950s, journalist Doris Thompson, in an attempt to gather histori-cal and biographical background for dedicating a Calam-ity Jane roadside park, began to dig into town and county records and to interview longtime residents about Martha Canary and her family in the Princeton area. Thompson's research and interviews turned up the most thorough infor-mation then known about Calamity's origins in north-central Missouri. This spadework corrected misinformation appearing in Aikman's book of the 1920s and the Paine essays of the 1940s and 1950s. As Thompson put it, in the dedication of the Calamity Jane Park, "Princeton at least is joining Deadwood and other towns in the West with markers commemorating the once famous character of the West, Calamity Jane."

By 1960, Calamity's ostensible connections with Wild Bill Hickok had solidified, particularly in Jean Hickok McCormick's widely circulated stories and manuscripts and in films such as *The Plainsman* and *Calamity Jane*. That reputed linkage, not supported by any strong factual information, continued into the following decades. William Elsey Connelley, author of the biography *Wild Bill and His Era* (1933), tried to quash rumors of a Wild Bill and Calamity romance, but otherwise his treatment of Calamity ran to the romantic and included contrived conversations said to be hers but without historical basis. Not until the sound, diligent work of Englishman Joseph Rosa in the 1960s and thereafter did Wild Bill receive the through biography he deserved—and readers got much more dependable information on the Wild Bill–Calamity story.

At the end of the 1950s no coherent, ongoing single image of Calamity Jane had come into focus. Rather, divergent and changing images dominated the scene. Historians and biographers wrestled with the chaotic, differing stories about Calamity's life. Fictionists and moviemakers, though accepting some of Calamity's rough, uncouth side, were more interested in peddling romantic stories about her. And for nearly twenty years the variant story of Jean Hickok McCormick as the daughter of Calamity and Wild Bill had troubled and diverted many Calamity tellers. If these diverse, often shifting images dominated the period from 1930 to 1960, an even sharper shift transformed Calamity images after 1960. A New Grey Calamity bounded on the scene, influencing—indeed transforming—much of what was written and filmed about her up to about 1990.

9

A New Gray Calamity, 1960 to 1990

When Pete Dexter's gritty novel *Deadwood* appeared in 1986, it raised a storm of comment. Had the author decided to trot out all of Calamity Jane's shortcomings and none of her positive actions? Had Dexter decided to reshape Calamity into a new gray heroine whose attitudes and actions condemned her? Four years later famed western novelist Larry McMurtry's *Buffalo Girls* (1990) also depicted Calamity in decidedly antiheroic terms, as a drunken and possibly hermaphroditic woman. What was happening to Calamity Jane? Had she fallen into the clutches of a new group of cultural crucifiers bent on creating new negative legends about her?

Three decades or so later, these questions remain valid. But they must be addressed in context. In the 1960s the United States experienced what journalist Malcolm Gladwell calls a "tipping point." From early in the decade until well into the 1970s and beyond, the United States was roiling in controversies, challenges, and changes. The assassinations of President John F. Kennedy in 1963 and of his brother Robert in 1968 and civil rights leader Martin Luther King, Jr., in the same year shocked the nation. So did the Vietnam War and the antiwar dissent that boiled up vis-à-vis the war. The riots that broke out in Chicago during the Democratic nominating convention in 1968 and President Richard Nixon's resignation in 1974 as a result of the Watergate imbroglio added to the public discontent. Student and feminist activists, the hippy movement, and newly spawned ethnic/racial organizations stirred new yeasty elements into the mix.

These traumatic shifts transformed many Americans' attitudes about the present—and the past. Patriotism and positive reactions to the country's social and cultural institutions drooped, and in some cases these shifts gave rise to dark reinterpretations of the present and the past.

The sociocultural changes beginning in the 1960s, not surprisingly, reshaped interpretations of the American West. One historian speaks of these shifting interpretations as illustrations of a "postregional" West, in which increasingly gray stories of ethnic and racial prejudice, mistreatment of women, and environmental degradation pushed aside previous regional emphases on place and its shaping power on people and identity. Western novels such as Thomas Berger's *Little Big Man* (1964), Robert Flynn's *North to Yesterday* (1967), and John Seelye's *The Kid* (1972) illustrated the exploding postregional stresses on violence, on ethnic and racial topics, and on new roles for women. Some of the same topics received major attention in Western films such as *A Fist Full of Dollars* (1964), *The Wild Bunch* (1969), and *Little Big Man* (1970). Western historians likewise participated in the transformation, gradually transitioning away from earlier narrative and romantic storytelling to more analytical/evaluative studies of Native Americans, Chicanos, women and family, and environmental history. By the end of the 1980s, these new historical trends had coalesced into what became known as the New Western history, with Patricia Nelson Limerick's *Legacy of Conquest: The Unbroken Past of the American West* (1987) as an early, pivotal example.

These sociocultural transformations clearly molded the images of Calamity Jane between 1960 and 1990. English author J. T. Edson whipped out nearly twenty novels from the 1960s to the 1980s featuring a non- if not an anti-romantic Calamity as a central or supporting character. Pete

Dexter's novel *Deadwood* and McMurtry's *Buffalo Girls*, much more sophisticated literary works than Edson's popular novels, also painted Calamity as a new gray figure. So did the TV movie *Calamity Jane* (1984). Biographers and historians were more hesitant, however, to move in these new directions. In fact, no book-length biography of Calamity appeared in these decades, even though several had been published in the previous generation.

The New Gray Calamity did not dominate the entire scene. In fact, Jean Hickok McCormick's false story as Calamity's daughter still fascinated and enticed many followers, as aptly revealed by the role of Jane Alexander in *Calamity Jane* (1984); the later biography by Stella Foote, *A History of Calamity Jane* (1995); and Libby Larson's musical cycle *Songs from Letters* (1989).

But of all the trends emerging in the three decades from 1960 to 1990, the rise of a Gray Calamity was the newest and most significant.

J. [John] T. [Thomas] Edson was an unusual candidate for becoming the most prolific writer about Calamity Jane since Edward L. Wheeler, the one-man dime novel factory of the late nineteenth century. A British postman, Edson began scribbling in his spare time, found success, and turned to full-time writing in the early 1960s. From the 1960s into the 1990s, he turned out more than 130—perhaps as many as 150—novels. He seemed proud that on one occasion he completed a full-length novel in eleven days and rarely took more than six weeks to complete one.

A self-assured author, Edson told one source that he did not much care about the historical accuracy or literary value—or lack thereof—of his novels. He was writing entertainment for steak and potato readers, not for scholars, especially not for picky literary critics. He defended his more than one hundred Westerns as "action-escapism-adventure fiction." He wrote this kind of novel "for a living," making sure it appeared first in "paperback publication—where the money is." He added, "I do not consider writing westerns in any way beneath my dignity, [so] I insisted upon using my own name and not a pseudonym."

Edson revealed that he knew little about Calamity Jane and that he was willing to create an imagined life to use in his fiction. Yet he acted as if he were writing historical fiction by including several footnotes in many of his novels that sometimes were historical, sometimes sheer fantasy. He had available to him the recent works by Jennewein (1953) and Sollid (1958), but he seems not to have used those sources.

Edson's treatment of Calamity resembled his approach to other recognized historical characters such as Wild Bill Hickok, Belle Starr, and Ella "Cattle Kate" Watson. He uses a historical fact or two, but nearly all his descriptions of people and events come from his own imagination rather than from verifiable documents. For example, in a two-to-three page appendix he included in several novels, Edson speaks of Charlotte Canary as the mother of "Mary Jane Canary" and, after being widowed, sending her children to a convent in St. Louis to be raised. At sixteen Martha escapes, hides away in a caravan headed west, and begins a new life in Texas. After serving as a cook for a short time, Edson's Calamity learns to ride challenging mounts, manipulate a long whip, and handle handguns. Most of the places where Calamity lives in Edson's novels—namely ranches and small towns in Texas and the Southwest—are places where Calamity never visited.

Edson wrote nearly a dozen novels in his Calamity Jane series, and he also included her in several other novels outside the series and in anthologies of short fiction as a major or supporting figure. The series novels first appeared in the mid-1960s and stretched on into the 1980s. The heroine of the these novels is an attractive (but not beautiful) woman, sexually voracious, a moderate drinker and smoker, a stout but well-built woman, and romantically intertwined with more than two or three handsome and virile heroes. In molding this ostensibly factual character, Edson excised, for the most part, Calamity's drunkenness, possible prostitution, general waywardness, and aging. Rather, his Calamity is young, robust, competitive, and rarely defeated in any area.

Trouble Trail (1965), the first installment of the Calamity Jane series, illustrates well the Calamity Jane figures in Edson's numerous novels about her. Calamity drives a wagon with an overland trail group, now on the Great Plains but bound for the Far West. Within hours, she proves her superb skills with a whip, her bravado as a girl/woman/manlike driver, and her joyous "couplings" (off-scene, of course) with the rough but heroic scout Beau Resin. Calamity is both feminine and manly. She's sexy and alluring: "the round full swell of her breasts straining against its material [her blouse], the shirt's upper three buttons lay open and revealed there was little other than girl under the cloth." The same comely young woman holds her own with the men, using her rapier-like whip to drive off a rapist, injure an attacking Indian, and head off other foes. Her reputation has already preceded her: the name Calamity Jane turns heads and catches the breath.

In this opening installment of the Calamity Jane series, Edson makes clear what he will emphasize in a dozen or more volumes. Most of the competitions will be among women—sharp-tongued vixens, yes; but also brutal fist-fights in which four women, including Calamity, smash one another, while nearly ripping off one another's clothes. Was he titillating his male readers with his graphic descriptions of exposed women's figures after such brutal fights? Perhaps. For certain, his plots in the Calamity Jane series moved in directions vastly different from those in the Westerns of Luke Short and Louis L'Amour, the two leading American writers of Westerns at the time. No depictions of Calamity as a saloon brawler had appeared previously, except in the rumored wrestling match with Madame Bull Dog in Livingston where that stout lady threw Calamity out of a saloon. Edson's inordinate interest in class divisions among men and among women in this novel also sets the work aside from most American traditions in the Western.

Another novel in the series, *The Cow Thieves* (1965), shifts scene to a Texas county beset with a remuda of vicious cattle rustlers. Calamity plays a sidekick role to a young, stud-like Texas Ranger, Danny Fog, who sets out to crack the rustling ring. Calamity rides nonstop throughout the novel. Threatened with rape and murder in the opening scene, she survives and gallops through a series of escapades, escaping violence from male and female opponents and bedding down two or three times with Fog. Portrayed again as a young, vivacious woman with a foul mouth, handy with reins, Calamity also wields a colt and hidden belly gun with amazingly adept skill.

Edson invokes history glancingly. He repeats his imagined story of Calamity's background, mentioning her mother Charlotte, the convent in St. Louis where the children were sent, and the escape west of the sixteen-year-old—all before the story gets underway. A similar use of fabricated history occurs when Edson introduces Wyoming rancher Ella Watson as a saloon owner and rustler and at the end of the novel mentions her involvements in rustling and her violent demise in frontier Wyoming. Obviously, Edson is more interested in guns—all makes and models—saddles, a multitude of brands, and whips than he is in the specifics of history, including Calamity's life.

In a later novel in the series, *Cold Deck, Hot Lead* (1969), Calamity has grown. She is taller and stouter—and even bustier. Red-headed with a well-turned figure dressed in buckskins, she is attractive and freckled, but not beautiful. She hangs out with the boys, and is already a living legend in a Kansas cowtown, especially in its saloons and dives. Edson says of his heroine, "Happy-go-lucky, living each day to the full, Calamity Jane had won the admiration and friendship of many people." Or later, "Calamity Jane might be a touch hot-headed, a mite tactless and somewhat reckless at times, but she could be relied upon to keep her eyes open and take notice of anything interesting she saw." Still later, in referring to marrying and settling down, Calamity says, "I'd hate like hell for *that* to happen." Edson, of course, was well off base in the latter statement since the real Calamity wanted to marry, did legally marry once, and often spoke of "husbands," who were not officially her spouses.

Surprisingly, considering what happens in other segments of the Calamity Jane series, there are no "couplings" here. But she is involved in perhaps the most vicious barroom brawl of her life—with another woman. For five full pages, Edson recounts the slug-by-slug battle between Calamity and Sal Banyan, ending up with both exhausted, Calamity's breasts bared, and Sal in an insensible heap. Partially recovered, Calamity resumes her role as part owner in a saloon and as an inveterate gambler. "She acted as charming and demure as a schoolmarm being interviewed for a prosperous position," Edson writes, "if one could imagine a schoolmarm standing with a foot on a bar rail, cigar in hand and a glass of whiskey ready for drinking."

One of the last volumes in the Calamity Jane series, *Calamity, Mark and Belle* (1980), revealed much about Edson as a hack writer. It demonstrated how he revised and reprinted earlier writing, which his publishers marketed worldwide, and what changes were made over time in his portraits of Calamity Jane. In 1965 in *Troubled Range*, Edson included a Part I section entitled "The Bounty on Belle Starr's Scalp." Fifteen years later, in revised form, that section appeared in *Calamity, Mark and Belle* (1980). Meanwhile, *Troubled Range* appeared under new imprints in 1979 and 1990. Although Edson's revised some of these pages, adding footnotes in

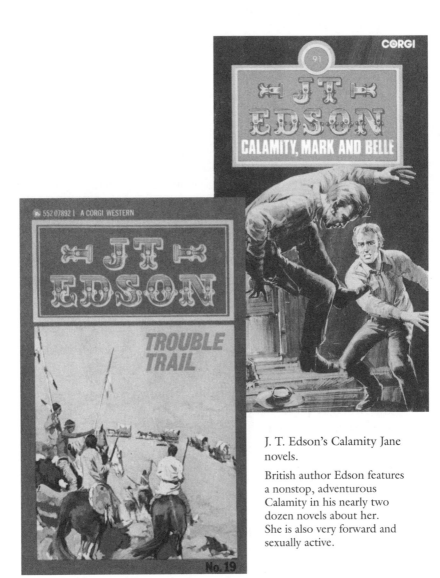

J. T. Edson's Calamity Jane novels.

British author Edson features a nonstop, adventurous Calamity in his nearly two dozen novels about her. She is also very forward and sexually active.

some and omitting them elsewhere, his *Calamity, Mark and Belle* features his trademark emphases.

Calamity comes on scene buttressed by her usual background. Freed from a convent at sixteen where her mother had sent her, she marches west and in two years becomes an accomplished wagon driver, a whip wielder, and renown in much of the Plains West. Edson exhausts his list of adjectives in describing Calamity: she is young, pretty, red-haired, sexy, well-endowed, raunchy, promiscuous, foul-mouthed, adventuresome, courageous, forever-young, and much more. In *Calamity, Mark and Belle*, she is the sidekick of a blond giant from Texas, Mark Counter, handsome and powerful, as are most of Edson's heroes. The plot, moving in other directions in the first half, follows familiar tracks in the second half. Mark and Calamity, trying to carry out an assignment from Mark's ranch boss, soon become "coupling" partners. But a few scenes later, that cad Mark steams up his blankets with Belle Starr.

Again, most of the conflicts occur between women. After catty verbal battles, Calamity and Belle (she's a six-foot blond in this novel) engage in a titanic saloon battle for nearly eight pages, until they lie exhausted in a draw, the combatants left in nothing but their sweaty underwear.

The action takes Mark and Calamity to Elkhorn, Montana, a boomtown where the sheriff already recognizes Calamity as "Wild Bill's girl." Several others in Elkhorn also know about Calamity; she's become a legend throughout much of the interior West in two years or less. The novel ends with two appendixes, one on Calamity and one on Mark Counter. The history narrated illustrates Edson's imagined West and Calamity, rather than the actual region or person.

Not much changed in the dozen or so volumes in J. T. Edson's Calamity Jane series and in the other novels about her outside the series. She never moved past her early twenties, was well known in many subregions of the West, captivating and sexy. Although handy with whip, gun, and, if need be, her fists, Calamity retained her curvaceous figure and attracted men like Mark Counter, Danny and Dusty Fog, and the Ysabel Kid. Nearly all of her violent conflicts are with equally alluring and daring—and physically strong—women. The vast audience of Edson's readers, including those of his two dozen or so novels featuring Calamity Jane, helped his Westerns to sell well around the world in English-speaking countries. Even though Edson's fictions were mostly innocent of factual history, they kept Calamity's name continuously before a huge reading public.

Popular fiction, strikingly similar to Edson's novels, proliferated during the 1960 to 1990 period. Major paperback publishers launched several series described as "Adult Westerns," featuring plots overflowing with violence and explicit sex scenes. For the most part the series volumes, although carrying the same author's name, were produced by a stable of house-hired writers. Not surprisingly, most of the adult series included novels about Calamity, often featuring her in the Deadwood area and partnered with Wild Bill Hickok. These sex-and-violence Westerns added considerably to the New Gray Calamity image emerging in these decades.

The most voluminous of the Adult Western series, supposedly authored by one writer, Jake Logan, was actually the product of many hands. Launched in mid-1970s by Playboy Books and then taken over by Penguin Books, the Jake Logan series numbered more than four hundred volumes by 2010. One critic, also an author of volumes in the series, thought that *Dead Man's Hand* (1979) was one of the best in the entire series. Written by Donald McCaig, the novel features the superhero John Slocum, the central protagonist in the Jake Logan series. He is a magnificent John Wayne type, a man of hyperviolence and sensuous sex appeal. Calamity comes on scene as a sexual toy of the machismo men, eventually simultaneously taking on Slocum as a lover

Adult Westerns.

Several major publishers issued books termed "Adult Westerns," featuring numerous sexually explicit and violent scenes. These Westerns illustrated a New Gray Calamity who emerged from the 1960s onward.

and also Wild Bill Hickok, on the same night, in the same blankets. "Women bore the hell out of me," Calamity says in anger; "never liked 'em," but "the men don't. Not strong men." The Jake Logan series volumes, obviously aimed at salacious male readers, overflow with men fighting other dangerous and violent opponents and women too often little more than servicing the phallic heroes. A twenty-page gunfight near the end of the novel adds to the masculinity of the heroes—John Slocum and Wild Bill Hickok—and the rascality of the villains, even while showing Calamity and other women as little more than sex subjects of their men. Logan/McCaig provides bits of history lite, but truncates and scrambles the chronology of Calamity's life and the events of Deadwood.

Other sex and violence series included Westerns featuring Calamity characters as minor and unimportant as those in some of the Edson and Jake Logan novels. These decidedly masculine works often feature testosterone-fueled protagonists, violent gun and fistfights, and hard riding. Women like Calamity are corseted into sexual beings, satisfied to steam the sheets of their male companions; they do not marry or become mothers. Such Westerns provide only very limited historical settings for Calamity and furnish but two or three facts about her life, some of them wrong.

Among these Westerns are *Longarm in Deadwood* (1982) and Jackson Cain's *Hellbreak Country* (1984). The Longarm volume, said to be authored by Tabor Evans (another house name), features another crusty, fast-gun artist Custis Long, a federal marshal who beds several women. In fact, the opening pages have him scared out of the bed of a wife cuckolding her early-returning husband. The Calamity figure is a drunken nymphomaniac, trying to seduce Longarm and other men who come to her attention. The novel presents a negative and distorted picture of Calamity, as a filthy, ugly, clap-ridden, and hopeless liar.

An equally erotic and distorted historical Calamity appears in *Hellbreak Country*. Calamity and Wild Bill are electrical lovemakers in more than one scene, as is Calamity and the novel's lead character, Torn Slater. The historical characters are equally hyped up with the author creating such ludicrous scenes as the James and Younger brothers chasing Calamity and her sidekicks toward the Custer debacle in Montana. Jackson Cain also places Calamity where she never was: with Custer, in Arizona, and among the Apaches. He likewise has Wild Bill choosing Calamity over Agnes Lake as his lover and brings Belle Starr on scene as another very sexual heroine. Cain seems driven to corral several of the magic Old West figures in one place at one time: Calamity, Hickok, Custer, the James and Younger brothers, and Belle Starr. The historical portraits in the afterword are but another revelation of how little the author knows about western history, including the life and career of Calamity.

A similar sex-driven Calamity appears in Dorothy Dixon's *Yellowstone Jewel* (1983), volume 9 in the Leather and Lace series. Again, Calamity is Wild Bill's woman, and they engage in some magnetic lovemaking. But this novel provides one bit of refreshing change in the author's attempt to deal with Martha as a young girl with her parents, Robert and Charlotte. Near the end of her teen years Martha loses her virginity to Lieutenant Somers and flirts with becoming a prostitute, but it is Hickok who captures her. She meets him in Abilene, where she competes with Agnes Lake for his attention. Later they take up in the northern Rockies where they left off in Kansas. Calamity finds Wild Bill critically wounded and nurses him back to health; they spend the long winter in one another's arms. Then Wild Bill leaves again, only to return to Deadwood, where their lovemaking resumes, even though Hickok is now a married man. Dixon follows the helpful biographical information of such writers as Duncan Aikman and White Eye Anderson and notes Calamity's willingness to help sick miners and families, but then she undermines that historical information through her numerous misstatements and false assertions. Her Calamity is indeed an unromantic, gray figure driven by an excessive, often-expressed lust for Wild Bill.

The most notable Calamity novel within—but still at odds with the Edson–Jake Logan–Longarm tradition—is *Deadwood: Stagecoach Station 11*. Said to be the product of author Hank Mitchum, the novel actually came from the pen of D. B. Newton, a prolific writer of Westerns and author of eight volumes in the Stagecoach series. Newton's novel, well-plotted and based on selective strong sources, presents Calamity as swearing but not excessively profane and reaching out in friendship to another young woman. Calamity, asserts one of Wild Bill's supporters, was "drunk as usual, crying and carrying on about her and Bill—how he'd been her man, and she promised to stay true to him forever." Newton does not overplay the Hickok-Calamity connection, instead depicting Calamity as drawn to Hickok but also looking to and pushing her own myth. The author balances domestic romance with steady, staccato gunplay. More a ballad of blood than a drama of hyped sexuality, Newton's *Deadwood* parts company from many of the Adult Westerns of the time.

Although the Adult Westerns gained a good deal of popularity in the 1960s and 1970s, with some of the series still in existence in 2014, two other novels gained even more attention and remain more influential in the shaping of the legends surrounding Calamity Jane. Pete Dexter's *Deadwood* and Larry McMurtry's *Buffalo Girls* were widely read, gained thousands of readers, and both were eventually made into movies. They were influential in adding to the New Gray Calamity figure emerging after the 1960s.

Dexter's *Deadwood* proved to be an early launching point in his career. Two years after its appearance, he won a National Book Award for his next novel *Paris Trout* (1988).

Perhaps because of an early violent incident that nearly took his life, Dexter seemed attuned to violence, a theme at the center of most of his fiction. He also, early on, turned to parody and satire in his novels.

Parody and satire, more than violence, rule in *Deadwood* and in Dexter's depiction of Calamity. In his novel she smells like the ripe mules and horses she rides. Nor is she much cleaner than the filthy tents and lean-tos where she flops. Calamity is so rancid that a fresh crop of mold grows unnoticed on her neck. No man pays much attention to her, even though fornication and sexual violence are rife in Dexter's Deadwood. Unwashed, unloved, and underappreciated, she seems less a woman than a two-legged screaming eagle bent on shooting off toes, bragging of her "husband" Wild Bill, and outdrinking all others, men and vile drunkards included.

Only when smallpox breaks out does Calamity serve a purpose. God made her, she and the author imply, to minister to the sick. Ironically, she carries the pox germs while aiding others, often helping to heal those inflicted with her germs. In this regard, Dexter portrays Calamity ambivalently, not as a devil of death but as a much-flawed angel of mercy causing the spread as well as the cure of the disease.

Overall, Dexter dishes out too little of a complex Calamity. He serves up small portions of the ambivalent heroine—the man/woman; the on-the-move tramp/resident squatter; the mother/dissolute female. Overall, Dexter's Calamity is a flat, one-sided figure of parody instead of a full-bodied, round character of memorable fiction.

As a result, the Calamity of *Deadwood* is unbelievable— perhaps as much from the limits of parody as from the weaknesses of the novel and its heroine. Dexter's satirized characters are attempts at countering earlier excessively sentimental images. Instead of a wandering picara, Calamity becomes a drunken, filthy, promiscuous antiheroine. She and other figures are ludicrous, hyperbolic caricatures. Wild

Pete Dexter's *Deadwood*, 1986.

Dexter's novel, which attracted widespread attention and
became the source for movies, satirized Calamity Jane as a
foul-smelling, drunken prostitute. Unfortunately Dexter's
overly active penchant for parody undermined the value of
his otherwise well-written novel. Courtesy Paul Andrew
Hutton.

Bill is going blind, unable to urinate, worried, obviously not the heroic figure legendmakers tried to travel. His pard, Charlie Utter, is similarly ineffectual, frozen in his emotions for Bill. Charlie feels little or anything for Mrs. Langrishe, whom he beds once a week in her third-story bedroom. Only with Agnes Lake, Wild Bill's widow, does Charlie fashion a warm connection, and that at a distance—and in his mind.

These excesses in character mockery lead to a simply stated question: once the earlier, too simplistic, and romantic legends about Calamity, Wild Bill, and their supporting cast have been roundly lampooned through satire and parody, what remains in the novel? Not much. The abundant energy, humor, and attractiveness of Dexter's *Deadwood*, once lavishly expended in countering Wild West images, leave too little for memorable characterizations or probing sociocultural comment. This is a problem, generally, in western fiction. Few western novels correcting previous stereotypes retain sufficient literary power to be remembered for their artistic excellence. Perhaps Walter Van Tilburg Clark's *The Ox-Bow Incident* (1940) and H. L. Davis's *Honey in the Horn* (1935) come closest to these dual achievements, but they, too, fall short in comparison with the strongest western fiction of Willa Cather, John Steinbeck, and Wallace Stegner.

Larry McMurtry's *Buffalo Girls* illuminates the author's evolving reactions to a frontier West as well as similarities to Dexter's *Deadwood*. McMurtry's literary career, nearly thirty years in existence in 1990, exhibited clear lines of development, particularly in his attitudes toward an overly mythologized Old West. In novels such as *Horseman, Pass By* (1961, better known in its cinematic version, *Hud*, 1963), *The Last Picture Show* (1966), and *Lonesome Dove* (1986), McMurtry betrayed an ambivalent attitude toward the Old West, embracing realistic, hard-bitten cowboys and cattlemen, small-town roustabouts, and other frontier protagonists, but also undercutting long-held myths about a masculine, demanding Wild West. By the end of the 1980s, he was writing counterclassics like *Anything for Billy* (1988), painting Billy the Kid as a violent but crying and wandering, uncertain boy/man. *Buffalo Girls* followed up this demythologizing trail.

Calamity plays a major role in McMurtry's *Buffalo Girls*. Aging, increasingly out of step with changes in the West, and unable to find new moorings, she symbolizes a closing frontier, a once-heroic past disappearing into nostalgic haze. Throughout, decline, despair, and death exude from the novel.

McMurtry's Calamity comes on stage trying to understand how her West not only has vanished but is now being embalmed in Buffalo Bill's phony Wild West show. Like her old mountain men friends, Jim and Bartle, who search for the last beaver in the West, like the elderly Native American No Ears, and like her best friend Dora Du Fran, madam and frustrated lover, Calamity is forced to exist in a West of memory. We also come to realize that she has imagined a daughter to whom she addresses her tearful laments. To that conjured-up daughter, Calamity writes early on: "I *am* the Wild West, Janey, no show about it, I was one of the people that kept it wild, why should I want to make a spectacle of myself before a bunch of toots and dudes?" But she does, joining Buffalo Bill's Wild West, which she asserted she would never do. Calamity's problems are exacerbated, McMurtry suggests, because she may have suffered from the frustrations of a hermaphroditic condition.

McMurtry depicts Calamity as a failure in nearly all of her endeavors. Unable to adjust to a closed frontier, she boozes and cries her way through much of the novel. She falls off the stagecoach in Cody's Wild West, she cannot use a gun (and thus is unable to compete with Annie Oakley), and fails to *do* anything but live off others, especially Dora. McMurtry also implies how little space or acceptance

Larry McMurtry, *Buffalo Girls*, 1990.

McMurtry also depicts his heroine as a New Gray Calamity, dramatizing her as a tearful, out-of-time western wanderer. The author expertly shows the impact of a closing frontier and the emergence of Buffalo Bill's Wild West arena show on the novel's major characters.

existed in the Old West for a woman like Calamity, without husband, children, or calling. Although this novel, too, suffers from the excessive grayness and ambiguity that undermine Dexter's *Deadwood*, McMurtry raises significant cultural questions about the impact of a closing frontier. As mountaineer Bartle Bone discerningly puts it, "'What Wild West? If Billy Cody can make a poster about it there ain't no Wild West.'" *Buffalo Girls* is also revelatory about the narrow, constricting roles forced on women in an imagined West. McMurtry moves beyond Dexter in not limiting his fiction to satirizing earlier cultural stereotypes.

Calamity Jane (1984), starring Jane Alexander, was the most important film released on the subject after 1960 and before 1990. The movie illustrated not only the staying power of the Jean Hickok McCormick story but also the increasing tendency among Calamitists to create an ambivalent character, rambunctiously masculine and less assertively feminine. The film likewise foreshadowed other later movies such as *Buffalo Girls* (1995) and *Wild Bill* (1995).

Alexander's Calamity, for the most part, lives out the major story elements in the Hickok McCormick diary and letters. The plot deals with the years stretching from Calamity's first meeting with Wild Bill, her mating with him, and their marriage. The birth of daughter Janey follows, the writing of the diary, and the later meetings with Janey—all are based on unsubstantiated, if not entirely false, evidence.

Several scenes in the movie feature actions known to be untrue. The information about Wild Bill's close links to Calamity—all of it is nonhistorical. Nor is the information about a daughter Janey true. Equally mistaken is the assertion that Calamity went to Buffalo in 1901 to meet with Buffalo Bill Cody. And the final scene of Calamity writing while seated in an arena and dreaming of going with Buffalo Bill and his Wild West show lacks confirming evidence.

If the thematic emphasis on Calamity Jane as Hickok's wife and mother of their daughter wants in substantiation, a second emphasis on Calamity as a strong, independent woman is on much stronger ground. In the movie she assertively drives a stagecoach (maybe), dresses in buckskins (sometimes), and put critics and snobbish onlookers in their places (often). Still, behind these scenes we also see how weak Calamity is, how gone to drink. And her desire for independence clashes with her lust for a partner. Hickok is it, when Calamity often dreams of a mate, but he moves on after their tryst, leaving her lonesome and depressed. The film repeatedly depicts Calamity as entirely and continually in love with Wild Bill—from early mating, to hugging him in death, and to telling Buffalo Bill she wants to be buried next to Hickok.

Alexander ambivalently portrays another clash of desire and actuality. Her Calamity is caught between her drive toward self-sufficiency and, simultaneously, her wish to be a traditional pioneer woman. When her dreams of motherhood falter or fall off track, she backslides to excessive drinking, carousing, and sometimes whoring. The central tension between independence/dependence is on target for understanding the historical Calamity, even if the finely wrought pull here is based on faulty and sometimes nonexistent evidence.

Other proof for Alexander's depiction of Calamity is more substantial. Her drunkenness and possible prostitution, for example, are clearly attested. So is her relationship with Clinton Burke and maybe her helping as a ministering angel in the smallpox epidemic in Deadwood. Even though the movie's stress on Calamity's participation in Cody's Wild West show is wrong, the film's mention of Calamity's going east with eastern author Brake is correctly depicted.

Most of the "interior" Calamity in the film comes from her chats with Janey/Jean. In these conversations, Calamity speaks of her mistakes and inadequacies. On one occasion,

Calamity Jane, 1984.

This made-for-TV Western follows the Jean Hickok McCormick storyline. Jane Alexander plays a Calamity of antisocial actions but also one deeply in love with Wild Bill Hickok. Courtesy James D. McLaird.

she tells a startled Janey (who does not know that Calamity is her biological mother), "What I know about wifeing you could stuff in a saddlebag." Or, even more sensationally, she also shares with Janey, "Well, I guess it's the same for us ladies here or there. You either get paid for washing a man's drawers or for pulling them down."

Independent, unpolished, and ultimately tragic, Calamity barely holds on in a life overflowing with frustrations and defeats. Disappointed in love and motherhood, she nonetheless retains her courage and honor in the face of stinging failures. In her unvarnished and gritty actions, Alexander's Calamity, foreshadowing even more realistic images in coming movies, illustrates the large distances between her and Doris Day's Calamity of the 1950s. She clearly represents the new, varied Calamitys increasingly coming on scene after 1960.

During these decades a few local and regional historians, adding local details to Calamity's story, enlarged information on her. The diligent and thorough research of long-time Montana historians shines through in Bill and Doris Whithorn's *Calamity's in Town: The Town Was Livingston* (1974?). The fifty-page pamphlet includes sixteen photographs and forty-one newspaper stories and notices. The photos furnish a wide-ranging portrait of Calamity, showing her in buckskins but also in pioneer women's dress. The same is true of the collected journalistic accounts, depicting her as a wandering drunk but also as a lover of children, a companion of men and families. The Whithorns' own text (pp. 40, 44–45) replicates this balanced approach to Calamity, with comment on her excessive drinking, the suspect claims in her autobiography but also her admiration for little people. Sadly, however, parents—aware of Calamity's downsides—were often reluctant to allow their offspring to be near her.

Irma H. Klock, in a booklet of thirty pages, *Here Comes Calamity Jane* (1979), focuses on Calamity in Deadwood and western South Dakota. A specialist on the Black Hills area, Klock consulted a wide variety of sources and wrote a brief, balanced account of Calamity's career and character. One major difficulty: Klock tried to weave together information from vastly different sources, for instance embracing (without citing) Jean Hickok McCormick's diary and letters and the more veracious research of Jennewein. Unfortunately, Klock seems not to have used the most significant secondary source then available: Roberta Beed Sollid's analytical study of Calamity. Even though wobbling back and forth between divergent accounts, Klock avoided the one-sided interpretations of Calamity as a Wild West woman or solely as an angel of mercy on the opposite extreme.

British writer Andrew Blewitt proved, meanwhile, that in a very abbreviated essay of just nine oversized pages a careful writer could judiciously address several of the major topics of concern in dealing with Calamity Jane. Drawing on a wide survey of published books and essays, the Englishman furnishes a balanced, probing account of Calamity. His essay "Calamity Jane" (1963) deals with Calamity's birth date and first years, her wanderings in Wyoming, South Dakota, and Montana, her good deeds as a nurse, her "husbands" and possible children, her faltering last years, and bits on her treatment in popular culture. What Blewitt achieved seemed beyond so many writers before about 1950: one need not be taken in by Calamity's stretchers, a careful researcher should sift out impossible assertions by careless journalists and memoirs, and a biographer must admit that some questions cannot be answered because of insufficient evidence. Writing just before the New Gray Calamity began to emerge, Blewitt accepted the erratic and dark sides of Calamity without turning her into a devilish drunk and harlot.

In these decades, readers were also treated to the most thoroughly researched and appealingly written studies of the Black Hills and Deadwood in the works of historian Watson Parker. First in his revised doctoral dissertation, *Gold in the Black Hills* (1966) and later in *Deadwood: The Golden Years* (1981), Parker contributed pioneering and still very useful overviews of these subjects. For the first time, those wanting diligent, illuminating accounts of the Black Hills and Deadwood had them at their fingertips.

Parker, though knowledgeable about the places and people of the Hills, was decidedly unfriendly to Calamity. Calling her "the notorious harlot" and that "notorious bawd" in his first volume, he asserted, without the slightest proof, that she likely "got her name" because "her paramours were generally visited by some venereal 'calamity.'" He also cited several negative opinions of observers: she was "about the roughest looking human being" in the Hills, "built like a busted bale of hay." Parker agreed, too, that talk about a Wild Bill–Calamity tryst was groundless. He had to admit, however, that Calamity probably nursed sick miners in the smallpox epidemic that struck Deadwood in mid-1876 (most sources say summer 1878).

Fifteen years later in the best history of the town to date, *Deadwood*, Parker repeated much of his critical commentary about Calamity. Naming her Martha "Calamity Jane" Cannary Burke, he thought she probably helped "smallpox victims" because she was "a woman of generous inclinations," but he also sided with critics that concluded "that if she indeed cured any smallpox victims, she probably gave them the great pox in return." (Parker conceded in his footnotes that his conclusions about Calamity's "calamities" are "entirely my own invention, the surmise of an old medical NCO.") In Parker's vignette, Calamity is a "boozy old bawd" who patronizes bars, drinks far too much, and, once over the brim with liquid refreshment, howls up the streets of Deadwood. Regrettably, too, Parker gets several facts wrong in his minibiography of Calamity. But what Parker achieves most are credible, scholarly studies providing valuable contexts for Calamity's several years in the Black Hills and Deadwood.

If no full-length biography of Calamity was published between 1960 and 1990, biographies of Wild Bill appeared just before and during these decades. More than one included sections on Calamity. Journalist and popular historian Richard O'Connor, after producing successful biographies of Jack London and Sinclair Lewis, turned out *Wild Bill Hickok* in 1959. O'Connor's stirringly written but lightly researched biography dealt glancingly with Calamity Jane, primarily in a chapter entitled "Calamity Jane and Other Fables." Regrettably, O'Connor follows falsehoods in Calamity's autobiography and the distortions of Duncan Aikman. Conversely, he seems not to have consulted Paine and Jennewein and quotes far too many of the wildest stretchers without questioning them. In addition, he goes astray in asserting that the dime novelists created the Calamity-Hickok affair rather than pointing the finger at journalists and filmmakers. Even his details go awry when he contends Calamity and the Hickok-Utter party arrived in Deadwood in mid-April, three months before they came. Generally, he makes too much of Calamity's connections with Wild Bill, failing to query their source and facticity.

O'Connor's mistakes and limited research are more than corrected in Joseph G. Rosa's *They Called Him Wild Bill: The Life and Adventures of James Butler Hickok* (1964, 1974). Fifty years after its first appearance, the Rosa volume remains the most thorough, dependable biography of Wild Bill. Englishman Rosa deals concisely and clearly with the Hickok-Calamity connections that so many popularizers—especially moviemakers and novelists—exaggerate excessively. Along the way, regrettably, Rosa is taken in by Clarence Paine's faulty research on Calamity's origins and his wild idea about Calamity being a hermaphrodite. Nonetheless, Rosa makes substantial contributions by drawing on the memories of White Eye Anderson, before those recollections were edited and published, in correcting the faulty contentions that Wild Bill and Calamity were closely connected. Even more thoroughly, he debunks the claim of Jean Hickok McCormick to be the offspring of Hickok and Calamity. Indeed, Rosa's careful and substantial research should have scotched the bed-sharing stories of the Wild West duo, but the sensational idea did not go away, continuing to grab and convince readers and viewers during the next half century.

Another important juncture in writing about Calamity came about in the 1970s. James D. McLaird, a professor of history at his alma mater Dakota Wesleyan University, published his first writings about the subject, beginning a forty-year career eventuating in the definitive biography, *Calamity Jane: The Woman and the Legend* (2005). "Initially," McLaird writes, he "did not plan to write a biography of Calamity Jane." Rather, he intended "only to determine how Calamity became famous," separating "fact from fantasy in her life's story."

In the 1970s, in the early stages of his authorial journey, McLaird coedited two reprinted books and cowrote explanatory introductions to both volumes. These tasks, accomplished with Lesta V. Turchen, provided evidence of McLaird's thorough research even at the launching of his Calamity voyage. The prefatory materials in *The Black Hills Expedition of 1875* (1975) explain the background to the Jenney-Newton expedition and note Martha/Calamity's tangential and unauthorized role with the group. Similar contextual information appears in the McLaird-Turchen introduction to Mrs. William Loring Spencer's novel *Calamity Jane, A Story of the Black Hills* (1887, 1978). The prefatory section, in addition to summarizing the career of

Spencer, furnishes interesting tidbits of commentary on the novel's plot and its relevance for understanding the "development of the Calamity Jane legend."

Of greater eventual significance, even though the author downplays its importance, is the first wide-reaching essay McLaird published on Calamity in 1984, "Calamity Jane: The Development of a Legend." The most revealing statement in McLaird's pioneering essay is his assertion that "the real person who was known as Calamity Jane really doesn't deserve a biographical study." Since "the woman known in history as Calamity Jane is entirely secondary in this study," McLaird focused instead on "the legend of Calamity Jane." McLaird dealt first with the books by Jennewein and Sollid, which he considered "serious biographies," and with the writings and opinions of Calamity's contemporaries. Second—and third—he discussed the rise of the unhistorical Calamity and the importance of the legends surrounding her for a larger understanding of both the historic and mythic Calamity. Foreshadowing his later emphases, McLaird draws heavily on the writings of American Studies scholars Henry Nash Smith and Kent L. Steckmesser to elucidate the shifting meanings, over time, of the legendary Calamity. Revealingly, McLaird's emphases would transition through the years when he realized that to examine the Calamity legends he had to know more about the factual Calamity. That discovery and McLaird's dogged research to uncover every available fact about Martha Canary and Calamity Jane were but prologue to the most important book yet written on Calamity.

Building on the expanding biographical information available on Calamity, very useful brief entries on her were appearing in encyclopedias and other reference guides to the American West. The best of these entries was by Howard R. Lamar, editor of the helpful reference work on the region *The Reader's Encyclopedia of the American West* (1977, updated as *The New Encyclopedia of the American West* in 1998). One of the country's leading western historians and author of the best study of the early northern West, *Dakota Territory: A Study of Frontier Politics* (1958, 1997), Lamar carefully sifted the facts and sources on Calamity's life and showmanship. Discounting the Hickok McCormick story, as well as Wild Bill's reputed connections with Calamity, Lamar also critically examined Calamity's own braggadocio, showing that many of her claims were patently false. To Lamar's credit, while providing a sound abbreviated biography, he admits that in the mid-1970s facts about her birth date and place, early life in the West, and possible roles as a scout were still in dispute. Now readers had a sound, factual reference entry that provided the capsule information they needed.

By the end of the 1980s, biographical-historical writings had added much to an understanding of Calamity Jane's life. Building on the strong publications of Clarence Paine, J. Leonard Jennewein, and Robert Beed Sollid, writers such as Watson Parker and Joseph Rosa had further clarified Calamity's connections with Deadwood and the Black Hills and her links with Wild Bill Hickok. In his earliest publications, James McLaird added other details filling in gaps in Calamity's story and also prefiguring the facts-versus-fiction of his later writings on the subject.

But in some ways the mushrooming images of a New Gray Calamity gained more headway than the declared truth-tellers in the race to reveal Calamity's story. Edson, authors of the sex and violence Westerns, and well-known novelists Pete Dexter and Larry McMurtry gathered many more readers than the biographers and historians. And even they were still holding on to the Jean Hickok McCormick story of the Calamity–Wild Bill twosome.

More segments of Calamity's story remained to be uncovered. No one yet had dealt clearly with census, marriage, and land records treating the Canary clan. Calamity's several "husbands" were yet to be named and described. Her daughter, Jessie, still was a mystery. These and other lacunae, all to be addressed in the next quarter century, meant that much of the Calamity story was still under wraps in 1990.

10

A Complex Calamity, 1990–Present

In the quarter-century following 1990, a variety of Calamity Janes marched across the stages of global culture. Most appeared in the United States, but a surprising number appeared outside U.S. borders. The complexity of and the continuing changes in these images are particularly noteworthy. It would be difficult to reduce the treatments of Calamity to two or three trends; they were more varied than that. Some image-makers advanced new feminist interpretations of Calamity, as did the directors of two movies, *Buffalo Girls* (1995) and *Wild Bill* (1995); others, like the HBO *Deadwood* moviemakers, preferred a New Gray Calamity; still others continued to treat Calamity as a bona fide Wild Woman of the Old West, while others, like biographer James McLaird, aimed at a full, historically sound life story of a complex woman of the pioneer frontier. A few others stuck with the outdated Jean Hickok McCormick story, while more than a few created imaginary Calamitys, with little or no ties to the historical woman. One conclusion remained true, however: historians, biographers, novelists, journalists, and filmmakers still found Calamity Jane an intriguing subject; there was no dearth of new treatments of this complex and ever-changing western woman.

The film *Buffalo Girls* (1995), based substantially on Larry McMurtry's novel of the same name published five years earlier, immediately won attention, in part as a feminist interpretation of Calamity Jane and the Old West. As McMurtry had done in his fiction, this motion picture followed the increasingly discredited Jean Hickok McCormick story.

Despite its unfortunate links to the McCormick documents, the cinematic *Buffalo Girls* epitomizes the more realistic Calamity Jane appearing in many films, biographies, and novels after the 1960s. In its treatment of sexuality, gender relationships, maternal desire, and a disappearing Old West, the film abandons the earlier, much more romantic treatments of Calamity. In other ways, in its treatment of Calamity's connections with famed historical figures (or her distance from them), such as Wild Bill, Buffalo Bill, and Annie Oakley, the movie plays fast and loose with historical facts.

Like Wild Bill, the two old mountain men, Bartle Bone and Jim Ragg, and No Ears and Sitting Bull as Indians, Calamity (played by Angelica Huston) represents an Old West vanishing over the horizon. The Wild West of the characters' earlier years is gone, now being replaced by pageantry and showmanship. Calamity and the others rightly conclude that the frontier must have closed, because Billy Cody is now frequently dramatizing it as the now-gone past in the U.S. East and Europe. "We've seen some glory days, you and me," Calamity tells one of the mountaineers.

Calamity is a reluctant participant in the new arena West. She seems willing to take part only when she realizes that a trip to England will allow her to see her daughter Janey (conceived with Wild Bill), whom she has given up for adoption to an Englishman and his wife. The film takes advantage of Calamity's trip to England to contrast her as a buckskin-clad Westerner trying to navigate polite English society. In addition, when Billy Cody says he wants to make Calamity "famous," she retorts "I am famous." Later, when she joins the Cody show, she tells Buffalo Bill "I'm gonna let you make me immortal," since she is already famous. On

Buffalo Girls, 1995.
This made-for-TV movie, starring Anjelica Huston as Calamity Jane and Melanie Griffith as Calamity's best friend and bordello madam Dora Du Fran, is based largely on the Jean Hickok McCormick story and Larry McMurtry's novel of the same name. Her frontier having closed, Calamity writes letters to and finally visits her daughter, Janie, whom she has given away to a sea captain now living in England. Courtesy Paul Andrew Hutton.

another occasion, when Cody calls her "an original," she fires back, "My reputation is all I got, and it's not for sale." But she also admits, "I got nowhere left to go."

The film dramatizes several intriguing gender relationships. Calamity and Dora Du Fran (Melanie Griffith) are very intimate girl friends, much like the parallel close friendship between the two old trappers. A good deal of heterosexual activity also takes place—in Dora's bordello, between Dora and cowboy Teddy Blue—and in Calamity and Wild Bill's tangles before the film's opening scenes. But Calam can be one of the boys too, a fitting and warm companion to the mountain men and No Ears. She can run around the West, hike into dangerous spots, and, evidently, be safe from any sexual harassment.

If the film provides intriguing, suggestive insights into Calamity's life and actions, its treatment of historical facts is not to be trusted. As we have already seen, the Hickok McCormick story line was a false one on which to base any film. And its chronology of the year 1876 is distorted so that the plot can include Wild Bill and Calamity's participation in the Custer affair. The sequence of happenings in Deadwood and Buffalo Bill's Wild West travel schedule are similarly wrenched out of order.

Probably many viewers were more interested in the film's maternal Calamity than they were in the false facts given about her. Huston plays a warm woman wishing for an intimacy with men and women, which, for the most part, eludes her. "Never knew of what it was to be loved by a man," Calamity writes to her supposed daughter Janey; or, as Dora says of Calamity, "No man has ever loved her." "What do you want?" Hickok asks Calamity, and she tells him you "never will, Hickok," understand what I want.

The mother-daughter relationship between Calamity and Janey depicted in the film fits well with an increasing interest in that domestic theme in American thinking and writing. Previously, little was known about Calamity's womanly side; now, it seemed to some Calamity followers that they had glimpses of the supportive motherly woman she might have been. Near the end of the film, as Dora is dying after a difficult, debilitating childbirth, she emotionally wills the child to Calamity, telling her, "You raise her for me; she's going to need a good mother." And in the final words of the film Calamity writes to Janey: "I'll always be your mother, Calamity Jane."

Similar themes appear in *Wild Bill* (1995), with Jeff Bridges starring as Wild Bill and Ellen Barkin as Calamity. Pete Dexter's novel *Deadwood* is a credited source for the

Wild Bill, 1995.
Ellen Barkin's Calamity Jane is a hybrid western woman, loving her independence but emotionally needing Wild Bill Hickok as a lover and companion. Calamity is a warm-hearted female in a heathenish man's world. Courtesy Paul Andrew Hutton.

movie, which also accepts much of the Jean Hickok McCormick plot. Like *Buffalo Girls*, released in the same year, *Wild Bill* promotes a strongly feminist rendition of Calamity.

Since Wild Bill is the central figure in the film, not much of Calamity's past is spoken of, only the "good times" she and Hickok had previously. Bill's past, including his conflicts with David McCanles at Rock Creek Station in 1861, his killing of David Tutt in 1865, and his intimate relations with the mysterious Susannah Moore (Diane Lane), are mentioned; but his connections with Sarah Shull and his marriage to Agnes Lake Thatcher in spring 1876 are omitted. Hickok's relationships with women play an important role in the film because they figure centrally in Calamity's thoughts about Bill and her own feminine actions.

Calamity, speaking on many gender topics, provides a woman's voice at the center of the film. Clearly, she retains her love—in fact her lust—for Wild Bill; but she also has much to say about men-women relationships, about sexuality, and about the significance of these relationships. In several scenes she enters the narrative by speaking about three man-woman connections. First and foremost, hers with Wild Bill. She would like to think it was love, but she's willing to have it in any form, including making love on a saloon table. Frequently, she feels bad that Bill seems to take her for granted and doesn't want her, doesn't want to bunk with her. Too often, she thinks, she has to begin the encounters because he won't.

Calamity frets much, too, about Hickok's intimacy with Susannah Moore. Is she Bill's real love, illustrating a pure thing she wishes hers with Bill would be? Calamity is both taken with and uncomfortable with talk about this relationship because it seems more than she has been able to establish and maintain with Wild Bill.

Calamity's conversations with "the Kid" about men and women also include much of her reflections about male-female links. In these comments, Calamity seems to be talking to Bill as she converses with the Kid. Perhaps Calamity is speaking about herself and about Susannah Moore when she intimates that Bill has taken advantage of women. He emotionally disagrees with her comments.

The Calamity of *Wild Bill* is a female nurturer in a heathenish guy world. She looks after Wild Bill's health and is worried about what's happening to him. As something of a saloon housewife, she cleans up and serves up necessities. She keeps up with the Kid and his affairs and explains things to him, even though later she hates him for possibly being involved in Bill's death. If Wild Bill is the Big Man of the world and the Kid is trying to gain revenge, Calamity is the whore with a soul and social conscience.

In short, Calamity's role in this film fits into and breaks with previous cinematic Calamitys. Once again, she is a mixture of a mannish woman who wants to be with the boys and yet loved as a woman. Although we see her in buckskins, with a single braid, hat, suspenders, shirt, and pants, she is not the dirty and foul Calamity of Dexter's novel who seems to have bundled with a skunk. Ellen Barkin's Calamity is much more willing to talk about class and gender, about women's roles in a Wild West, than most previous Calamitys. She would have seemed out of time in Doris Day's era. Here is another example of the New Gray Calamity reflecting on love, sex, class, and gender.

The HBO made-for-TV *Deadwood* probably attracted more viewers than any other Calamity-portraying venue gathered in the years following 1960. The show, lasting three seasons (2004–2006) and featuring thirty-six episodes, proved unusually fascinating for television audiences. It also illustrated how much a New Gray Calamity Jane had come on scene and how a gifted and controversial writer and producer such as David Milch could bring to life an innovative and different kind of Western series.

Deadwood arrived in unexpected fashion. Milch had proposed a series on Nero's Rome, but the HBO mavens urged him, instead, to travel his themes in a different time and place. So it happened. Intrigued with telling the unfolding story of American history, Milch chose to focus on the first year or so (1876–77) of white settlement in Deadwood. Community-building—in all its complex, confusing, and stuttering steps toward organization—was to be the central theme of *Deadwood*.

In several interviews and commentaries on the HBO series, Milch clarified some of his intentions. First, he wanted to meld historical facts and imagined characters and events, thus avoiding being a "slave to history." He trotted out familiar characters such as Al Swearengen [*sic*], Seth Bullock, Wild Bill Hickok, Calamity Jane, and several others, and dealt with events like the assassination of Hickok, the smallpox epidemic in the Hills, and the local election of 1877. Alongside these historical characters and events were imagined or composite characters, Doc, Trixie the prostitute, and several Chinese figures. On occasion, Milch and his actors claimed the episodes were "historically accurate."

But, for the most part, historical inaccuracies were more common than facts. For instance, the series skews the early lives of Swearengen and Bullock to fit them more smoothly into the cinematic themes being promoted. Swearengen was not raised in a horrendous orphanage and was a married man, Bullock was married and a father when he arrived in Deadwood, and he and his partner Sol Star did not duel with Swearengen, the bellicose operator of the Gem Theater, to obtain their building site. Preacher Smith did not die from a brain tumor. These, and dozens of other inaccuracies, betray Milch; the series is an undependable source of Deadwood and Black Hills history.

Milch achieves much more in a second, larger purpose: to show how a nascent settlement, lacking *law*, attempts to establish *order*. In its first months, Milch says, Deadwood was an "outlaw community." *Deadwood*, according to its chief spokesman, replicates the archetypical American historical story in its "impulse toward community." To achieve this thematic goal, Milch, the executive producer, shows how dictatorial tyrants like Swearengen of the Gem and Cy Tolliver of the Bella Union bully their workers, their sex slaves, and most other residents of the town. Seth Bullock tries to bring another kind of order—and law—with his badge, fists, guns, and volcanic temper. Doc, Preacher Smith, the territorial politicians of Yankton, and the newspaper editor embody other avenues toward community-building. The preacher, speaking at the burial of Wild Bill, gives them St. Paul's recipe for unity: they are all of one body, the eye cannot separate itself from the foot, they must all work together.

As strong and persuasive as these community themes are, *Deadwood* often undermines its own thesis through its excesses. Violence is overblown, for example. Perhaps Milch's previous work in cop shows shines through in his inordinate stress on murder and mayhem in the HBO series. The most thorough historical research estimates thirty-four murders occurred in Deadwood and the Black Hills in the years from 1875 to 1879, and more if killings in Indian conflicts are included. Milch's offhand comment that a murder occurred every night in Deadwood can be dismissed as a from-the-hip exaggeration, but he also depicts the Gem Theater/Saloon as a den of death. Also, if that murder rate had occurred, the town would have been without residents in about five years. Over the three seasons of the series, about a dozen murders alone take place in Swearengen's private rooms and other parts of the Gem. Generally, in fact, the series reveals little understanding of the historical development of western mining camps and cowtowns. Sometimes Milch's excessive essentializations derail his treatment of Deadwood. On one occasion, supporting the film's widespread use of pro-

310

fanity, he baldly asserts "that's . . . the way they talked in the West." Few if any authorities on western history would venture such an outrageous generalization since evidence on how residents across the vast West spoke—what words they used, if they were outrageously profane (as are many characters in *Deadwood*)—is lacking. Quite simply, most of the producers, editors, and actors, including Robin Weigert as Calamity Jane, seemed little acquainted with the specifics of Deadwood and the history of the American West in the 1870s.

The mishmash of strengths and limitations of *Deadwood* is mirrored in the show's handling of Calamity Jane. Jane CAN-ery, as she is called, appears in major or minor roles in about three-fourths of the thirty-six episodes. She is described ambivalently, as a profane drunkard but also as a nurse of the sick and a lover of children, with more emphasis on the darker than lighter side of her character. But other segments of the historical Calamity remain off-scene. We learn nothing about her background, her activities outside Deadwood and the Hills, and her part-time work as a dance hall worker. Withal, Calamity Jane, although vividly portrayed, comes across as a narrow, truncated figure.

No one should hesitate about portraying Calamity as cursing drunk. Nor should one question her errands of mercy. But some of these characteristics are overdone in the HBO program. Calamity is so often inebriated and isolated from the community that she cannot function as a dancer and entertainer, which in reality she did. Too much under the bottle, she is unable to serve, too, as a helper in the pesthouse. Berating herself, Calamity says she's too drunk to help care for a little orphan girl whose family has been killed and who needs Calamity's help. (On other occasions she overflows with love and attention for this little girl.) In addition, Calamity's hatred for and avoidance of Swearengen are so intense here that one would not guess that the historical Calamity worked in the Gem for several months.

The drunkenness means Calamity cannot work, as her historical counterpart did.

Like so many other creators of cinematic and literary Calamitys, David Milch has trouble with the Wild Bill–Calamity relationship. Milch begins, as do recent biographers and historians, by showing Calamity coming into Deadwood with Hickok, Charlie Utter, and several others. To his credit, Milch avoids Calamity's outrageous claim that she cornered Hickok's killer, Jack McCall, with a cleaver and led his capture. But the producer exhibits outright silliness too. Contemporary sources did not refer to Calamity as "Hickok's woman," as several scenes do here. As already seen, earlier information did not claim the two were close friends or intimate—or more than acquaintances, in fact. But Milch rushes into a morass of vulgar unbelievableness when he asserts: "I don't think he ever banged her . . . [but] she told everyone he did." No serious writer or biographer—at the time, or since—has Calamity saying she and Hickok were bedmates.

Weigert performs superbly as Calamity. Beyond the numerous scenes of drunkenness and numerous bursts of profanity, a few other interesting hints of Calamity's character emerge, especially in the second and third seasons. She becomes a defender of children, sides with individualistic Doc and Charlie, though often swearing at them like a programmed robot. Even more intriguing is Calamity's growing friendship and love for Joanie Stubbs, a prostitute who has escaped the brutal ownership of Cy Tolliver. As Milch discerningly notes, Calamity, so fearful of intimate friendships with men or women, is won over by Joanie's understanding that she and Calamity are mutually outside of and isolated from the camp's dominating men and elite women.

Regrettably, however, the depiction of Calamity in *Deadwood* is, like the historical setting itself, so condensed that it limits the needed full portrait of her. Conversations and

Calamity Jane in HBO's *Deadwood*, 2004–2006.

Talented actress Robin Weigert expertly plays a drunken Calamity wandering the streets of Deadwood. Although David Milch, the program's producer, claimed the series was historically accurate, it was not—neither in its general outlines nor in its depiction of Calamity. Courtesy Paul Andrew Hutton.

stream-of-conscious murmurings provide flashes of Swearengen's, Tolliver's, and Bullock's backgrounds and previous experiences; we get similar bits about Joanie's and Trixie's pre-Deadwood years. But we get no such prefatory information about Calamity's years before she came to the Black Hills; nor do we get hints of her later roles as mother, wife, and pioneer woman. Even when Weigert was interviewed about her role in the series, she showed no knowledge—in fact, no seeming interest—of the historical Calamity. In short, though the *Deadwood* series captured millions of viewers and its depiction of Calamity was cheek-and-jowl with other Gray Calamitys, the movie did not move much beyond a rather circumscribed portrait of her. All the more disappointing since the program had such an amazing following.

The last hurrah for full-length books adhering to the Jean Hickok McCormick line came with Stella Foote's *A History of Calamity Jane: Our Country's First Liberated Woman* (1995). Foote and her husband, Don C. Foote, longtime residents of Billings, Montana, had established an amusement park and gathered "Treasures of the West" as part of a museum and heritage center in eastern Montana. Hearing of Hickok McCormick's story and desiring to display in their museum the reputed diary and letters of Calamity, the Footes purchased them and offered McCormick much-needed part-time employment in the Wonderland Museum.

Not surprisingly, Foote accepts the authenticity of the diary and letters and employs them as a central source for her skip-and-run biography of Calamity. Her efforts are not successful—for a number of reasons. First, the jumbled chronology of the McCormick-Calamity documents does not mesh well with the incomplete but more thorough chronology available in the best-documented stories about Calamity. Foote either overlooks or purposely omits all census, marriage, and other statistical records available to her in the mid-1990s. (She cites only the land purchases and sales of the Canary families in Mercer County, Missouri, in the 1850s and 1860s.) In addition, the author's reach often exceeds her grasp in bald, mistaken statements. Consider but four errors: (1) Foote says there are no marriage certificates for Calamity; (2) she asserts that Calamity was in Chicago at the World's Fair as part of Buffalo Bill's Wild West show; (3) she misfires on Calamity's "husbands" George Cosgrove and Robert Dorsett and discounts Jessie Elizabeth as her daughter; and (4) and she is incorrect in arguing that Calamity gave up drinking for several years. The largest problems, however, come from her uncritical acceptance of the fraudulent McCormick story, meaning that she states Wild Bill and Calamity married, that Calamity served with Custer, and that she traveled with Buffalo Bill. Page after page of long block quotes from newspaper and other published sources also detract from the author's efforts. Some of these long quotations deal with Calamity and her checkered life; too many do not.

By the mid-1990s several secondary sources, the early ones by Roberta Beed Sollid and J. Leonard Jennewein and the later ones by James D. McLaird and Richard W. Etulain, should have encouraged Foote to ask more evaluative questions about the McCormick documents. Indeed, Foote's inability or refusal to question obviously incorrect information in the documents undoubtedly played into the hands of critics. Careful research had called into question many facets of the Calamity-McCormick story, but because Foote did not address these queries, she gained several negative reviews and, in the end, contributed to the demise of a story line that had fascinated readers and moviegoers for a half century.

If the HBO *Deadwood* series illustrates the recent distorted, sensational images of Calamity, the solid, exhaustively researched essays and books of James D. McLaird epitomize the opposite in interpretations of her during the past generation. Beginning in the 1970s and 1980s, McLaird issued preliminary essays and other brief pieces. In the following decade or so, he published a handful of first-rate essays on Calamity, which eventually became parts of the two very important books he published on her in 2005 and 2008.

Three essays published in the 1990s illustrate McLaird's thorough research and balanced, defensible conclusions. "Calamity Jane: The Life and Legend" (1994), "Calamity Jane's Diary and Letters: Story of a Fraud" (1995), and "Calamity Jane and Wild Bill: Myth and Reality" (1998) were finger pieces for, and eventually became key parts of,

McLaird's path-breaking volumes appearing a decade later. The first of the essays focuses on the final hectic months of Calamity's declining life. This valuable piece illustrates McLaird's prodigious research as well as his balanced, thorough depiction of Calamity's closing days. Using information from dozens of newspapers in Wyoming, Nebraska, and especially Montana and South Dakota, McLaird reveals how far he had moved beyond previous biographers in examining, week by week, journalistic accounts of Calamity's aimless wanderings from November 1902 until her death in August 1903. No previous scholar had so diligently plundered newspaper stories about Calamity.

McLaird also avoids the too-often one-sided conclusions of others and, instead, embraces more complex views of Calamity. A drunk and probable prostitute of boisterous and untoward actions—yes, by all means; but also a woman who wanted to marry and be a good mother, be respectable (and respected), and help the sick and needy. In addition, McLaird clearly reveals—and accepts—the diversity of opinions journalists and others expressed about Calamity. Some viewed her as a hopeless inebriate and beggar; others saw her as a warm, sympathetic woman despite her weaknesses. McLaird, as he would in his subsequent writings, embraces a *both-and* rather than an *either-or* perspective and thus portrays Calamity as a multifaceted instead of a one-dimensional character.

McLaird's essay on Calamity and Wild Bill proved to be a précis of the comparative biography he published on the two Old West worthies a decade later. Deftly summarizing their careers, their six-weeks acquaintance in summer 1876, and the scattered and conflicting research on their characters, McLaird proved again how much new information he had turned up. His sifting and comparing of newspaper, rare book, and memoir information gave readers a measured account, one they could rely on in treating either or both figures. Unfortunately, too many popularizers repeatedly told the same stories about Calamity and Wild Bill without consulting what McLaird had put forth in his valuable essay.

But the most significant of McLaird's essays in the 1990s was his remarkably thorough treatment of the Jean Hickok McCormick story that had fascinated followers of Calamity and Wild Bill for a half century. McLaird's essay in *Montana* should have settled for all time the fraudulence of McCormick's story—particularly when he enlarged upon his earlier findings in his 2005 full-length biography. Unfortunately, many Sunday supplement and digital scribblers have failed to learn from McLaird's turning-point piece.

"Calamity Jane's Diary and Letters: Story of a Fraud" not only provided the most complete background story about Jean Hickok McCormick to date; it also proved, point by point, why her claims about a Calamity Jane diary and letters were entirely fraudulent. Pulling together findings from a plethora of rich sources, McLaird logically demonstrated that the diary and letters, as well as Hickok McCormick's assertions about those documents, were a bundle of lies. As one of the most important handful of essays ever written about Calamity Jane, McLaird's piece destroyed the Hickok McCormick stretchers.

As important as the Hickok McCormick background was for an understanding of her attempts to fool the public as Calamity Jane and Wild Bill's daughter, even more significant was McLaird's proof that no one should place any reliance on the diary and letters for further research on Calamity. He accomplished this by proving that many statements in the documents were false. Even more damning, he demonstrated that loose-leaf pages were being added, probably by Hickok McCormick, as she met and interviewed people about Calamity thirty years and more after Calamity's death. And he proved that someone changed (again, probably Hickok McCormick) parts of the diary and letters as well as stories about the documents along the way, especially after doubters questioned their authenticity.

Why had Hickok McCormick set out on her fraudulent path? McLaird speculates that she hungered and thirsted after notoriety; she wanted to be someone, somebody. Replacing her own nondescript background with a life linked to two western legends would give her the desired headlines. A quick appearance on a national radio program and at two or three other gatherings, as well as coverage in several widely read newspaper stories, gave her much public notice, even though it quickly melted away. She also achieved some financial payoff for the notoriety, using her connections with the *We the People* staff to provide support for substantiating her successful claims for welfare assistance. Even if the documents were undoubtedly forgeries, Hickok McCormick gained, in some measure, what she may have wanted to achieve in claiming to be the daughter of Calamity and Wild Bill.

These essays and McLaird's expanding research came to full fruition in his extensive biography, *Calamity Jane: The Woman and the Legend* (2005). Published more than a century after her death, McLaird's thorough, measured, and thoughtful book is, by far, the most important publication on Calamity. It is a tour de force of diligent, far-reaching scholarship.

The outstanding achievement of McLaird's book is his exhaustive research. His bibliography lists nearly 150 newspapers, with especially thorough coverage of periodicals in South Dakota, Montana, and Wyoming, and also several national and even international newspapers. The author plundered all the pertinent manuscript collections, including those of earlier researchers on Calamity. Nor did he overlook any of the germane published primary and secondary essays and books.

McLaird draws on this monumental research to address the most controversial subjects of Calamity's life and legendary career. His extensive coverage not only treats the subjects themselves but also the varied interpretations of the controversies over time. For example, his discussions of Calamity's correct birthday (1 May 1856, probably), birthplace (Princeton, Mercer County, Missouri), and the Canary family history are particularly extensive, showing which conclusions are valid, which off the mark and to be dismissed. Utilizing this comprehensive approach means that McLaird could chop out the cluttering underbrush of misconceptions—for example, the Jean Hickok McCormick fable, the wrong views of Calamity's origins, the exaggerations of Calamity herself, and the misleading conclusions on the Calamity–Wild Bill relationship—and plant and nourish a new crop of correct assertions. If subsequent researchers examined closely McLaird's text and notes, they could avoid the noxious weeds of unsubstantiated rumors, falsehood, and downright lies that littered the Calamity landscape.

In approaching his subject, McLaird eschewed, for the most part, theoretical or new interpretive approaches. He did not plunge into the tangled thickets of theorizing that characterized so many psychobiographies published from the 1970s onward. Nor did he resort to a feminist interpretation of Calamity, as valuable as that approach and other theories might be.

McLaird's interpretative framework owed most to the American Studies myth-and-reality school that came to the fore in Henry Nash Smith's classic work, *Virgin Land: The American West as Myth and Symbol* (1950). Quite simply, Smith convinced scholars and generalists that attempting to dismiss ideas about the West as misleading "myths" or falsehoods was a dead-end approach; instead, researchers ought to examine these ideas—whether they were factual or fictional—to see how they had originated, changed over time, and shaped subsequent views. In much of his thorough book, McLaird travels the myth-and-reality path, especially as it is employed in Kent Ladd Steckmesser's well-known volume, *The Western Hero in History and Legend* (1965). After devoting the first two-thirds of his biography to a corrected version of Calamity's life, in which he shows the influential roles of journalists, dime novelists, and Calamity herself in shaping legends about her, McLaird contributes three long chapters tracing the varied interpretations of Calamity in the century following her death. As the author notes in his introduction, Calamity's "importance rests not on the similarity of her life to that of other frontier women, but on the manner in which her life was reshaped to fit a mythic structure glorifying 'the winning of the West.'" That being the case, "the growth of the Calamity Jane legend needs revisiting as much as the life of Martha Canary."

The contributions of McLaird's turning-point biography are two. For the first time we had a full-scale, dependable account of Martha Canary's life. We were also given an overview of the legends that grew up around her, during her lifetime and in the following decades. After the publication of McLaird's biography, no one could say we lacked a thorough, trustworthy life story of Calamity Jane. But, unfortunately, as we shall see, not all writers in the next decade or so benefitted as much from his volume as they should have.

Three years after the appearance of his biography of Calamity, McLaird published *Wild Bill Hickok and Calamity Jane: Deadwood Legends* (2008). The author's discussion of Calamity, drawing from his definitive biography of her, concisely summarizes his exhaustive research findings. Along the way, his bits-and-pieces approach pulls together the best brief biography we have of Calamity. After devoting his first two chapters to Wild Bill's rise to fame, McLaird turns to a section on Wild Bill and Calamity, two chapters on Calamity's apotheosis, and a final chapter and conclusion comparing the legends of the two characters.

McLaird also advances a provocative thesis. It was Hickok and Calamity's contacts with early popularizers that did most to launch their careers: Wild Bill's in the George Ward Nichols essay "Wild Bill," in *Harper's New Monthly Magazine* in February 1867, and Calamity's in H. N. Maguire's *The Black Hills and American Wonderland* (1877). Neither of these accounts possessed outstanding historical accuracy, but they captured thousands of readers—and attracted other popularizers. In Calamity's case, Edward L. Wheeler and his more than thirty dime novels. Even though Hickok and Calamity professed to detest journalists and their hyped stories, they seemed, in McLaird's words, to relish "the opportunity to tell their stories to the press." And convincing themselves of the truth of the exaggerated tales—or talking themselves into the veracity of the hyperbolic yarns—they enthusiastically participated in the expansion of those imagined stories.

McLaird presents a complex Calamity. Particularly of note are the jostling images of a young woman dressed as a dancer, waitress, and entertainer in Deadwood saloons and the buckskin-clad rider and teamster among workers and soldiers, usually dressed as a man. Equally rewarding is McLaird's tracing of the evolving notoriety of Calamity from a young waif, to a local celebrity, to a nationally recognized dime novel heroine, and on to a notorious wanderer and distressed, aging woman.

The author's extensive and helpful footnotes cite the significant sources on Calamity, especially the numerous obscure newspaper references. Also of note is McLaird's assertion that Calamity's statements often showed "how much she wanted the public's acceptance." Although not often advanced in biographical accounts of Calamity, this contention offsets the numerous one-sided, sensationalist arguments through the years that Calamity was solely a devil-may-care, freedom-loving wild woman who always did as she wished, thumbing her nose at a homogenizing society.

The final chapter is of particular value for those interested in the Wild Bill–Calamity relationship. McLaird catalogues and evaluates the false previous accounts of Calamity and Hickok as very close friends or lovers. If subsequent novelists and filmmakers begin with this chapter, they might be much less likely to distort the true stories of the two Deadwood legends.

In the near-decade since the publication of McLaird's comprehensive biography in 2005, other authors have not moved notably beyond his contributions. Nor have they made good use of his prodigious research in their own recent essays and books.

The only book-length biography of Calamity since McLaird's is Linda Jucovy's *Searching for Calamity: The Life and Times of Calamity Jane* (2012). Jucovy's study curiously balances achievements and limitations. Exceptionally well written and appealingly organized, the new book is quite limited in its research and strongly contests conclusions eminently more defensible than hers.

Jucovy bases her derivative volume on most of the strongest primary and secondary sources dealing with Calamity. She admits to being "indebted to previous writers, . . . especially James D. McLaird, for their dogged efforts to discover . . . information." The author's research is limited primarily to published books and essays, with a few references to newspapers and manuscript materials. But readers will enjoy—and profit from—the maps Jucovy provides of Calamity's tireless travels, the scraps of context she furnishes, and the clear, general story she tells about Calamity.

Jucovy exhibits, early on, a healthy skepticism about many of the Calamity stories. Well she should since many are unreliable as historical sources. But the author's skepticism sometimes gets out of hand, leading her to question far too many sources. Indeed, the excessive doubting undermines some of her contributions. Several of her conclusions are wrongheaded, indefensible. For example, she contends that Calamity must have been born in 1852 "because of the relatively convincing anecdotal evidence," and because census records are often flawed (in this she is disagreeing with the 1860 census, which indicates Calamity was born in 1856). Had Jucovy checked other census and marriage records in Iowa and Missouri, she would have seen the strongest evidence points to 1856 as the correct birth date. Charlotte Burge Canary, Calamity's mother, was born in 1840 and married to Robert in 1855; she could hardly have given birth to Martha at age twelve in 1852, three years before marrying Robert. The author also questions whether Calamity was in Coeur d'Alene, Idaho, and Spokane, Washington, in 1884 and in the Klondike in 1898. She dismisses such possibilities as "reminiscences of old timers" or not "first hand." Again, more thorough research in newspapers of the time should have corrected most of the author's doubts about Calamity's travels. Additional examination of newspaper reports and other evidence might have kept Jucovy from asserting that "there is no clear evidence that Calamity ever referred to the girl [Jessie] as her 'daughter.'" She can reach that incorrect conclusion only by dismissing the crucial interview of Calamity with M. L. Fox in the *Illustrated American* (1896) as a falsified get-up "of press agents for the dime museum chain that had recently signed Calamity to a contract." There is not a shred of evidence for that strange conclusion, and Jucovy seems unaware too that Fox, a recognized reporter, wrote other (even negative) stories about Calamity.

Jucovy could have stood on more solid—but also risky—ground in her contention that Calamity was a supremely independent woman determined to stand on her own, be her own boss, and keep true to her own liberty-leaning lodestar. Careful, extensive examination of Calamity's life and career might sustain this illuminating view, but the author too often bounces off this assertion to move on to other topics. And in dismissing the Fox interview and other such evidence, Jucovy overlooks countertrends—that is, Calamity's love for Jessie, her desire to be a good mother, her wish for husbands, and her longing to be a traditional pioneer woman. Rather than a singular, life-long passion to be in all ways set apart from societal expectations, Calamity wobbled back and forth in one of the central tensions of her life—wanting separation and yet marriage, motherhood, and acceptance. Although in many ways an interesting, well-written biography, Jucovy's work misses, because of the author's limited research and excessive skepticism, an opportunity to depict Calamity as a more complex woman.

Surprisingly, even though the best biographical accounts of Calamity have appeared since 1990, and the HBO *Deadwood* TV garnered headline attention, first-rank novelists have been hesitant to take on Calamity as a fictional subject. Still, the Edson novels, mostly published before 1990, continued in wide circulation, the Adult Westerns stayed on scene, and a few other novels dealt with Calamity.

Typical of the sex-and-violence Adult Westerns was J. R. Roberts's *Return to Deadwood*, number 146 in the Gunsmith series (1994). Early on in the novel, Calamity writes a letter requesting that the Gunman, Clint Adams, a friend of the late Wild Bill, come to Deadwood to help her. Adams thinks that Jane is still in love with Hickok after his assassination. Roberts, one of the several pennames of prolific writer Robert Randisi, spins a story of sex, violence, and mystery. The Gunman beds several willing women, kills off several unwilling competitors, and helps Calamity regain money stolen to support her daughter's schooling. Drinking excessively and wrongly jailed as a murder suspect, Calamity plays a sideline role as the Gunman mows down his opposition between steamy bedroom scenes. The author hints that Calamity represents an older Deadwood now long gone, but his own shaky plot suggests that the Deadwood of the 1890s remains a violent and amoral place.

Bill Brooks's novel *Deadwood* (1997), the work of a talented writer, nonetheless is as tied to the sex-and-violence formula as the Adult Westerns featuring Calamity. Quint McCannon, a gunman nearly on a par with Wild Bill Hickok, rides into Deadwood to solve a mysterious string of murders of prostitutes. Calamity enters the scene as a mannish teamster, "a mistake of nature. . . . There was nothing in her gait or manner to suggest womanly qualities." During the next weeks, she appears "horribly drunk" and reeking of a drug that miners used to fend off body lice. "Her breath as sour as a kraut," she tries to get McCannon to buy a drink for her and her miner lover. Or, if the hero wishes, she'll abandon the miner, and they can go up to his crib "and have us a sweet time." Or another occasion, Calamity, carrying a heavy liquid load and swearing profusely, "smelled the way no woman should smell, worse than any muleskinner." Brooks's Calamity seems straight out of Pete Dexter's *Deadwood*.

Calamity turns tricks, gets lugubriously drunk, is often childlike and bawling; but mostly she wobbles up and down the Deadwood streets and into its saloons. She often reminds Quint that she and Bill were married. Although Calamity was working as a waitress and entertainer in the dance halls of Deadwood for two or three years in 1876–79, she's mainly a senseless drunk in Brooks's novel. Then, in the final pages, Calamity, without a clear motivating reason for doing so, decides she will leave off her drunken ways, reform, forget her unreasonable attachment to the memory of the deceased Hickok, and take up with a drummer and go with him to Denver. Overall, the depiction of Calamity here is narrow, superficial, and unbelievable.

Before 1990, but especially afterwards, authors of children's and adolescent books found Calamity Jane an attention-catching subject. Their varied treatments of the controversial actions of Calamity were particularly intriguing in light of the expected readers of these volumes.

In 1992, the Disney Press published *Calamity Jane at Fort Sanders* in its American Frontier series. Coauthored by Ron Fontes and Justin Korman and touted as "a historical novel," the book presents a highly fictionalized Calamity Jane who hauls on the reins of a hell-bent stagecoach in the opening scene and later rides like a whirlwind, disguised as a man and serving as an army scout, falling reluctantly into a conflict with friendly Indians. The nonstop frenetic action, at a galloping pace, must have attracted adolescent readers. A dash of humor, poking fun at the nabob Nellys ruling Piedmont, Wyoming, for chasing Calamity out of town, spices the lively narrative. As Calamity rides on, she calls out to a societal termagant, "Don't get your bloomers in a bunch, you old lemon!"

Fontes and Korman portray Calamity as a twenty-one-year-young woman who outmans masculine competitors in her abundant courage, sense of adventure, and hero(ine)ism. "Nobody tells me what to do!," Calamity snaps at her critics. Playing on that independence card, the authors fashion an appealing work more imagined than factual. But the image of the youthful Calamity, sanitized here without a hint of her drunkenness and possible prostitution, fits comfortably within the legend of Calamity as a devil-may-care adventuresome female.

In the same year, biographer Doris Faber produced the best of the children's books published thus far in her *Calamity Jane: Her Life and Her Legend*. The author pic-

Calamity Jane in books for children and young adults.
Late in the twentieth century, authors for children and young adults featured Calamity Jane in several works. Doris Faber's book was an outstanding biography for younger readers.

tures Calamity as a lively pony girl, who, once she grows up, is unable to find herself and becomes an alcoholic. Faber makes clear that Calamity likes men; she seems always to be around them. But she is not referred to as a prostitute.

The author achieves her major purpose: to show how Martha Jane Canary [*sic*] became Calamity Jane, how life became wedded to legend. Additionally, Faber questions Calamity's veracity, the McCormick diary and letters, and the story of Wild Bill and Calamity's attachment. Still, Faber falls victim to a good deal of misinformation while establishing that, early on, Calamity gained a reputation as a feisty, assertive, and independent young woman.

Most of all, Faber embeds Calamity's story in an adventuresome Old West. When it changes and becomes more settled, Calamity cannot find her place in the transformed region. Overall, Faber provides a Dexter-McMurtry Calamity for kids. The adventuresome tomboy on one side, the alcoholic carouser on the other.

By the end of the twentieth century, readers, viewers, and a variety of other participants in popular culture had a veritable smorgasbord of Calamity Jane representations spread before them. In addition to the previously mentioned biographical-historical, literary, and cinematic treatments, a plethora of other images were on scene. They often varied from cultural to economic symbols, from clothing styles to restaurant names. The name of Calamity Jane had become so well known that nearly everyone in the United States, and in many other countries as well, recognized her and some of the representations associated with her name. She became the brand of dozens and dozens of ideas and items.

Consider, for example, the other dramatic images of Calamity in TV shows, dramas, and one-person presentations. Over time several TV series, especially popular Westerns, featured a Calamity Jane episode, with a guest star playing her role. For instance, *Bonanza*, *Death Valley Days*, *Wild West*, and *Tall Tale* included Calamity appearances. The most ballyhooed of the recent Calamity Jane TV shows was the animated *Legend of Calamity Jane* (1997). Created in France and distributed in England, the cartoon series was intended for an American pre-adult audience. This Warner Brothers series, according to one billing, wanted to depict "a self-sufficient woman who follows her heart and fights for her convictions in the Wild West." Along with fellow westerner heroes and heroines such as Wild Bill Hickok and Indian Quanah Parker, as well as her imagined partner Joe Presto, Calamity (in the voice of Barbara Scaff) takes on evil-doers, ex-Confederates, crooked government agents, and gangs of thieves. Calamity is an agent of justice and honor in a threatening and threatened Old West, but working in a wider world too. As one journalist put it, "Though the story has an American perspective, it is not overly Americanized." But the series never seemed to catch on in the United States. Only three of all the episodes were broadcast in the United States before they abruptly disappeared.

Dramas about Calamity, presented from California to New England, were also staged outside the U.S. in France, England, and Canada. Some were little more than replays of Doris Day's romantic musical *Calamity Jane* (1953). Others were much more innovative in form and content. One of the most unusual plays was *Sonofabitch Stew: The Drunken Life of Calamity Jane* (1995), a one-woman show that played to enthusiastic audiences in western Canada. It featured two settings: that of Calamity in the nineteenth century and that of Janet Payne, a contemporary professor of women's studies alienated from a masculine-dominated citadel of academics. Both Calamity and Payne are presented as women thumbing their noses at homogenizing societies bent on fencing them in. Instead, the raucous, independent women drink, cuss, and belch and fart themselves away from those wishing to encircle them. Although actress Deb Pickman (playing Calamity and Payne) incorrectly stated that no previous play or movie had portrayed Calamity as a free-wheeling, vernacular spirit—*Calamity Jane* (1984), with Jane Alexander, and *Buffalo Girls* (1995), with Anjelica Huston, had already done that—her performance, wrote one journalist, was "a portrait of a hellion, a revisionist look at history, and a satire of academia rolled into one." Pickman was convinced that the play, through its feminist emphases, would provide a "power fantasy for women," a perspective too often missing from accounts of the past. Portraying Calamity as "the legendary hell raiser[,] as the true tough-talking, masculine woman that she truly was," Pickman added, would allow a Wild West woman to speak to modern audiences.

Other dramatic venues in the 1980s and 1990s included one-woman impersonations of Calamity. Marianne Donnelly (Massachusetts), Diane Moran (Missouri), Anne Pasquale (New York), Leah Schwartz (Missouri), and Dianne Gleason (Arizona, Montana, et al.) were five such speakers. Three others captured even more attention. Former teacher and librarian Glenda Bell touted herself as an authentic Calamity, making more than 2,000 presentations of Calamity and averaging 150 shows during some years between the late 1980s until 2004. Bell presented Calamity as a homespun "Wild West Legend" and a "Western Woman Wildcat" and spun tales of Calamity's many "humorous ups

Calamity Jane impersonators.
Beginning in the 1970s, several women began to travel as Calamity impersonators. The best known of these presenters was Glenda Bell, who depicted Calamity as lively and unorthodox, but hardly immoral.

and downs." In the first years, Bell traveled with a companion, "Barb Wire" (Barb Fisher), who set the stage for the later Calamity presentation ("The Whole Shebang"), but more recently Bell has made solo talks on "Researching Calamity Jane." Bell's interpretation of Calamity runs decidedly toward the Wild West. In spring 2013 she told an interviewer that "the stereotype of the cigar-smoking, tobacco-chewing, sure-shooting, tough old broad is based on [the actual] Calamity." But even well after James McLaird turned up solid facts about Martha's name and birth date, Bell chose to tell audiences, wrongly, that Calamity was born as "Martha Jane Cannary" and "around 1848." Nor does Bell tell audiences that Calamity bore two children, was legally married to Bill Steers in 1888, and took part in 1884, 1896, and 1901 shows, but not in Buffalo Bill's.

Dr. Joyce Therier, a faculty member at Emporia State University in Kansas, also gives Calamity presentations. Therier likes to describe herself as an "academic being a rowdy woman." Rather than being a research-and-writing historian, she has majored in oral presentations, including dozens on Calamity. She attempts in her performances to show the differences between mythic and factual representations of the West. Not surprisingly for a professor who places heavy stress on oral history, Therier emphasizes thoroughly oral accounts and newspapers. She also uses, unfortunately too much, Calamity's suspect autobiography and the Jean Hickok McCormick diary and letters. Her research seems stuck in an earlier era, stressing now-discounted sources rather than the stronger essays and books published since 1990.

The third of the best-known presenters, Norma Slack Haskell, has family ties to Calamity. The great-great-grand-niece of Calamity (and the great-great-granddaughter of Calamity's younger sister, Lena, and her husband, Johnny Borner), Haskell portrayed the Wild West woman at the Laramie Wyoming Territorial Park for more than ten years, as well as in numerous other venues across the West. Her great-great-aunt Calamity Canarie (the spelling the Borners alone have used), says Haskell, was a "modern day lady born before her time." A warmly patriotic American much devoted to her family heritage, Haskell wants to portray Calamity as the "Wildest Woman in the West," but also one sympathetic to the poor and unhappy. Haskell is an outstanding horsewoman, an appealing singer, and snappy with her bullwhip.

Unhappily, Haskell's grasp of historical facts is off-track. She told an interviewer that Calamity was the daughter of "a Methodist minister and his wife . . . [who] joined a group of Mormon families . . . [but who were] killed during the journey" west. Haskell also incorrectly claims Calamity took part in Buffalo Bill's Wild West show. Plus, she is unwilling to admit that her relative was, at times, a hopeless drunk and perhaps a prostitute. Although Haskell's riding, singing, and other presentations have brought her acclaim, she has followed much too closely her family's mistaken memories (or reshaped past) and thus provides a flawed historical portrait of her ancestor.

It is of note that community celebrations of Calamity's heritage have never been numerous. Indeed, only three towns have launched well-publicized Calamity celebrations. At first, Princeton, Missouri, seemed more reticent about than proud of being the birthplace of Martha Canary/ Calamity Jane. Not until the mid-twentieth century did Princeton do much to acknowledge Calamity's beginnings in its environs. Almost reluctantly, local newspapers began to publish stories about Martha's first years and call attention to the Canary family's history in northern Missouri. Spurred on, Princeton began its Calamity Days in the 1960s, sponsoring, over time, parades, barbecues, rodeos, and a Miss Calamity Jane contest. Other events include an Old West "Calamity Jane Shoot Out Gang," a melodrama about Calamity, a car show, and a Bluegrass Jam Session.

The third weekend of each September has now become a Calamity Days Fall Festival. Revealingly, the celebration includes very little about Calamity herself, although in some years a special issue of a local newspaper has been published with bits of information about her.

As early as the late 1950s, Livingston, Montana, thinking of itself as one of Calamity's "homes" (and it was), tried to organize a Calamity Jane pageant to celebrate her life in the Livingston area. An ambitious graduate student at the University of Montana even wrote a three-act pageant as his master's thesis, hoping it would be used in Livingston. But town leaders were hesitant. How were they to lionize a

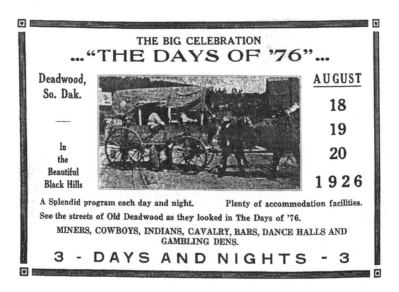

Days of '76.

Launched in 1924, Days of '76 remains an annual community celebration in Deadwood, South Dakota. Part tourist come-on and part romanticized history, the extravaganza features parades and competitions and celebrates Black Hills pioneers and such notorious former residents as Calamity Jane and Wild Bill Hickok. From the *Sunshine State* 7 (June 1926).

woman who was so often intoxicated and guilty of antisocial actions while there? Later, a watered-down approach won out. The town would sponsor a yearly Calamity Jane Rodeo and a Calamity Jane Look-A-Like Contest, but nothing much would be hinted about Calamity's controversial side.

Deadwood, South Dakota, proved the community most willing to celebrate Calamity, Hickok, and others of the '76 generation. With a keen eye and thirst for tourists, residents of Deadwood began to celebrate the Days of '76 as early as the 1920s, a celebration that continues today. When beginning the planning for the Days of '76 celebrations, conservatives warned against trotting out a "wild Deadwood" of saloons, fights, and bordellos. But those pushing for a lively Old West celebration gradually won out; tourists coming to the annual festivities seemed much more interested in a Wild than a Mild West. Calamity and Wild Bill, in rather ahistorical roles, proved to be central figures in the Deadwood community celebration. Calamity's drinking, possible prostitution, and other errant behaviors were pushed aside in the depiction of her as Wild Bill's pard. Tourists—and the Days of '76 as well—wanted Calamity front and center but not as a disreputable, foul-mouthed frontier wild woman. The lively events and content of the yearly celebration continue to draw hundreds, if not thousands, to Deadwood to embrace and applaud the Old West while they also participate in the gambling widespread in the celebrated town.

In another field, clothing entrepreneurs have also capitalized on Calamity's name for their wares, running the gamut from the leisurely informal to the stylish elite. Perhaps the most ubiquitous clothing items are Calamity Jane t-shirts and sweatshirts. Some are adorned only with Calamity's name or picture, but others shout out interpretations. One such line states "I figure if a girl hankers to be a legend, she ought to go ahead and be one," said to be a quote from her. Another says "If I punch your button . . . will you spank me?" Other stores feature Calamity jeans and denim shorts, tank tops, lingerie (including thongs and bikinis); but others offer Calamity wedding dresses and more formal wear. There are Calamity Jane clothing stores across the country, especially in or near such places as Alpine and Laramie, Wyoming, and Spokane, Washington. One of the most intriguing is the Calamity Jane Vintage line of clothing in Calgary, Canada, whose offerings include canvas trench coats, dresses, boots, lingerie, and wedding dresses. They cater to the "fashionistas" and emblazoned on their webpage is "Be What You Want to Be."

No less widespread are the restaurants carrying Calamity's name. Calamity Jane cafés are situated around the United States, from the Northeast to the Northwest, although, interestingly not many are located in Calamity's areas of South Dakota, Montana, and Wyoming. Calamity Jane's Hamburger Restaurant of Sandy, Oregon, features a rustic, informal atmosphere with an astounding variety of huge burgers. The Calamity Jane restaurant in the Georgetown area of south Seattle attempts to "celebrate the spirit of our namesake." Its webpage asserts that "Calamity Jane helped settle the Wild West and today we continue her tradition of rowdy women and straight shooting." The café will serve up "great grub," with no dishes proving to be calamities. In faraway Eagle's Nest in northern New Mexico, a Calamity Jane restaurant features New Mexico food in an 1890s hotel built from stolen railroad ties. Its offerings of green chile stew, burritos, and enchiladas would likely have struck Calamity as foreign. In Las Vegas, Calamity Jane's restaurant, in a hotel and gambling hall, certainly would have given Calamity an at-home feeling. Perhaps the most unusual of these institutions is the Calamity Jane Saloon in the Basque area of southern France. Its publicity indicates the establishment will "cultivate the meaning of the heroes of the American West." The walls of the restaurant feature a western décor and display several photographs of Old West personalities and scenes.

Many others have capitalized on Calamity's notoriety. One writer, Kathleen Bacus has adopted Calamity's name for her series of romantic suspense novels, titling them the Calamity Jayne Mysteries. Her heroine, a modern, rambunctious young woman, has nothing to do with the historical Calamity. Others use Calamity's name for racehorses and show dogs, names of pets, for artworks, and footwear. Athletes adopted her name too, and famed golfer Bobby Jones, naming his putter Calamity Jane, transformed the golf club into the world's best-known club. A webpage "Women in Sports," reprinting Calamity's autobiography, promised that in sports competitions "women will find the courage and daring to follow their goals." An advertisement for the Indiana University's Women's Ultimate Frisbee team was even more explicit and caught the varied implications of Calamity's divergent identities. "Give 'em Hell, Give 'em Fear!" one part rang out. Another section was more thoughtful: "Calamity Jane Ultimate is rooted in respect, teamwork, and love of the game. When you become a Jane, you not only join an athletic group of girls with a history of successes, but a sisterhood of women you can rely on whether you're on or off the field."

By the early twenty-first century, Calamity Jane's name had come to represent a hodgepodge of diverse meanings. Most of these signifiers were clearly separate from the nineteenth-century woman whose name they traveled. True, biographers, historians, and some filmmakers and novelists may have focused primarily on the well-known and notorious western female. But other entrepreneurs, cultists, and purveyors of popular culture had found a catchy brand that could capture buyers, attendees, and hangers-on. Much as dime novelist Edward L. Wheeler had in the nineteenth century, others of the late-twentieth and early twenty-first centuries discovered or rediscovered that the name Calamity Jane snapped up attention. Like the names of leading sports figures, political leaders, others of the past, and the newest sensation on the morning TV or evening news shows, Calamity's name grabbed buyers, curiosity-seekers, and tourists. She had become a powerful magnet of popular culture. That was not likely to change soon.

Conclusion

Pondering a Life and Legends

In early 1896, Calamity Jane launched herself on the road with the Kohl and Middleton touring group. On the trip she was touted as the original Wild West woman. At the same time, her newly published autobiography *Life and Adventures of Calamity Jane, By Herself* was chock-full of amazing feats she claimed to have accomplished as an amazon of the Old West. In the same months, M. L. Fox, a woman journalist, conducted a notable interview with Calamity that revealed her maternal instincts as a devoted mother and her desire to be an acceptable—and accepting—pioneer woman. Still others at the time praised Calamity for her kindness, generosity, and aid to the needy and poor.

These three divergent views of Calamity Jane had all emerged, evolved, and hardened before her death in 1903. The view that she was an unorthodox woman of the Wild West dominated comments about Calamity. If expanded, this interpretation pointed to Calamity's drinking, possible prostitution, and unacceptable social behavior. The second perspective argued that despite her aberrant actions, Calamity was an aspiring pioneer woman desiring a husband, wanting to care for her daughter Jessie, and wishing for a stable home. The third point of view, perhaps advanced as a balance to the first conclusion, repeatedly pointed to

Calamity's help with sick and down-and-out people as strong evidence of her being a kind-hearted woman.

Journalists, dime novelists, and other observers competed with one another in putting forth these competing interpretations. In the next century, so did biographers, novelists, filmmakers, and other interpreters. Male newspaper reporters, journalist H. N. Maguire, and dime novelist Edward L. Wheeler did most to solidify the image of Calamity Jane as a Wild West woman. Besides writer Fox, the novelist Mrs. William Loring Spencer and Dora Du Fran did most to portray Calamity as a person with clear womanly feelings. Other journalists and acquaintances were the main sources of accounts emphasizing Calamity as kindly and openhanded.

These three conclusions about Calamity traveled widely and continuously from her death into the early twenty-first century. They hardened into legends, with sometimes less and less evidence to sustain the conclusions but more and more accretion of emotion and subjectivity to carry them forward. Along the way, too, other elements were added, broadening the conclusions but frequently distorting them factually. For example, most of the moviemakers organized their films around Wild Bill Hickok–Calamity Jane stories; although not historically sound, they proved very appealing to audiences. *The Plainsman* (1936), *Calamity Jane* (1953), and *Calamity Jane* (1984) were luminous examples of the draw of Wild Bill–Calamity stories. Jean Hickok McCormick's startling claim in 1941 that she was the daughter of Hickok and Calamity obviously was based on her desire to be "somebody," but it also built on and advanced the Hickok-Calamity legends.

The legends of Calamity as a pioneer woman and a good, generous person fanned out less widely, but they too persisted. The Maguire and Newson accounts and the dime novels in the 1870s, alongside their depictions of Calamity as something of frontier hellcat, also saluted her efforts in helping needy people. Later, Dora Du Fran's memoir, Doris Day's romantic role in the musical *Calamity Jane*, Jean Hickok McCormick's spurious documents, and Noley Mumey and Glenn Clairmonte's biographies variously treated Calamity as an often-generous woman who desired motherhood and loved children.

Two other questions deserve consideration: what was it that transformed Martha Canary into the legendary Calamity Jane, and are the form and content of Calamity legends likely to change? First the transformative steps. By 1875, Martha Canary, newly dubbed Calamity Jane, emerged on the scene as a very unusual woman in Wyoming and South Dakota. Rather than a daughter, sister, and young wife and mother—the roles the times expected—she traveled about fearlessly without family or spouse. She smoked, chewed, drank, did men's work, and, if in a group, it was often with men, such as railroad workers and soldiers. Those unorthodox actions brought her out of the crowd and into the spotlight of attention for journalists and other writers. By 1875–76 they were outing her as a sensational woman/man of the frontier, particularly when she claimed also to be army scout, bullwhacker, and stagecoach driver. The images of Calamity, chiefly in the writings of male writers, appearing first in newspapers in the northern West, went national in 1876–77 and caught the attention of dime novelist Edward L. Wheeler.

Wheeler, like all dime novelists, needed a female figure for a heroine in his Deadwood Dick series. The very limited bits he had heard about the young Calamity Jane were a smooth fit for his popular fiction. He did not want a fainting female from the East but a lively, durable heroine from the frontier. Beginning with the handful of details he knew about Calamity, Wheeler greatly inflated her story into escapade after escapade of frenetic action. Once a nationally recognized dime novel heroine, Calamity never again was Martha Canary, the Missouri farmer's daughter. Journalists,

Conclusion

publicists for her Kohl and Middleton and Pan-American Exposition presentations in 1896 and 1901, and Calamity herself in the autobiography and peddled photographs continued and enlarged her already legendary reputation in the last years of her life. By her death in 1903, Calamity Jane was already a widely known and recognized legend of the American West.

The steady if stuttering steps by which Calamity became a frontier legendary figure paralleled those of others who traveled similar paths. The early unusual deeds of George Custer, Wild Bill Hickok, and Billy the Kid in male circles drew large, sustained attention to them. Whether as military leader and Indian fighter, as lawman and gunman, or outlaw and gunslinger, the triumvirate quickly gained newspaper headlines and were soon launched in dime novels and exaggerated biographical accounts. The quick turnaround in male dominions from extraordinary actions to frontier demigods was swift and certain—and similar to what happened to Martha Canary/Calamity Jane in 1875 to 1877.

Calamity's swift steps to legendary status also resembled those of another legendary western woman, Belle Starr (Myra Belle Shirley, 1848–89). Also born in Missouri, Starr was raised in Texas and as a young woman began associating with a series of male companions (mostly nonhusbands) who busied themselves with raiding and selling horses not theirs. Riding with them, Belle became known as the "Bandit Queen." After upsets with her first men, Belle organized her own raids and gangs of thieves. In and out of court and prison and still in her early forties, Belle was gunned down from behind by an unknown assailant.

Newspapers speedily headlined Starr's exploits as those of a sensational Wild Woman of the West. Following on the heels of the headlines were dime novels and popular biographies filling their pages with Belle as a Calamity-like figure. Before her death in 1889, she was already a legend. Belle's unusual actions as a woman, her involvements in dramatic events, and her quick appearance in journalistic and sensational stories made her, like Calamity Jane, a legend in her own time. Calamity's path to the pantheon of Old West legendary figures was remarkable similar to Belle's.

Will legends about Calamity change in the near future? Perhaps, but probably not. When the Jean Hickok McCormick story emerged with its path-breaking new ingredients in 1941, novelists, filmmakers, and not a few biographers incorporated that plot into their stories of Calamity. Conversely, even when the best studies of Wild Bill Hickok showed he had little or no contact with her and seemed to want to avoid her, popular culture faddists continued linking Hickok and Calamity in marriage and in the birth of a daughter, or at least in a torrid love affair.

In recent contacts with Deadwood, I have rediscovered the staying power of western legends. Publicity coming out in town-sponsored publications and events still retails Calamity images that the latest and strongest biographies have proven inaccurate. Incorrect information about her birth date, age, and name remain on her graveyard marker. Then, a trip to the tourist town added to my convictions about legends rarely changing. I stood near the graves of Calamity and Wild Bill in the Mount Moriah Cemetery. The revealing setting of a huge bronze statue of Wild Bill and only roundabout entrance to Calamity's grave (without sculpture) through or around Wild Bill's site suggests that Calamity has been sidelined in her popular competition with Hickok in Deadwood. A tour guide in the cemetery voiced the usual stereotypes. He asserted that Hickok had killed a hundred or more men and that Calamity was nothing but a hellcat of the wildest kind. Afterwards, I asked persons at two kiosks booking the tours what their guides were reading. None knew of Rosa's biography of Hickok or of McLaird's of Calamity. I realized again how strongly the Wild West legends, including those about Calamity, were fastened like leeches on the minds of many Americans and that many popularizers were not much interested in examining the most up-to-date, complete, dependable sources for their information.

Still, readers should be aware of missing information about Calamity. Future biographers have unanswered questions facing them. Perhaps thorough research will solve some of these conundrums. We know little of the Canary family, before the life of Grandpa James and during their journey from Virginia to Missouri in the first half of the nineteenth century. The lives of Calamity's sister Lena, brother Elijah, and daughter Jessie remain, for the most part, mysteries. So do the relatively "silent years" of Calamity's life from 1870 to 1875 and 1890 to 1895. We know little about her "husbands," such as George Cosgrove, Billy Steers, Clinton Burke, and Robert Dorsett. What do census, marriage, and death records tell us about them? Are there other jail or legal records for Calamity, since she so often brushed up against such institutions? These and other questions remain unanswered. Perhaps if they and other gaps are filled, we may get new perspectives on Calamity, but they are not likely to throw off kilter the major legends about her.

As we move well into the second century after Martha Canary exploded on the scene as Calamity Jane, one conclusion seems certain. She will not disappear. Whether as a Wild West female, an aspiring pioneer woman, or a kind and generous vagabond, Calamity will remain on the scene. Judging from recent treatments of her legends, she is likely to be traveled as the epitome of the independent woman finding her own way. Probably novelists and moviemakers will find new ways to configure her story, undoubtedly biographers and historians will continue placing her in the limelight of the frontier West, and the general public will remain fascinated with the legends of Calamity Jane, the lively, unorthodox woman of the Old West.

Essay on Sources

This study is based on a near-exhaustive examination of manuscript and published sources dealing with Martha Canary/Calamity Jane. Full citations for the collections, the books and essays, newspapers, novels and movies, and other materials appear in the accompanying bibliography. Here only the most pertinent sources receive comment; the bibliography lists many more items.

ARCHIVES AND LIBRARIES

The largest collections of manuscript materials are on file in several archives and libraries. These include, in Wyoming, the American Heritage Center in Laramie, the Wyoming State Archives in Cheyenne, and the Buffalo Bill Historical Center in Cody; in Montana, the Montana Historical Society in Helena; and in South Dakota, the Clarence S. Paine Papers at the Center for Western Studies at Augustana College in Sioux Falls, the South Dakota State Historical Society (particularly the Lloyd McFarling Collection) in Pierre, and the J. Leonard Jennewein Collection at the McGovern Library at Dakota Western University in Mitchell. Other important collections on Calamity Jane are at the public libraries and archives of Denver, Billings, Montana, Lander, Wyoming, Deadwood, South Dakota, and the library and county courthouse in Princeton, Missouri. Also important are the unpublished research guides William R. Whiteside prepared for the scholarly study of Calamity Jane. Copies of these lists are in the writer's collection.

REFERENCE WORKS

The pioneering bibliography for Old West subjects is Ramon F. Adams, *Six-Guns and Saddle Leather: A Bibliography of Books and Pamphlets on Western Outlaws and Gunmen*, rev. ed. (1969). Although Calamity was neither an outlaw nor a gunman, Adams annotates, with his essentialist conclusions, numerous books dealing with her. I have also made use of the handy bibliographical lists on the leading Old West figures in Kathleen Chamberlain, comp., *Wild Westerners: A Bibliography* (1998). The most extensive bibliographical listings on Calamity Jane are in James D. McLaird, *Calamity Jane: The Woman and the Legend* (2005). See the numerous references in his text and in the exhaustive bibliography, pp. 337–63. A less extensive but annotated listing of key Calamity sources appears in J. Leonard Jennewein, *Calamity Jane of the Western Trails* (1953), 40–47; and McLaird, *Wild Bill and Calamity Jane* (2008), 157–66.

GENERAL BOOKS AND ESSAYS

Every reader interested in Calamity Jane should begin with James D. McLaird's two books, *Calamity Jane: The Woman and the Legend* (2005), and *Wild Bill Hickok and Calamity Jane: Deadwood Legends* (2008). I have relied heavily on these two volumes, especially the first. No one should overlook his essays, particularly the path-breaking "Calamity Jane's Diary and Letters: Story of a Fraud" (1995). Still useful are the brief, no-nonsense views of J. Leonard Jennewein in his pamphlet *Calamity Jane of the Western Trails* (1953) and also the more extensive and analytical examination in Roberta Beed Sollid, *Calamity Jane: A Study in Historical Criticism* (1958). Librarian Clarence S. Paine's three essays, published as part of his biography-in-the-works (never completed), are still useful, even though he was too tied to the Jean Hickok McCormick story and his mistaken view of Calamity's alleged hermaphroditism. See his "She Laid Her Pistol Down; or, the Last Will and Testament of Calamity Jane" (1946), "Calamity Jane: Man? Woman? or Both?" (1947), and "Wild Bill Hickok and Calamity Jane" (1952). A brief overview of Calamity's life appears in Richard W. Etulain, "Calamity Jane: Independent Woman of the Wild West" (1997). Etulain's abbreviated treatments of Calamity's depictions in western history and literature include the afterword, to Sollid's book *Calamity Jane* (1995), *Telling Western Stories* (1999), and "Calamity Jane: The Making of a Frontier Legend" (2003).

Conversely, I have been cautious in my use of several other sources. Calamity's flawed autobiography, *Life and Adventures of Calamity Jane, By Herself* [1896], contains too many exaggerations and downright lies to be wholly embraced. Also readers should avoid using the falsified Calamity–Jean Hickok McCormick materials in *Calamity Jane's Letters to Her Daughter, Martha Jane Cannary Hickok* (1976) and in earlier form in Nolie Mumey, *Calamity Jane: 1852–1903* (1950)—except as examples of fraudulent stories about Calamity. Two other flawed biographies of Calamity must be used with caution because they too accept the Hickok McCormick story: Glenn Clairmonte, *Calamity Was the Name for Jane* (1959) and Stella Foote, *A History of Calamity Jane: America's First Liberated Woman* (1995).

BEGINNINGS TO 1875

A few sources are key for the scattered information on Martha Canary and her family up to 1875, when she became Calamity Jane. The U.S. censuses from 1820 to 1860 include information on Grandpa James and Grandma Sarah Canary and their children in Ohio from 1820 to 1850. Other census and marriage records in Iowa reveal backgrounds for Martha's mother, Charlotte Burge Canary, and her marriage to Robert Wilson (Willson) Canary in 1855. Still other records in the Princeton (Mercer County) Missouri archives, the census of 1860, and land and probate records furnish information on Martha, her parents, and her relatives in the late 1850s and early 1860s.

Published information on the Ohio and Missouri years dealing with the Canary family and Martha is skimpy. Later in the twentieth century, Princeton newspapers printed bits and pieces on Martha and her family, some of which came in retrospective stories. These stories were a mix of valuable information and a surprising number of errors, chiefly concerning Calamity's experiences farther west.

The first book to deal with Martha's early years (along with comment on her later life) was Duncan Aikman, *Calamity Jane and the Lady Wildcats* (1927). A muckraker of the first order interested in the unorthodox behavior of several Wild West women, journalist Aikman interviewed older residents in the Princeton area about their half-century and more memories of Martha and the Canary family. He also added, whole cloth, stories for which there was absolutely no evidence. Far too many later writers—and scholars—accepted his imagined yarns without examining them carefully.

Only two strong pieces of evidence deal with Martha's life after the Canarys left Missouri, probably in 1864, and before she came on scene as Calamity Jane in 1875. A brief story about the Canary family's tumble into trouble appeared in the *Montana Post* on the last day of 1864. Five years later, her name is listed in a special pre-territorial census of what became Wyoming, placing her in the railroad town of Piedmont. Calamity herself and sister Lena's family shoveled out other information about Martha's earliest years in Utah and Wyoming (ca. 1867 to 1875), but those fragments are so filled with error that they are of limited use to the historian or biographer. Other rumors, without strong support, place Martha in the early mining towns of Wyoming—for example, Miner's Delight and South Pass City—either before or after her brief stay in Piedmont.

Not much is known about Martha's life from 1870 to 1875. The wrong-headed stories from the Lena Canary Borner family provide helpful information on Lena and brother Elijah's lives but misfire badly on the Canary family origins and their first years in the West. Perhaps future diligent research in obscure sources will turn up more information on this "silent" period of Martha's life.

THE DEADWOOD YEARS (1875–1881)

If dependable sources on Martha's pre-1875 years remain skimpy, numerous important ones have appeared dealing with the next half-dozen or so years of her life. Contemporary and later studies helpfully fill sociocultural contexts for these very active years when Martha Canary became Calamity Jane and catapulted onto the national scene. In *The Black Hills Expedition of 1875* (1975), Lesta Turchen and James D. McLaird furnish valuable information on the Jenney and Newton party that brought Calamity to the Black Hills in 1875; and a recent good source for General George Crook, with whom Calamity traveled twice to the north in 1876, is Charles M. Robinson, *General Crook and the Western Frontier* (2001). Neither this source nor most others on the Crook expeditions are able to establish convincingly the exact role Calamity played in these trips north. Was she an actual scout, as she and some others claimed, a driver, or a camp follower? No one seems to know.

The best account of Calamity's first contact with Wild Bill Hickok and her first days in Deadwood is William B. Secrest, ed., *I Buried Hickok: The Memoirs of White Eye Anderson* (1980). Still the fullest treatment of Wild Bill, with some discussion of his relationship with Calamity, is Joseph G. Rosa, *They Called Him Wild Bill: The Life and Adventures of James Butler Hickok*, rev ed. (1974). The strongest but not entirely convincing assertion that Calamity became a prostitute in these years is in L. G. (Pat) Flannery, *John Hunton's Diary*, 6 vols. (1956–70).

By 1875–76 journalists from the Black Hills, and national correspondents as well, were featuring the strange new woman, Calamity Jane, in their stories. Newspapermen became the major source of information on Calamity from this time forward to the end of her life. But the most useful account of the years after 1875 is in McLaird, *Calamity Jane* (2005).

Horatio N. Maguire's *The Black Hills and American Wonderland* (1877) and his *The Coming Empire* (1878) and journalist Thomas McLean Newson's published play *Drama of Life in the Black Hills* (1878) were the first books to deal with Calamity in Deadwood. Later, two memoirs by Deadwood pioneers added biographical information, as well as very extensive portraits of the cultural contexts surrounding her. For that, see John S. McClintock, *Pioneer Days in the Black Hills* (1939) and Richard B. Hughes, *Pioneer Years in the Black Hills* (1957). The most helpful of the later scholarly studies of the Black Hills and Deadwood are the two books by Watson Parker, *Gold in the Black Hills* (1966) and *Deadwood: The Golden Years* (1981).

More than any other source, the Deadwood Dick dime novel series of Edward L. Wheeler brought Calamity to the attention of the nation's readers of popular fiction. Extensive information on Wheeler and dime novels in general, as well as on his Deadwood Dick series, is included in Albert Johannsen, *The House of Beadle and Adams and Its Dime and Nickel Novels* (1950). For other discussions on dime novels and Calamity's role as a dime novel heroine, see Daryl Jones, *The Dime Novel Western* (1978), Henry Nash Smith, *Virgin Land: The American West as Symbol and Myth* (1950), and Bill Brown, ed., *Reading the West: An Anthology of Dime Westerns* (1997).

WANDERING THROUGH WYOMING AND MONTANA

The best sources on Calamity's scurrying about in Wyoming and Montana, and South Dakota as well, are the stories in regional newspapers. Many of these stories are available on microfilm or in digital format in the library and archival sources mentioned above; and the clipping files at the Montana Historical Society, the American Heritage Center, and the South Dakota State Historical Society (in the McFarling Collection) are especially full. Some of the pertinent newspaper stories are reprinted in Nolie Mumey, *Calamity Jane*, and extensively cited in the books and essays of James D. McLaird.

Among the later memoirs with information on Calamity is Dr. Will Frackelton, *Sagebrush Dentist* (1941). Pamphlet-sized accounts by local historians also add fragments of useful information. In this regard, consult Irma Klock, *Here Comes Calamity Jane* (1979), Bill and Doris Whithorn, *Calamity's in Town: The Town was Livingston, Montana* (n.d.), and Ellen Crago Mueller, *Calamity Jane* (1981).

CALAMITY AS WIFE AND MOTHER

Calamity spoke early and often about her "husbands" to journalists, but not much hard information is available on these men. Fortunately, William R. Whiteside of Cottage Hills, Illinois, retired professor and indefatigable researcher, has turned up valuable information in census, marriage, and death records for most of Calamity's so-called husbands: George Cosgrove, Bill Steers, Clinton Burke, and Robert Dorsett. These invaluable guides are listed in the bibliography under "Manuscripts." Roberta Beed Sollid includes information she gained in interviews with elderly men who knew some of the "husbands," in her *Calamity Jane*. Calamity's legal marriage to Steers is confirmed in a Certificate of Marriage, County of Bingham, Territory of Idaho, 30 May 1888, copy in Fremont County Pioneer Museum, Lander, Wyoming.

M. L. Fox's crucially important interview, "Calamity Jane," published in *Illustrated American*, 7 March 1896, p. 312, contains valuable insights on Calamity's desires for motherhood and family stability. For a fictional source portraying Calamity's womanly feelings, see the novel by Mrs. William Loring Spencer, *Calamity Jane: A Story of the Black Hills* (1887). In her autobiography, Calamity herself speaks of marrying Burke, not Steers, and says he was the father of her daughter, Jessie, born in 1887. But she was with Steers at that time and did not meet Burke until later.

In the 1930s and 1940s, Calamity's daughter, Jessie Elizabeth Oakes Murray, identifying herself as Calamity's granddaughter or niece, wrote several letters to newspapers and archives in the northern West soliciting information about persons she thought to be her parents. Some of those letters are on file in the South Dakota State Historical Society. In addition to the sources mentioned above dealing with Jessie Hickok McCormick, see the files on her at Fort Collins Pioneer Museum in Fort Collins, Colorado, and in the Paine Collection at Augustana College in Sioux Falls, South Dakota. The best abbreviated treatment of Lena Canary Borner is Jean A. Mathisen, "Calamity's Sister" (1996). I am also indebted to Jan Cerney, who is researching Elijah Canary, for additional information on him.

CALAMITY AS PERFORMER

Information on Calamity as a performer in the Hardwick, Kohl and Middleton, and Pan-American Exposition is primarily from newspapers. Journalists in Montana and South Dakota were the chief sources on all three adventures, but other stories appeared in Minneapolis, Chicago, and Buffalo, New York, papers. I have learned about dime museums in Andrea Stulman Dennett, *Weird and Wonderful: The Dime Museum in America* (1997) and the Pan-American Exposition in http://panam1901.org. Not much is known, however, about Josephine Winifred Brake, the New York journalist and author who invited Calamity east to take part in the exposition. Frederick Cummins and his Indian Congress are discussed in Richmond C. Hill, *A Great White Chief* (1912).

FINAL YEARS

Several writers provide fragmentary accounts of Calamity in the last years of her life, from her return to Deadwood in 1895 until her death in 1903. Estelline Bennett furnishes positive snapshots of her youthful reactions to Calamity, published more than thirty years later in *Old Deadwood Days* (1928). The remembrances of Mrs. Osborne Pemberton about attending school with Calamity's daughter in 1895 are an important source for understanding the difficulties both mother and daughter faced in this period; they are in the Jennewein Collection at Dakota Western University and the Oral History Program at the University of South Dakota, Vermillion. Lewis R. Freeman's account of his bizarre meeting with Calamity in May 1901 was first printed in *Sunset Magazine* in July 1922 and then in his book *Down the Yellowstone* (1922).

Events in the final year of Calamity's life are expertly summarized in James D. McLaird, "Calamity Jane: The Life and the Legend" (1994). Bordello madam Dora Du Fran (under the pseudonym D. Dee) adds her unique perspective on Calamity's last days in her memoir published thirty years afterwards, *Low Down on Calamity Jane* (1934).

CALAMITY JANE IN HISTORY AND LEGEND

All of the major novels, movies, and biographies so important for illustrating the making and remaking of Calamity's legends are listed in the text and in the bibliography. But a few studies that have shaped how I have treated the making of such legends should be mentioned.

For more than a half century, my thinking and writing have been influenced by Henry Nash Smith's classic work *Virgin Land: The American West as Symbol and Myth* (1950). More recent works in a similar mold are Kent Ladd Steckmesser, *The Western Hero in History and Legend* (1965) and William H. Goetzmann and William N. Goetzmann, *The West of the Imagination* (1986). Two of my own books inform what is said here: Richard W. Etulain, *Re-imagining the Modern American West: A Century of Fiction, History, and Art* (1996) and *Telling Western Stories: From Buffalo Bill to Larry McMurtry* (1999).

For information on J. T. Edson and the sex-and-violence Westerns, I have relied on the discussions in Geoff Sadler, ed., *Twentieth-Century Western Writers*, 2d ed. (1991). Still a valuable source on Western films is Edward Buscombe, ed., *The BFI Companion to the Western* (1988). Several books have been compiled on the HBO production of *Deadwood* (2004–2006), but I have relied primarily on the recorded interviews with David Milch, Robin Weigert, and others included with the CD versions of the thirty-six segments.

For a companion volume examining the legendary accounts of Wild Bill Hickok, including stories about Hickok and Calamity, see Joseph A. Rosa, *Wild Bill Hickok: The Man and His Myth* (1996).

Finally, not to be overlooked is James D. McLaird's thorough coverage in his two books of the legends that grew up and clustered around Calamity, *Calamity Jane* (2005) and *Wild Bill Hickok and Calamity Jane* (2008). I have drawn much from these two volumes.

Bibliography

MANUSCRIPTS

American Heritage Center. University of Wyoming, Laramie, Wyoming.
Buffalo Bill Historical Center, Cody, Wyoming.
Center for Western Studies. Augustana College, Sioux Falls, South Dakota, Clarence S. Paine Collection.
George McGovern Library. Dakota Wesleyan University, Mitchell, South Dakota, J. Leonard Jennewein Collection.
Harold B. Lee Library. Brigham Young University Library, Provo, Utah.
Homestake Adams Research and Cultural Center, Deadwood, South Dakota.
Mercer County Court House, Princeton, Missouri. Land and probate records, Circuit Court files.
Montana Historical Society, Helena, Montana. Vertical files.
South Dakota State Historical Society, Pierre, South Dakota. Lloyd McFarling Collection.
Whiteside, William R. Working Papers. These research compilations list research sources—newspapers, census, biographical-historical, manuscript, and others—available for the topics indicated. They are superb finding guides for all researchers. "Family of James Canary of Virginia," 14 July 1997; "Canary Families in Iowa," 7, 15 August 1998; "1875," 5 September 1998; "Family of Elijah Canary," 5 September 1998; "Hardwick's Great Rocky Mountain Show: Chicago," 2 October 1998;"Calamity Jane and General Crook, 17 December 1998; "The

Bibliography

Trip West," 1998; "Cosgrove," 13 November 1999; "Canary Marriages: Idaho," November 1999 to January 2000; "Could Calamity Jane read and/or write?" 1 January 2000; "Thomas McLean Newson Newspaper Articles: Deadwood, SD," 26 June 2000; "Madam Bull Dog," 24, 26 June 2000; "The Unknown (Smith) Bloxsom," 30 June 2000; "Calamity Jane in the Coeur d'Alenes," 12 July 2000; "Calamity Jane Tobacco Spitting Incident: Two Versions," rev. 16 August 2000; "Robert Dorsett," 2001, rev., 16 May 2013. Copies in author's files.

Wyoming State Archives and Research Division, Cheyenne, Wyoming.

LIBRARY COLLECTIONS

Deadwood Public Library, Deadwood, South Dakota.
Denver Public Library, Denver, Colorado.
Parmalee Public Library, Billings, Montana.
Princeton Public Library, Princeton, Missouri.

BOOKS: BIOGRAPHIES AND HISTORIES

Abbott, E. C. (Teddy Blue) and Helena Huntington Smith. *We Pointed Them North: Recollections of a Cowpuncher.* 1939. Reprint, Norman: University of Oklahoma Press, 1955.

Adams, Ramon F. *Six-Guns and Saddle Leather: A Bibliography of Books and Pamphlets on Western Outlaws and Gunmen.* Rev. ed. Norman: University of Oklahoma Press, 1969.

Aikman, Duncan. *Calamity Jane and the Lady Wildcats.* New York: Henry Holt, 1927.

Annin, Jim. *They Gazed on the Beartooths.* Vol. 2. Billings, MT: Reporter Printing, 1964.

Bankson, Russell A. *The Klondike Nugget.* Caldwell, ID: Caxton Printers, 1935.

Bennett, Estelline. *Old Deadwood Days.* 1928. Reprint, Lincoln: University of Nebraska Press, 1982.

Bourke, John. *On the Border with Crook.* New York: Charles Scribner's Sons, 1891.

Briggs, Harold E. *Frontiers of the Northwest: A History of the Upper Missouri Valley.* 1940. Reprint, New York: Peter Smith, 1953.

Brininstool, E. A. *Fighting Red Cloud's Warriors: True Tales of Indian Days When the West Was Young.* 1926. Reprint, New York: Cooper Square Publishers, 1975.

Bibliography

Brown, Jesse, and A. M. Willard. *The Black Hills Trails: A History of the Struggles of the Pioneers in the Winning of the Black Hills.* Edited by John T. Milek. Rapid City, SD: Rapid City Journal Company, 1924.

Brown, Mark H. *The Plainsmen of the Yellowstone: A History of the Yellowstone Basin.* New York: G. P. Putnam's Sons, 1961.

Brown, Mark H., and W. R. Felton. *Before Barbed Wire: L. A. Huffman, Photographer on Horseback.* New York: Henry Holt, 1956.

Buscombe, Edward, ed. *The BFI Companion to the Western.* New York: Atheneum, 1988.

Calamity Jane's Letters to Her Daughter, Martha Jane Cannary Hickok. Lorenzo, CA: Shameless Hussy Press, 1976.

Casey, Robert J. *The Black Hills and Their Incredible Characters.* Indianapolis: Bobbs-Merrill, 1949.

Chamberlain, Kathleen, comp. *Wild Westerners: A Bibliography.* Albuquerque: Center for the American West, University of New Mexico, 1998.

Circus Memoirs: Reminiscences of George Middleton. Los Angeles: G. Rice and Sons, 1913. Reprint, Chicago Historical Society, 2006.

Clairmonte, Glenn. *Calamity Was the Name for Jane.* Denver: Sage Books, 1959.

Cloud, Barbara. *The Business of Newspapers on the Western Frontier.* Reno: University of Nevada Press, 1992.

Connelley, William Elsey. *Wild Bill and His Era: The Life and Adventures of James Butler Hickok.* New York: Press of the Pioneers, 1933.

Copies of Calamity Jane's Diary and Letters. N. p.: Don C. and Stella A. Foote, 1951.

DeBarthe, Joe, ed. *The Life and Adventures of Frank Grouard.* St. Joseph, MO: Combe Printing Company, 1894.

Dee, D. [Dora Du Fran]. *Low Down on Calamity Jane.* Rapid City, SD: n.p., 1932.

Dennett, Andrea Stulman. *Weird and Wonderful: The Dime Museum in America.* New York: New York University Press, 1997.

Dolph, Jerry, and Arthur Randall. *Wyatt Earp and Coeur d'Alene Gold! Stampede to Idaho Territory.* 2d ed. Post Falls, ID: Eagle City Publications, 2000.

Drago, Harry Sinclair. *Notorious Ladies of the Frontier.* New York: Dodd, Mead, 1969.

1860 Federal Census for Mercer County, Missouri. Chillicothe, MO: E. Ellsberry, 1900(?); reprint, 1980.

Eisele, Wilbert E. *The Real Wild Bill Hickok: Famous Scout and Knight Chivalric of the Plains.* Denver: William H. Andre, 1931.

Bibliography

Etulain, Richard W. *Beyond the Missouri: The Story of the American West*. Albuquerque: University of New Mexico Press, 2006.

———. *Re-imagining the Modern American West: A Century of Fiction, History, and Art*. Tucson: University of Arizona Press, 1996.

———. *Telling Western Stories: From Buffalo Bill to Larry McMurtry*. Albuquerque: University of New Mexico Press, 1999.

Faber, Doris. *Calamity Jane: Her Life and Her Legend*. Boston: Houghton Mifflin, 1992.

Fisher, Vardis, and Opal Laurel Holmes. "Camp Angels." *Gold Rushes and Mining Camps of the Early American West*. Caldwell, ID: Caxton Printers, 1968.

Flannery, L. G. (Pat), ed. *John Hunton's Diary*. 6 vols. Lingle, WY: Guide-Review, 1956–70.

Foote, Stella. *A History of Calamity Jane: Our Country's First Liberated Woman*. New York: Vantage Press, 1995.

Frackelton, Dr. Will. *Sagebrush Dentist*. Edited by Herman Gastrell Selly. Chicago: A. C. McClurg, 1941.

Freeman, Lewis R. *Down the Yellowstone*. New York: Dodd, Mead, 1922.

Furlong, Leslie Anne. "Gold-Dust and Buckskins: An Analysis of Calamity Jane as a Symbol of Luck and Womanhood in the Black Hills." PhD diss., University of Virginia, 1991.

Gilfillan, Archer B. *A Goat's Eye View of the Black Hills*. Rapid City, SD: Dean and Dean, 1953.

Greenwood, Grace, ed. "Diary of D. M. Holmes." In *Collections of the State Historical Society of North Dakota*. Vol. 5. Edited by O. G. Libby. Grand Forks: [State Historical Society of North Dakota], 1923, 23–84.

Haines, Aubrey L. *The Yellowstone Story: The History of Our First National Park*. Yellowstone Park, WY: Yellowstone Library and Museum Association, 1977.

Hill, Richmond C. *A Great White Indian Chief: Thrilling and Romantic Story of the Career, Extraordinary Experiences Hunting, Scouting and Indian Adventures of Col. Fred Cummins*. N.p.: Col. Fred T. Cummins, 1912.

History of Harrison and Mercer Counties, Missouri: From the Earliest Times to the Present. St. Louis: Goodspeed Pub. Co., 1888; 2d ed., Princeton, MO: Mercer County Historical Society, 1972.

History of Mercer County, Missouri. Rev. ed. N.p.: n.p., 1911.

Holbrook, Stewart H. *Little Annie Oakley and Other Rugged People*. New York: Macmillan, 1948.

Holmes, Burton. *Burton Holmes Travelogues, with Illustrations from Photographs By the Author*. Vol. 6. New York: McClure Co., 1901.

Bibliography

Homsher, Lola M., ed. *South Pass, 1868: James Chisholm's Journal of the Wyoming Gold Rush.* Lincoln: Nebraska State Historical Society, 1960.

Horan, James D. *Desperate Women.* New York: G. P. Putnam's Sons, 1952.

Hughes, Richard B. *Pioneer Years in the Black Hills.* Edited by Agnes Wright Spring. Glendale, CA: Arthur H. Clark Co., 1957.

Hutchens, John K. *One Man's Montana: An Informal Portrait of a State.* Philadelphia: J. B. Lippincott, 1964.

Jennewein, J. Leonard. *Calamity Jane of the Western Trails.* Huron, SD: Dakota Books, 1953.

Johannsen, Albert. *The House of Beadle and Adams and Its Dime and Nickel Novels: The Story of a Vanished Literature.* Norman: University of Oklahoma Press, 1950.

Jones, Daryl. *The Dime Novel Western.* Bowling Green, OH: Popular Press, 1978.

Jucovy, Linda. *Searching for Calamity: The Life and Times of Calamity Jane.* Philadelphia: Stampede Books, 2012.

Kime, Wayne R., ed. *The Black Hills Journals of Colonel Richard Irving Dodge.* Norman: University of Oklahoma Press, 1996.

Klock, Irma H. *Here Comes Calamity Jane.* Deadwood, SD: Dakota Graphics, 1979.

Kuykendall, Judge W. L. *Pioneer Days: A True Narrative of Striking Events on the Western Frontier.* N.p.: J. M. and H. L. Kuykendall, Publishers, 1917.

Lackman, Ron. *Women of the Western Frontier in Fact, Fiction and Film.* Jefferson, NC: McFarland, 1997.

Lamar, Howard Roberts, ed. *The New Encyclopedia of the American West.* 1977; New Haven, CT: Yale University Press, 1998.

Life and Adventures of Calamity Jane, By Herself. N.p.: [1896]. Reprint, Fairfield, WA: Ye Galleon Press, n.d.

Linn, Joe Dale. *Linn's 1976 History of Mercer County, Missouri: Illustrated and Including a Family Index.* [Marceline, MO]: Walsworth, 1976.

Maguire, H. N. *The Black Hills and American Wonderland.* Chicago: Donnelley, Lloyd and Company, 1877.

————. *The Coming Empire: A Complete and Reliable Treatise on the Black Hills, Yellowstone and Big Horn Region.* Sioux City, IA: Watkins and Snead, 1878.

Malone, Michael P., et al. *Montana: A History of Two Centuries.* Rev ed. Seattle: University of Washington Press, 1991.

McClintock, John S. *Pioneer Days in the Black Hills: Accurate History and Facts Related by One of the Early Day Pioneers.* Edited by Edward I. Senn. Deadwood, SD: privately printed, 1939.

Bibliography

McGillycuddy, Julia B. *McGillycuddy, Agent: A Biography of Dr. Valentine T. McGillycuddy.* Stanford, CA: Stanford University Press, 1941.

McLaird, James D. *Calamity Jane: A Life and Legend.* Norman: University of Oklahoma Press, 2005.

———. *Wild Bill Hickok and Calamity Jane: Deadwood Legends.* Pierre: South Dakota State Historical Society Press, 2008.

Mercer County Pioneer Traces. Vol 1. Princeton, MO: Mercer County Genealogical Society, 1997.

Miller, Darlis. *Captain Jack Crawford: Buckskin Poet, Scout, and Showman.* Albuquerque: University of New Mexico Press, 1993.

Mills, Anson. *My Story.* Edited by C. H. Claudy. Washington, DC: Byron S. Adams, 1918.

Milner, Joe E., and Earle R. Forrest. *California Joe, Noted Scout and Indian Fighter.* Caldwell, ID: Caxton Printers, 1935.

Montana: A State Guide Book. New York: Duell, Sloan and Pearce, 1941.

Moulton, Candy. *Valentine T. McGillycuddy: Army Surgeon, Agent to the Sioux.* Norman, OK: Arthur H. Clark, 2011.

Mueller, Ellen Crago. *Calamity Jane.* Laramie, WY: Jelm Mt. Press, 1981.

Mumey, Nolie. *Calamity Jane, 1852–1903: A History of Her Life and Adventures in the West.* Denver: Range Press, 1950.

Nelson, Bruce. *Land of the Dacotahs.* Minneapolis: University of Minnesota Press, 1946.

Newson, Thomas McLean. *Drama of Life in the Black Hills.* Saint Paul, MN: Dodge and Larpenteur, 1878.

O'Connor, Richard. *Wild Bill Hickok.* Garden City, NY: Doubleday, 1959.

Parker, Watson. *Deadwood: The Golden Years.* Lincoln: University of Nebraska Press, 1981.

———. *Gold in the Black Hills.* Norman: University of Oklahoma Press, 1966.

Rezatto, Helen Graham. *Tales of the Black Hills.* Aberdeen, SD: North Plains Press, 1983.

Robinson, Charles M., III. *George Crook and the Western Frontier.* Norman: University of Oklahoma Press, 2001.

Rogers, Cameron. *Gallant Ladies.* New York: Harcourt, Brace and Co., 1928.

Rogers, W. B. *Rogers' Souvenir History of Mercer County, Missouri and Dictionary of Local Dates.* Trenton, MO: privately printed, 1911; Princeton, MO: Joe D. and Mary Casteel Linn, 1980.

Rosa, Joseph G. *They Called Him Wild Bill: The Life and Adventures of James Butler Hickok.* Rev. ed. Norman: University of Oklahoma Press, 1974.

Bibliography

———. *Wild Bill Hickok: The Man and His Myth.* Lawrence: University Press of Kansas, 1996.

Ross, Nancy Wilson. *Westward the Women.* New York: Alfred A. Knopf, 1944.

Secrest, William B., ed. *I Buried Hickok: The Memoirs of White Eye Anderson.* College Station, TX: Creative, 1980.

Senn, Edward L. *Deadwood Dick and Calamity Jane: A Thorough Sifting of the Facts from Fiction.* Deadwood, SD: privately printed, 1939.

Shadley, Ruth. *Calamity Jane's Daughter: The Story of Maude Weir, A Story Never Before Told.* Caldwell, ID: Caxton Printers, 1996.

Shifting Scenes: A History of Carter County, Montana. Ekalaka, MT: Carter County Geological Society, 1978.

Smith, Henry Nash. *Virgin Land: The American West as Symbol and Myth.* Cambridge, MA: Harvard University Press, 1950.

Sollid, Roberta Beed. "Calamity Jane: A Study in Historical Criticism." Master's thesis, Montana State University, Missoula, 1951.

———. *Calamity Jane: A Study in Historical Criticism.* [Helena]: Historical Society of Montana, 1958. Reprinted, with a new foreword by James D. McLaird and new afterword by Richard W. Etulain, Montana Historical Society, 1995.

Spring, Agnes Wright. *The Cheyenne and Black Hills Stage and Express Routes.* Glendale, CA: Arthur H. Clark Co., 1949.

Steckmesser, Kent Ladd. *The Western Hero in History and Legend.* Norman: University of Oklahoma Press, 1965.

Stevenson, Elizabeth. *Figures in a Western Landscape: Men and Women of the Northern Rockies.* Baltimore, MD: Johns Hopkins University Press, 1994.

Thane, Eric. *High Border Country.* New York: Duell, Sloan and Pearce, 1942.

Tippets, Susan Thomas, comp. *Piedmont Ghost Town: Uinta County, Wyoming.* N.p.: 1995.

Trexler, H. A. *Missouri-Montana Highways.* Columbia: State Historical Society of Missouri, 1918.

Turchen, Lesta V., and James D. McLaird. *The Black Hills Expedition of 1875.* Mitchell, SD: Dakota Wesleyan University Press, 1975.

Watkins, John McLain. "Calamity Jane: A Pageant-Drama in Three Acts." Master's thesis, Montana State University, Missoula, 1961.

Whithorn, Bill, and Doris Whithorn. *Calamity's in Town: The Town Was Livingston, Montana.* [Livingston, MT]: [Enterprise], n.d.

Wilstach, Frank J. *Wild Bill Hickok: The Prince of Pistoleers.* Garden City, NY: Garden City Publishing Co., 1926.

Bibliography

Winters, N. A. *A Brief History of Mercer County, Missouri, Its Wealth, Resources, etc.: Together with Biographical Sketches of Many of Its Leading Citizens.* Princeton, MO: Princeton "Press" and "Telegraph" Offices, 1883; Reprint, Princeton, MO: J. D. and M. C. Linn, 1980.

Wolle, Muriel Sibell. *Montana Pay Dirt. A Guide to the Mining Camps of the Treasure State.* Denver: Sage Books, 1963.

Young, Harry (Sam). *Hard Knocks: A Life Story of the Vanishing West.* Portland, OR: Wells and Co., 1915. Reprint, with a new introduction by James D. McLaird, Pierre: South Dakota State Historical Society Press, 2005.

NOVELS

Brooks, Bill. *Deadwood.* New York: Pinnacle Books, 1997.

Cain, Jackson. *Hellbreak Country.* New York: Warner Books, 1984.

Cole, Judd. *Wild Bill: Dead Man's Hand.* New York: Leisure Books, 1999.

———. *Wild Bill: Santa Fe Death Trap.* New York: Leisure Books, 2000.

Dexter, Pete. *Deadwood.* New York: Random House, 1986.

Dixon, Dorothy. *Yellowstone Jewel: Leather and Lace #9.* New York: Zebra Books, 1983.

Edson, J. T. *Trouble Trail.* London: Brown Watson, 1965.

———. *Troubled Range.* 1965. Reprint, New York: Dell Publishing, 1969.

———. *The Wildcats.* London: Brown Watson, 1965.

———. *The Cow Thieves.* London: Brown Watson, 1965.

———. *The Bull Whip Breed.* London: Brown Watson, 1965.

———. *The Big Hunt.* London: Brown Watson, 1967.

———. *Guns in the Night.* London: Corgi Books, 1968.

———. *The Bad Bunch.* London: Corgi Books, 1968.

———. *Calamity Spells Trouble.* London: Corgi Books, 1968.

———. *The Fortune Hunters.* London: Corgi Books, 1969.

———. *The Small Texan.* London: Corgi Books, 1969.

———. *Cold Deck, Hot Lead.* London: Corgi Books, 1969.

———. *White Stallion, Red Mare.* London: Corgi Books, 1970.

———. *J. T.'s Hundredth.* London: Corgi Books, 1979.

———. *The Whip and the War Lance.* London: Corgi Books, 1979.

———. *Texas Trio.* London: Corgi Books, 1980.

———. *Calamity, Mark and Belle.* London: Corgi Books, 1980.

———. *J. T's Ladies.* London: Corgi Books, 1980.

Bibliography

———. *Cut One, They All Bleed*. London: Corgi Books, 1983.

Evans, Tabor. *Longarm in Deadwood*. New York: Jove Books, 1982.

Fontes, Ron, and Justine Korman. *Calamity Jane at Fort Sanders: A Historical Novel*. New York: Disney Press, 1992.

Hueston, Ethel. *Calamity Jane of Deadwood Gulch*. Indianapolis: Bobbs-Merrill Co, 1937.

Ihle, Sharon. *Wildcat*. New York: HarperPaperbacks, 1993.

Ingraham, Prentiss. *Buffalo Bill and Calamity Jane, or, A Real Lady from the Black Hills*. New Buffalo Bill Weekly, No. 177. New York: Street and Smith, 1916.

Logan, Jake. *Dead Man's Hand*. New York: Playboy Press Paperbacks, 1979.

McMurtry, Larry. *Buffalo Girls*. New York: Simon and Schuster, 1990.

Mitchum, Hank [D. B. Newton]. *Stagecoach Station 11: Deadwood*. New York: Bantam Books, 1984.

Reckless Ralph. "Calamity Jane: Queen of the Plains." Street and Smith's *New York Weekly* 37 (January 16–March 13, 1882). Reprinted in *The Queen of the Plains*. Log Cabin Library, No. 130. New York: Street and Smith, 1891.

Roberts, J. R. *The Gunsmith 146: Return to Deadwood*. New York: Jove Books, 1994.

Spencer, Mrs. William Loring. *Calamity Jane: A Story of the Black Hills*. 1887. Reprint, Mitchell, SD: Dakota Wesleyan University Press, 1978.

Wheeler, Richard. *Cashbox*. New York: Forge, 1994.

DIME NOVELS: DEADWOOD DICK SERIES

The thirty-three volumes in this series were published by Beadle and Adams and are also listed in Albert Johannsen, *The House of Beadle and Adams and Its Dime and Nickel Novels: The Story of a Vanished Literature*. This source includes additional information on the series and its author, Edward L. Wheeler.

Deadwood Dick, The Prince of the Road; or, The Black Rider of the Black Hills. 15 October 1877.

The Double Daggers; or, Deadwood Dick's Defiance. A Tale of Regulators and Road-Agents of the Black Hills. 21 December 1877.

Buffalo Ben, The Prince of the Pistol; or, Deadwood Dick in Disguise. 5 February 1878.

Wild Ivan, The Boy Claude Duval: or, The Brotherhood of Death. 26 March 1878.

The Phantom Miner; or, Deadwood Dick's Bonanza. A Tale of the Great Silverland of Idaho. 14 May 1878.

Bibliography

Omaha Olli, The Masked Terror; or, Deadwood Dick in Danger. 2 July 1878.

Deadwood Dick's Eagles; or, The Pards of Flood Bar. 27 August 1878.

Deadwood Dick on Deck; or, Calamity Jane, The Heroine of Whoop-Up. 17 December 1878.

Corduroy Charlie, The Boy Bravo; or, Deadwood Dick's Last Act. 14 January 1879.

Deadwood Dick in Leadville; or, A Strange Stroke for Liberty. A Wild, Exciting Story of the Leadville Region. 24 June 1879.

Deadwood Dick's Device; or, The Sign of the Double Cross. A Wild, Strange Story of the Leadville Mines. 22 July 1879.

Deadwood Dick as Detective. A Story of the Great Carbonate Region. 26 August 1879.

Deadwood Dick's Double; or, The Ghost of Gordon's Gulch. A Tale of Wild-Cat City. 13 January 1880.

Blonde Bill; or, Deadwood Dick's Home Base. A Romance of the "Silent Tongues." 16 March 1880.

A Game of Gold; or, Deadwood Dick's Big Strike. 1 June 1880.

Deadwood Dick of Deadwood; or, The Picked Party. A Romance of Skeleton Bend. 20 July 1880.

Deadwood Dick's Dream; or, The Rivals of the Road. A Mining Tale of Tombstone. 19 April 1881.

The Black Hills Jezebel; or, Deadwood Dick's Ward. 31 May 1881. Reprinted as *Deadwood Dick's Ward; or, The Black Hills Jezebel.* 30 March 1887.

Deadwood Dick's Doom; or, Calamity Jane's Last Adventure. A Tale of Death Notch. 28 June 1881.

Captain Crack-Shot, The Girl Brigand; or, Gypsy Jack From Jimtown. A Story of Durango. 20 September 1881. Reprinted as *The Jimtown Sport; or, Gypsy Jack in Colorado.* 1 February 1888.

Sugar-Coated Sam; or, The Black Gowns of Grim Gulch. A Deadwood Dick Episode. 18 October 1881. Reprinted as *The Miner Sport; or, Sugar-Coated Sam's Claim.* 14 March 1888.

Gold-Dust Dick. A Romance of Roughs and Toughs. 3 January 1882. Reprinted as *Deadwood Dick Trapped; or, Roxey Ralph's Ruse.* 24 April 1899.

Deadwood Dick's Divide; or, The Spirit of Swamp Lake. 8 August 1882. Reprinted as *Deadwood Dick's Disguise; or, Wild Walt, the Sport.* 17 July 1889.

Deadwood Dick's Death Trail; or, From Ocean to Ocean. 12 September 1882. Reprinted as *Deadwood Dick's Mission; or, Cavie, the Kidnapped Boy.* 9 October 1889.

Bibliography

Deadwood Dick's Big Deal; or, The Gold Brick of Oregon. 26 June 1883.

Deadwood Dick's Dozen; or, The Fakir of Phantom Flats. 18 September 1883.

Deadwood Dick's Ducats; or Rainy Days in the Diggings. 18 March 1884.

Deadwood Dick Sentenced; or, The Terrible Vendetta. A Nevada Tale. 15 April 1884.

Deadwood Dick's Claim; or, The Fairy Face of Faro Flats. 1 July 1884.

Deadwood Dick in Dead City. 28 April 1885.

Deadwood Dick's Diamonds; or, The Mystery of Joan Porter. 2 June 1885.

Deadwood Dick in New York; or, "A Cute Case." A Romance of To-Day. 18 August 1885.

Deadwood Dick's Dust; or, The Chained Hand. A Strange Story of the Mines. Being the 35th and Ending Number of the Great "Deadwood Dick" Series. 20 October 1885. Even though this is called the 35th volume in the series, it is actually the 33rd and final installment.

ESSAYS

Blewitt, Andrew. "Calamity Jane." *English Westerners' Brand Book* 5 (January 1963): 1–9

Brink, Elizabeth. "Clothing Calamity Jane: An Exercise in Historical Research." *True West* 37 (November 1990): 20–24.

Britz, Kevin. "Deadwood Days of '76: The Wild West Show as Community Celebration." *South Dakota History* 40 (spring 2010): 52–84.

"Calamity Jane as a Lady Robinhood." *Literary Digest* (14 November 1925): 46.

Crawford, John W. (Captain Jack). "The Truth about Calamity Jane." *Journalist* (5 March 1904): 333.

Douthat, Elva Pratt. "J. (James) Thornton Canary." In *Mercer County Pioneer Traces.* Princeton, MO: Mercer County Genealogical Society, 1 (1997): 150.

Eisloeffel, Paul J., and Andrea I. Paul. "Hollywood on the Plains." *NEBRASKAland* 68 (May 1990): 42–47.

———. "Hollywood on the Plains: Nebraska's Contributions to Early American Cinema." *Journal of the West* 33 (April 1994): 13–19.

Etulain, Richard W. "Calamity Jane." *Cowboys and Indians* 1 (July 1993): 30–33.

———. "Calamity Jane: Independent Woman of the Wild West." In *By Grit and Grace: Eleven Women Who Shaped the American West.* Edited by Glenda Riley and Richard W. Etulain. Golden, CO: Fulcrum, 1997, 72–92.

Bibliography

———. "Calamity Jane: The Making of a Frontier Legend." In *Wild Women of the Old West*. Edited by Glenda Riley and Richard W. Etulain. Golden, CO: Fulcrum, 2003, 177–95.

Forney, Gary. "Montana's Pioneer Editor: The Epic Career of Bozeman's First Newspaper Man [Horatio N. Maguire]." *Montana Pioneer* (June 2011).

[Fox, M. L.] "Calamity Jane." *Illustrated American* (7 March 1896): 312.

Freeman, Lewis R. "Calamity Jane and Yankee Jim, Historical Characters of the Old Yellowstone." *Sunset* 49 (July 1922): 22–25, 52, 54.

Giles, T. J. "Calamity Jane." In *Laurel's Story. A Montana Heritage*. Edited by Elsie P. Johnson. Laurel, MT: privately printed, 1979, 43–46.

Hilton, Frances W. "Calamity Jane." *Frontier Magazine* (September 1925): 105–109.

Hofstede, David." The Many Lives and Lies of Calamity Jane." *Cowboys and Indians* 9 (June 2001): 83–86.

Hope, B. W. "Joe Elliott's Story." *Annals of Wyoming* 45 (fall 1973): 143–75.

Mathisen, Jean A. "Calamity's Sister." *True West* 43 (December 1996): 23–30.

McInnes, Elmer D. "Wyatt Earp's Coeur D' Alene Comrade." *Old West* 32 (spring 1996): 50–53.

McLaird, James D. "Calamity Jane: The Life and the Legend." *South Dakota History* 24 (spring 1994): 1–18.

———. "Calamity Jane and the Black Hills Gold Rush in the Writings of William B. Lull." *South Dakota History* 28 (spring–summer): 53–65.

———. "Calamity Jane and Wild Bill: Myth and Reality." *Journal of the West* 37 (April 1998): 23–32.

———. "Calamity Jane's Diary and Letters: Story of a Fraud." *Montana The Magazine of Western History* 45 (autumn–winter 1995): 20–35.

———. "'I Know . . . Because I Was There': Leander P. Richardson Reports the Black Hills Gold Rush." *South Dakota History* 31 (fall–winter 2001): 239–68.

Mercer County Pioneer Press. *Calamity Jane Days*. Princeton, MO: Post-Telegraph, Don and LaVelle Sheridan, 1966. nos. 1–12 (1 October 1966–17 September 1977).

Nelson, D. J. (Dick). "Calamity Jane's Last Ride." Edited by Kathryn Wright. *The West* 17 (September 1973): 26–27, 61.

Paine, Clarence. "Calamity Jane. Man? Woman? Both?" *Westerners Brand Book, 1945–46*. (Chicago: Westerners, 1947): 69–82.

Bibliography

———. "She Laid Her Pistol Down; or, The Last Will and Testament of Calamity Jane." *Westerners Brand Book 1944.* (Chicago: Westerners, 1946): 9–21.

———. "Wild Bill Hickok and Calamity Jane." In *The Black Hills.* Edited by Roderick Peattie. (New York: Vanguard Press, 1952), 151–76.

Patterson, W. G. "'Calamity Jane,' A Heroine of the Wild West." *Wild World Magazine* 11 (September 1903): 450–67.

"Pioneer Profiles: John and Lena Borner." *Wind River Mountaineer* 5 (October–December 1989): 2, 32–34.

Pond, Seymour G. "Frontier Still Recalls 'Calamity Jane.'" *New York Times Magazine* (18 October 1925), 9.

Richardson, Leander. "Last Days of a Plainsman." *True West* 13 (November–December 1965): 22–23, 44–45.

Robbins, Peggy. "Calamity Jane: Hellcat in Leather Britches." *American History Illustrated* 10 (June 1975): 12–21.

Russell, John C. "Calamity Jane Lived Up to Her Name." *Wild West* 7 (August 1994): 42–48.

Russell, Ona. "What's in a Name Anyway: The Calamity of Calamity Jane." *American Studies* 35 (fall 1994): 21–38.

Spring, Agnes Wright, ed. "Diary of Isaac N. Bard (1875–1876)." *1955 Brand Book of the Denver Posse of Westerners.* [Denver:] Westerners, 1956, 1: 171–204.

Thorp, Raymond W. "White-Eye, Last of the Old-Time Plainsmen." *True West* 12 (March–April 1965): 6–10, 46, 48.

"True West Legends: Calamity Jane." *True West* 43 (July 1995): 31–34.

Ward, Josiah M. "A Wild West Heroine the Movies Overlook." *New York Tribune* (16 October 1921).

Whiteside, William R. "Martha Canary Family." In *Mercer County Pioneer Traces.* Princeton, MO: Mercer County Genealogical Society, 1 (1997): 151.

Wright, Kathryn. "The *Real* Calamity Jane." *True West* 5 (November–December 1957): 22–25, 28, 41–42.

NEWSPAPERS

Aberdeen (SD) *Daily News*
Anaconda (MT) *Standard*
Basin (WY) *Republican-Rustler*
Belknap (MT) *Enterprise*
Belle Fourche (SD) *Bee*
Billings (MT) *Daily Gazette Billings Gazette*
Billings Post

Bibliography

Bozeman (MT) *Avant Courier*
Buffalo (NY) *Evening News*
Buffalo (NY) *Morning Express*
Butte (MT) *Miner*
Casper (WY) *Tribune-Herald*
Castle (MT) *Whole Truth*
Cheyenne Daily Leader
Cheyenne Daily Sun
Cheyenne Democratic Leader
Chicago Inter-Ocean Cody (WY) *Enterprise*
Coeur d'Alene (ID) *Press*
Custer (SD) *Chronicle*
Dawson (NWT-Canada), *The Nugget*
Deadwood *Black Hills Daily Champion*
Deadwood *Black Hills Daily Pioneer*
Deadwood *Black Hills Daily Times*
Deadwood *Daily Pioneer-Times*
Deer Lodge (MT) *New Northwest*
Denver Post
Denver Republican
Denver *Rocky Mountain News*
Eagle (ID) *Coeur d' Alene Nugget*
Ekalaka (MT) *Eagle*
El Paso Times
Fort Pierre Weekly Signal
Frontier Index (several sites in Wyoming)
Gardiner (MT) *Wonderland*
Great Falls (MT) *Daily Leader*
Great Falls Tribune
Helena Daily Independent
Hot Springs (SD) *Star*
Ismay (MT) *Journal*
LaCrosse (WI) *Tribune*
Lander Wyoming State Journal
Laramie Daily Boomerang
Lead (SD) *Daily Call*
Lead Evening Call
Lewistown (MT) *Democrat*
Lewistown *Fergus County Argus*
Livingston (MT) *Daily Enterprise*
Livingston Park County News
Livingston Post

Bibliography

London Star
Miles City (MT) *Daily Press*
Miles City Daily Star
Miles City *Yellowstone Journal*
Minneapolis Journal
Montana News Association
New York Times
New York Tribune
Newcastle (WY) *News Letter Journal*
North Idaho News Network
Pierre Daily Capital Journal
Portland *Oregonian*
Powell (WY) *Tribune*
Princeton (MO) *Pioneer Press*
Princeton Post
Princeton Post-Telegraph
Princeton Telegraph
Rapid City (SD) *Black Hills Journal*
Rapid City Daily Journal
Rawlins (WY) *Carbon County Journal*
Rawlins Republican
Red Lodge (MT) *Picket*
Rock Springs (WY) *Miner*
Salt Lake City Tribune
Sheridan (WY) *Post*
Spearfish (SD) *Queen City Mail*
Spokane (WA) *Press*
Spokane Spokesman Review
Sturgis (SD) *Record*
Sundance (WY) *Crook County Monitor*
Sundance Gazette
Virginia City Montana Post
White Sulphur Springs Meagher Republican
Yankton (SD) *Press and Dakotanian*

FILMS AND TV PROGRAMS

Badlands of Dakota, 1941 (Frances Farmer as Calamity Jane)
Bonanza. "Calamity over the Comstock." 1963. NBC-TV
Buffalo Girls, 1995. CBS-TV (Anjelica Huston)
Calamity Jane, 1953 (Doris Day)
Calamity Jane, 1984. CBS-TV (Jane Alexander)

Bibliography

Calamity Jane and Sam Bass, 1949 (Yvonne De Carlo)
Deadwood (HBO), 2004–2006 (Robin Weigert)
In the Days of 75 and 76, 1915 (Freeda Hartzell Romine)
The Legend of Calamity Jane, 1997. (Voice of Barbara Scaff)
The Paleface, 1948. (Jane Russell)
The Plainsman, 1936 (Jean Arthur)
The Plainsman (remake), 1966 (Abby Dalton)
The Raiders, 1964 (Judi Meredith)
The Texan Meets Calamity Jane, 1950 (Evelyn Ankers)
This Is the West That Was, 1974. NBC-TV (Kim Darby)
Wild Bill, 1995 (Ellen Barkin)
Wild Bill Hickok, 1923 (Ethel Grey Terry)
Young Bill Hickok, 1940 (Sally Payne)

Index

Index

Index

Index

Index

Previous volumes of the Oklahoma Western Biographies